By Appointment to
Her Majesty The Queen
Builders & Decorators
Fairhurst Ward Abbotts Ltd

Diary
OF A
DECORATOR

COLIN DOUGLAS-FAIRHURST

Diary
OF A
DECORATOR

MEMOIRS

Cirencester

Published by Memoirs

MEMOIRS
PUBLISHING

Memoirs Books

25 Market Place, Cirencester, Gloucestershire, GL7 2NX
info@memoirsbooks.co.uk www.memoirspublishing.com

Copyright ©Colin Douglas-Fairhurst, June 2012
First published in England, June 2012
Book jacket design Ray Lipscombe

ISBN 978-1-909020-31-3

Printed in England

Diary

OF A

DECORATOR

Contents

Foreword
Acknowledgements
Introduction – the origins of FWA

FOREWORD

Upon witnessing the recent rapid and successful growth of FWA under its new management team, I set out to write this book in order to give to my grandchildren and others who might be interested the history of how it all began and to record some of the difficulties and amusing incidents encountered along the way.

ACKNOWLEDGEMENTS

I wish to record my heartfelt thanks for the tolerance shown by my wife Ann for over 50 years, especially during the early years of our marriage in the 1960s; also the forbearance shown by my whole family when living with me must have been extremely difficult during the regular recessions in the trade over those five decades. My grateful thanks too to my close colleague Alan Ward for his support over a 45-year period, and not least to Kathy Lynch, for almost 30 years of moral support when it was most needed.

INTRODUCTION

The origins of FWA

It was 1914 when my father, John Fairhurst, saw Lord Kitchener's famous poster declaring 'Your Country Needs You!' and responded by promptly signing on with the Army. He was one of many other young lads from his neck of the woods, Preston in Lancashire, to answer the call. He was persuaded to do so by his long-standing school friend, Fred Dewhurst.

Having been born on 14th December 1898, my father was not yet 16 years old when he called in at the local recruiting office. When asked how old he was he lied, as indeed did many others, and said he was 16.

At the initial brief interview he was asked if he had any experience with horses. He told me once that he had answered 'yes' to this question, because otherwise he might have been assigned to a more dangerous role. In fact the only steed he had ever encountered was the milkman's carthorse at the end of the road, but he thought the task of looking after them seemed like fun.

He ended up serving throughout the First World War in France. Although he and Fred saw many of their colleagues meet a sorry end in the trenches, they both survived.

As a young man, my father was very keen on sport and played football for Preston Schoolboys in the period 1910-1913. This was no mean feat, for at that time Preston North End was one of the premier football clubs in the country. In 1888/89 not only were they founder members of the newly-established Football League but they won the FA Cup. They were the first team to achieve the double, which they did at the first opportunity. In 1889/90 Preston North End were again League champions and they were runners-up in the following three seasons.

On leaving school in 1913, my father had started as an office boy with James Todd & Company, an eminent Preston firm of chartered accountants, so when the war was over both he and Fred applied to join James Todd's newly-opened German office in Koblenz. They were both usefully employed there doing junior audit work for two years, until in 1920 they decided to return to England.

The history of James Todd is interesting from the point of view of our firm. Todd himself was a reputable professional man-about-town from 1888, the year his firm was founded, until the outbreak of war in 1914. He was easily recognized by the expensive fur coat he wore as he was driven around the streets of Preston in his fine horse-drawn carriage. In fact Fred Dewhurst worked for a breakaway from this organization, James Todd & Company of Chichester, for over forty years. This branch acted as our firm's accountants and auditors from its registration in 1941 until the management buy-out in 2006. Even today in 2012, the original firm of James Todd & Company, still based in Preston, continues to advertise its accountancy services and to refer on its website to its date of formation in 1888.

When the Second World War started in September 1939, the powers that be decided on a compulsory call-up for all able-bodied men under 40. As my father was at that time coming up to 41, he declared, not unreasonably in my view, 'No thank you very much, I've done my stint and I'm very fortunate to have survived'. He carried on working in his own small accountancy practice, which he had named, straightforwardly enough, Preston & Company (although this sounded grand, he had only two employees), during the day and joining the night-time roster in Bromley to carry out fire-watching duties.

Coincidentally, the lookout position for central Bromley was on the small flat roof of his branch of the National Provincial Bank. His own small office was on the first floor.

Before moving to their house in West Wickham, near Bromley, in 1936, my parents were living on a modern housing estate in Heston, near what is now Heathrow Airport. This was when my father, on seeing large housing estates springing up all over Greater London, conceived the idea of people having the outside of their houses painted regularly every five years by paying a small sum every week. It seems that he borrowed the idea from the 'Man from the Pru', the area salesman for the Prudential Insurance Company, whose firm used the slogan 'sixpence per person per week'. Although he managed to sign up half a dozen homeowners to his scheme, the idea never really took off. His plan was to use the services of his nephew Tom in Preston, a part-time decorator. However Tom was disappointed to find that my father had no intention of contributing in a practical sense. He intended only 'to administrate by dealing with the book-keeping side of the business' as he put it. So after painting only two houses, a disillusioned Tom returned to Preston, leaving my father in the lurch.

Soon afterwards my parents decided to move south of the Thames to West Wickham in Kent, where I was born on 25th April 1937. In the spring of 1939, just a couple of months before my brother, John, was born and only a short time before war was declared in September 1939, they moved to a small newly-constructed detached house in

Hayes. Soon after the outbreak of war all areas of London, especially South London, became targets for intensive bombing raids. Many houses in our area were badly damaged, and some of them were wiped out completely.

After May 1941 the bombing raids became less frequent, as Hitler turned his attention to Russia. It was about this time that my father had a conversation with the bank manager downstairs. My father was what they used to refer to up north as someone who was 'never backwards in coming forwards', and, knowing him, on some previous occasion he must have made it clear to this manager that he would welcome any introductions that might lead to some business.

The manager took my father to one side and said 'Look, John, you know I said that if ever I was able to introduce you to someone in business it would be a person who was a bit special, and it would have been worth the wait?' He then took my father into his private office and introduced him to Frederick (Freddie) Love, a Chislehurst builder of high repute who had been responsible for building many large and prestigious Tudor-style houses during the 1930s in and around the Chislehurst Caves area. Today these are highly sought after homes of premier quality, marketed by estate agents as 'Love-built houses'.

My father began his business association with Freddie Love by preparing his accounts for the Inland Revenue. After a couple of months, Freddie asked my father if he had heard of a new invention which had recently been imported from America by a company called DeVilbiss. My father replied that the name meant nothing to him, but Freddie went on to say that he had seen an amazing demonstration.

He explained that the equipment used for spraying tar on the road was called a Four Oaks machine and was made by a firm near Birmingham. The tar was forced by compressed air out of a long lateral tube with four apertures to allow the sprays to overlap and cover about a ten-foot width. Mr DeVilbiss had used this concept to produce a single spraygun using air from a compressor to force a spray of paint at high speed, making the painting process very much faster than with a conventional brush. He went on to say that his foreman painter had described it as a dream come true for contractors wishing to camouflage aircraft hangars as part of the war effort.

My father was immediately intrigued. He discovered from an initial investigation that spraying paint on to a hangar roof, for instance, could be achieved at a rate of up to 200 square yards an hour compared to an average of only eight yards per hour with a four-inch brush. Of course, in practice, contractors were covering large areas of hangar roofs very quickly simply by pouring out cans of paint on to the corrugated iron roofs and spreading it out with a soft broom, but needless to say the resultant finish was deplorable. Using the new method the camouflage markings would be much neater, and the resultant finish would be much improved as well as more speedily achieved.

After further discussions, my father and Freddie Love agreed to form a company to carry out this work. My father thought up the idea of calling it Spraycraft Company Ltd, with himself and Freddie as the two directors and with a working capital of £100. My father once told me that when he broke the news to the bank manager the response had been 'starting up a company at a time like this? John, you must be mad!'

Freddie was very busy with his own business affairs and soon became little more than a sleeping partner. The company began trading on 30th August 1941, and my father approached both the Air Ministry and the War Department to be given an opportunity of quoting for suitable contracts.

After a while, as is usually the case, he was given a chance to submit a tender for a small job to see how he performed. The contract wasn't even a spraying job, but was to prepare and apply by brush two coats of black bitumen to a Nissen hut at Wrotham Camp in Seven Mile Lane near Maidstone in Kent. It must be remembered that my father was, essentially, a finance man and had little idea of the practical world of maintenance painting.

It appears that he read through the specification, and although he understood the rudiments of what was required, he did not foresee a small technical hitch. The preparation of the corrugated surface was simple enough with the use of wire brushes, but then came the time to apply the material. He did not realise this, but unless one ordered black bitumen in a suitable form for applying as paint it would be delivered to site (as indeed it was) in large black shiny lumps!

What should he do? The painter he had employed to carry out the work told him 'It'll have to be melted down, mate', so my father went back to his house in Hayes and, after a long argument with my mother, persuaded her to lend him the copper which she used to boil up the family's clothes on wash day. She was naturally most reluctant to part with her faithful copper, but she agreed to let him use it provided it came back clean.

I can immediately bring to mind, even as a four-year-old, the look on my mother's face when her copper was brought back and left in the garage at the end of the contract. It was completely ruined and totally covered in big lumps of gooey bitumen. It had to be dumped. Luckily the contract was financially rewarding enough to enable my father to go out and buy another copper.

As an indication of the thoroughness of the workmanship on this first contract, that particular Nissen hut was still visible from Seven Mile Lane on its base at Wrotham Camp until it was dismantled over 60 years later in 2005. When it was pulled down it was quite evident that the corrugated sheeting, although beginning to rust quite badly, had never been touched since my father's firm had painted it in 1941.

After that experience Spraycraft never looked back, and for the next twelve years it carried out an annual average of more than 20 large contracts. Several other spray painting contractors were established at about the same time but, to my knowledge, only two of them are still trading as independent businesses today, the other being Ian Williams from Cardiff. Spraycraft changed its name to the family name of John Fairhurst & Sons Ltd in 1962, and to Fairhurst Ward Abbotts Ltd in 1995.

One competitor which began trading shortly after Spraycraft in 1942 was a firm called Abbotts of Harrow Ltd, which later expanded considerably and opened offices in East London and Southampton. Unfortunately it went into receivership in 1992 and John Fairhurst & Sons were able to acquire certain assets and employees. In particular they were able to have novated to them a major contract for the painting of a huge area of roof steelwork at Waterloo Station.

My close working colleague Alan Ward was instrumental in the acquisition of Abbotts Painting Contractors, and I arranged for a new subsidiary company to carry on with the trade hitherto carried out by Abbotts. In recognition of the work Alan had put into the project, it was decided to call the new company Ward Abbotts Painting Ltd. The new company traded from a yard and offices near Dartford which had been purchased for the purpose by the Fairhurst Group Retirement Benefits Scheme.

After three years, however, we decided that our whole method of trading with several subsidiaries and branch offices under different names was too confusing for our clients. As Ward Abbotts Painting was the largest subsidiary, the new trading name for the Company from 1995 became Fairhurst Ward Abbotts Ltd (FWA).

As may be imagined, Spraycraft found it pretty hard going during the war years. With my father fire-watching most nights and continuing to run Preston & Company, his small accountancy practice, most contracts were on an ad hoc basis, as he was not in a position to offer full-time employment to anyone and had to do everything himself. He often used to say that he did four people's jobs.

The winter of 1946-47 was one of the coldest on record, and on one occasion my father turned his car upside down on an icy road in Norfolk, fortunately emerging with only a broken shoulder blade. The following summer Freddie dropped a bombshell by informing my parents that he, his wife Kathleen, and all the family had decided to emigrate to South Africa and accordingly he would like my father to buy him out. Freddie Love was quite a character, at times a real handful for his wife, so although it was of great concern for my parents, it was not at all untypical for Freddie to decide to go to South Africa the hard way. He and his family travelled overland in a small convoy of Jeeps through France and Spain, across the Straits of Gibraltar to Morocco and across the Sahara Desert, until, after many weeks, their adventure brought them to Durban, where Freddie lived for the rest of his life.

I recall hearing the story of how, some way down Africa, their tyre inner tubes could no longer be repaired from all the punctures suffered on the rough roads. Innovative and resourceful as ever, Freddie's family discovered a certain strain of wild grass that could be twisted into reasonable sized wads and stuffed into the tyres. This, apparently, was how they covered the last 2000 miles.

In the immediate post-war period, many of Spraycraft's competitors were expanding rapidly, including Abbotts of Harrow and Ian Williams Ltd from Cardiff. They say that every businessman gets one lifetime opportunity to go for the big time, and my father's chance came in 1948 on the premature death of Ian Williams. They had been trading for no more than about two years but were already making their mark in the painting contracting business. Ian's wife immediately assumed control of the business, whose annual turnover at that time was a little more than that of Spraycraft's, and my father was offered the chance to purchase the company for £4500. This was a considerable sum in those days, equating to the value of four average-sized houses. But my father turned it down, not least because he was very happy with what he had already achieved and for that reason had no ambition to expand. Over the ensuing six decades, Ian Williams Ltd went on to become the UK's largest privately- owned painting and maintenance contractors, with 18 offices spread throughout England and Wales!

From 1947 to 1953 Spraycraft really flourished. My father was truly proud when his firm was chosen to paint all the steelwork, inside and out, of the Queen's Flight 'C' type hangar at RAF Benson, near Oxford, as well as a large area of roof steelwork above the main engine plant at the Ford Motor Company factory in Dagenham.

The work was not always in the South East, for in 1949 he was even successful with his tender for painting two T2 type aircraft hangars at RAF Kinloss in the North of Scotland. Because he did much of the work himself in acting as estimator, supervisor and book-keeper, the company was very profitable, enabling him to send all his children to private schools except Derek, the eldest, who by then had left full-time education.

His efforts were rewarded further by being able to move from our small detached house in Hayes to Pelham Lodge, a very large detached Edwardian House in Bickley with six bedrooms and three bathrooms. Here in 1951 he was able to have a hard tennis court laid in a large open space at the bottom of the garden.

HM Government's massive spend on building repairs in the post-war era could not last forever, and in 1953 a moratorium was declared in respect of this type of expenditure. With little or no work about, my father had no alternative but to cease trading and pay everybody off.

I do remember the night he told us with a very sad face that he had been to North London that day and had arranged to sell all eight petrol compressors and associated spray equipment to a certain Benge Abbott, the founder of Abbotts of Harrow.

CHAPTER ONE

One Sat On A Time

I could not remember a time when creating awful puns was not a major part of my life. I had never intended the words 'one sat on a time' to have any humorous meaning - this was what I truly thought my mother was saying whenever she started to tell a bedtime story. It had of course begun with the very first time she had produced a book of nursery rhymes, for on the front cover, in graphic detail, was a rhyme alluding to a mouse running up a clock. The picture had clearly shown a grandfather clock with a mouse running up the side and another mouse, presumably waiting for it, at the top. From that moment, at the age of two until I started at primary school some three years later, every time a bedtime story had started with the customary opening words once upon a time, I interpreted the words as one sat on a time.

So convinced was I that all stories began with these words that I had an argument with my teacher and told her she was wrong. Then she explained what the opening words really were. After the laughter in the classroom had died down, I went into a sulk for the rest of the day.

I wasn't quite sure what made me think of this particular episode, but it was probably because I was in the local park watching small children with their parents throwing bread for the ducks. This was the first time I had ambled down to the park since bidding farewell to my colleagues at work. On previous occasions I had moved briskly and much more meaningfully, principally for the exercise. But I had retired five days earlier at the age of 69 after 52 years of work, the last 50 of which had been with the same firm, so I could see little point in wasting energy. I had felt a little nonplussed by having nothing much to do, so I had taken myself off to the park. I sat down on a bench dedicated to 'Emily Pritchard, who always enjoyed the view from here' and then returned to thoughts about my early life as a small child.

I have three very early recollections of the years before I started school at five. The first involved crawling on the grass in the garden of the house where I was born in West Wickham, and looking up wondrously at a huge pampas grass plant which to me seemed as high as the house. I was no more than about 10 months old at the time. The second event which has always stuck in my memory occurred at the age of about 20 months when I was sitting in a pram outside the front door of my family's new house in Hayes and saw a piece of old newspaper float in the wind above the pram and land in front of me within easy reach. I well remember tearing at it and putting a large piece in my mouth. Fascinated by the unaccustomed but intriguing taste of the printing ink, I started to chew it.

Shortly afterwards, my mother came outside to check on me and said 'you naughty boy, have you been eating that newspaper?' I shook my head, and as my mother advanced towards me to check that I was telling the truth, I managed to open my mouth sufficiently wide to satisfy her, while at the same time keeping the chewed-up piece of paper under my tongue and happily continued the chewing after she had returned indoors.

My third, quite vivid, recollection was of an incident when I was a little more than two years old, a few weeks before the outbreak of World War 2. My father and older brother and sister were getting ready to go to a fair on the local common. I had been listening to what they had been saying and, although unable to understand most of the words, it had dawned on me that they intended to go without me, implying that I was too young; it was then that I came out with, quite intentionally, my very first joke involving a play on words - 'Baby go fair - not fair'!

I continued to sit on the bench, reminiscing and watching two swans with six cygnets clamber up the bank, which resulted in the children retreating to a safer distance. I thought how peaceful this all was, and how fortunate young children are today taking peace for granted and knowing nothing of war. Things were so very different in my day when I was about their age. I can bring to mind that soon after the start of the Second World War, when we had been told the bombs were about to start dropping, my father had arranged for my mother, my younger brother John and myself to travel up to Blackpool, which was thought to be a much safer place to be. My elder brother and sister had been evacuated to Canada, or so my parents had thought – in fact their ship was sunk by a torpedo and they were rescued at sea. This was in the autumn of 1940, when I was three years old and John 15 months.

Whenever I see a typical four-storey seaside boarding house, my memory immediately returns to the time when my mother was pushing John in a pram along the back streets of Blackpool and I was under instruction to keep a firm hold of the pram's handle as she went from one boarding house to another seeking accommodation for the three of us.

The same sequence of events took place outside several establishments and it took almost an entire day. My mother would leave me on the pavement, with my brother in the pram, while she climbed the steps up to the front door. The door would be opened by a lady, invariably wearing some sort of headscarf, she would look over my mother's shoulder and her gaze would settle on the two young children waiting eagerly for the news that the long search for a room had ended. She would then shake her head and close the door, and my mother would come back down the steps with a tear in her eye.

Several times I asked her 'why can't we stay here, hasn't the lady got any room?' and my mother would reply that they did not take children. On one of these occasions, I looked up a particular flight of stairs and stared at the woman at the top and thought to myself 'just you wait, one of these days when I'm grown up, I shall be the one at the top of the stairs and deciding who I will take in and who I won't'.

Thus the seeds of ambition were sown outside a Blackpool boarding house. I am positive that it was that particular experience that has been the driving force all my life as I have done my utmost to succeed in the competitive world of business.

Towards the end of a long and incredibly tiring day, a lady finally took pity on our small bedraggled group and agreed to let us stay for a few days. Her name was Mrs Simpson. She was a really lovely lady and I became very fond of her.

Later on towards the end of the war, when warnings were being issued about a final German thrust with the impending launch of V2 rockets, I was sent with my family to the small village of Dickleborough near Diss in Norfolk. This did not last long, and we soon returned to our house in Hayes, Kent. During the stay in Dickleborough I recall catching snippets of a conversation between my parents, with my mother accusing my father of choosing the location because he would be near the many RAF and USAF bases where the vast majority of his work took place at that time as a specialist painting contractor carrying out essential camouflage work to aircraft hangars.

Soon things were hotting up too much even for my father. One afternoon on a country walk in Norfolk, we saw an enemy aircraft shot down. It spun out of control, a long plume of black smoke trailing from the tailplane, and crashed in flames in a cornfield only a few hundred yards from where we were walking. We went back home immediately.

The war was of course still raging. I will never forget seeing the tracer lights in the night sky somewhere over London as anti-aircraft fire attempted to bring down German bombers; adding to the spectacle were the darkened silhouettes of many barrage balloons. There was a period when the whole family kept being awakened, sometimes more than once in a night, by the air raid siren, to scuttle downstairs to safety in our Morrison shelter.

The Morrison shelter was named after Herbert Morrison (later Lord Morrison of Lambeth), who was the Minister of Home Security in the National Coalition Government during the war. He brought a sense of urgency and much-needed efficiency into all aspects of civil defence, in particular the National Fire Service. His Cockney humour, his understanding of ordinary people and his indomitable pluck did much to sustain the morale of everyone at that time. The famous shelter he promoted was issued to huge numbers of homes in the Greater London area and saved many lives.

The Morrison shelter was an indoor steel 'table' shelter, assembled from a kit of parts and bolted together inside the house. The steel top doubled as a table and there were wire mesh panels around the four sides, with an entry door through one of the panels. When the table was covered with a tablecloth and laid for a meal, you would never have guessed what lay underneath.

My elder brother Derek thought he was being very clever by always leaving it as late as possible before heading for the shelter. Everyone roared with laughter when one night he came tearing downstairs at the last moment and stubbed his big toe badly on the steel frame of the shelter. He had always suffered from an extremely bad temper. Fortunately I was too young to understand the meaning of all the expletives that filled the air.

The shelter, being inside the house, was generally only used at night time and was really only intended to be used as protection from falling ceiling joists and plaster, although there were many records of peoples' lives being saved when the whole house had collapsed around them.

A much more difficult type of shelter to construct was the Anderson shelter. This shelter was named after John Anderson (later Sir John), the then Home Secretary, who was responsible for air raid precautions. The shelters were made from straight and curved galvanized corrugated steel panels, which were bolted together. Six curved panels, bolted at the top, formed the body of the shelter, and the straight panels formed the ends, with a door located in one end.

The shelter was partially buried in the ground and provided with a concrete floor. There was usually a small drainage sump in the middle of the floor to collect any water that found its way inside. This type of shelter had been designed to accommodate up to six people, so it was just about big enough to accommodate my whole family.

During its construction, carried out by my father with assistance from neighbours, I can remember helping in my own small way by carrying partially-filled buckets of soil to the bottom of the garden.

As very young boys my brothers and I were fascinated by the unmanned V1 rockets, or 'doodlebugs' as everyone called them, which Germany had invented to bomb London and the suburbs towards the end of the war. Development of the V1 was carried out by Germany during 1942-3 and after successful tests, Hitler authorised full-scale development work on this 'pilotless airplane' in June 1942. It was constructed of plywood and sheet steel, so it didn't use scarce aluminium. Another advantage was that it burned low-grade petrol instead of aviation spirit and took only about 500 man-hours to manufacture (excluding the explosive and autopilot).

Right in the middle of the war, In September 1942, the time had arrived for me to start at the local primary school, Wickham Common School in Coney Hall near Hayes. I say 'local' although in fact it was situated about two miles from our house in Hayes and involved a good

45-minute walk. We used to joke about the unfortunate name of the school and said that only common people went there, and the area, Coney Hall, soon became known by us as Coney Hatch, after Colney Hatch Lunatic Asylum in what is now the London Borough of Barnet.

I well remember my first day at school, wondering what all those other little people like me were doing there. The standard of teaching, especially of English, geography and arithmetic, was very high, and I always seemed to achieve respectable marks when the frequent tests were conducted in those subjects.

One aspect of school life which I found difficult to come to terms with was the toilet arrangements. Before starting school I had been accustomed to going to the loo, other than for a quick pee, soon after breakfast. During term time, however, there was such a rush to get my brothers and me off to school that there never seemed to be time for this activity and as I was always on the verge of being late for assembly there was very often insufficient time when I got there. Even when I did have time at school, the toilets in the infants' department appeared to me quite disgusting compared to what I had been used to at home. On many occasions, therefore, I would not check in at the school but wander off into the woods opposite and make use of dock leaves instead of paper. Nobody knew where I was and, looking back now, it was an extremely dangerous and stupid thing to do. Even when, many times, where my end-of-term reports stated 'Times Absent' and the teacher had simply written the one word 'often', I was never questioned about this at home.

One event which always amused my mother took place during the last couple of years at this school when, at the age of nine or ten I would offer my two younger brothers a lift to school on my small bike. With John, eight, straddling the rear mudguard and David, six, balanced precariously on the handlebars, I would ride in this manner until we reached the main crossroads at Coney Hall, where we all had to dismount to cross the road safely. Several of our neighbours would recognise us and wave cheerily as we passed by - quite fast, as I recall, down one particular downhill section.

Very occasionally, especially if it was pouring with rain, our father would leave going into his office until a little later and give us a lift to school in his car. This was quite something, as very few families had cars in those days.

Although the lessons were made very interesting by the experienced teachers, all of us enjoyed break-time and we played all manner of games in the playground. It was a hard asphalt surface, so many were the times when my friends or I would take a tumble and require sticking plaster or bandages, especially when engaging in our favourite past time of 'bus ups'.

I have absolutely no idea why it was called bus ups, but it entailed two boys linking arms behind their backs and then confronting another pair of boys similarly entwined. The boys would then push or bash into each other until one pair was either knocked to the ground or gave in. I suppose an outsider would have considered this to be a very rough game, but we thoroughly enjoyed it.

There were three girls in my class, one with a Polish surname, who very sadly had no fathers; they had either been killed or gone missing in the war.

A few months after starting at Wickham Common School, I told my mother one morning that I was having pains in the stomach. She gave me some sort of painkiller for a couple of days, but when the pain got worse she called Dr Pearce, our local GP, and he realised at once that I had an enlarged appendix. I was rushed at once by ambulance to Farnborough Hospital, where I had immediate surgery. My parents were told that my appendix had burst as it was being removed. It left me with an enormous scar which has never really ever healed, even after 70 years. They were told they had nearly lost their little son. It was more than four weeks before I had recovered sufficiently to return home.

One afternoon in June 1944, soon after returning from school, I heard the terrible distinctive droning sound of a doodlebug. I looked up to see it in the sky some distance away, and ran as fast as I could from the front garden gate into the house to warn my mother, but because I was still keeping a watch on it I lost all sense of direction and ran straight into the corner of the brick wall near the front door. My mother rushed out on hearing my screams and an ambulance was immediately called.

Blood was gushing from my forehead, and my mother held the skin together until the ambulance arrived. Several stitches were necessary to join the gaping aperture, and to this day I still have a prominent scar on my left temple which I refer to as my 'war wound'.

During my years at school I was aware that my future might well lie working with my father in the small painting contracting firm he had started as a hobby business early in 1937. It was registered as Spraycraft Co Ltd in August 1941, and was part of the war effort to camouflage aircraft hangars.

Its success relied on a new invention from America - applying paint coatings with hand-held spray guns, an operation that cost about a tenth as much as applying paint by brush.

I was well used to hearing about some of the incidents my father had to deal with, especially some of the tricks the men on site used to get up to. On many occasions during the school holidays he would take me with him on his regular business trips, usually to RAF and USAF bases in East Anglia.

These trips would often take two or more days, and we would stay the night in a suitably located Trust House hotel. I cannot count the number of times I had to sit in the car on the edge of some isolated airfield while my father spent an hour or more in a site hut discussing prices and other contract matters.

I well remember one time where he came out to the car and said 'you're good at English, Colin – what to you make of this – I've just come out from discussing the wording on a contract with the Works Engineer – it's for that T2 hangar over there' and he indicated a large black shed over to our right. He then opened his brief case and produced a contract document. 'Take a look at this wording and see what you make of it'. He opened the document at a particular page and handed it to me. I read the section he pointed to and there was printed a short specification for surface preparation, the precise wording of which will stay with me forever: 'Prepare by mechanically wire brushing even to the greater extent of an area and then apply,' etc. etc.

He had underlined 'even to the greater extent of an area'. 'What do you suppose that means?' he asked. I said 'I'm not sure, it doesn't really make sense'. He said 'what they usually mean, and what we've been doing up to now, is to use mechanical wire brushes, as specified, and to chase off any loose paint back to a firm edge – this is normal practice. What the Works Engineer is expecting us to do is to use the wire brushes to completely strip the whole area, irrespective of whether or not the previous coatings are adhering soundly'.

I learned later that my father had gone to a higher authority for a ruling and was told that the procedure he was adopting was all that was required. Since that incident, at the age of 15, I have always been very wary of the precise wording of specifications and the like.

Another incident I recall his telling me about was the occasion, in about 1948, when he came up against a clerk of works at a certain RAF base in Norfolk with whom there was absolutely no rapport at all and in efforts to break the ice he would offer him a cigarette, as was his custom. This would always be refused, however, despite the clerk being a smoker. In short, every effort met with a stony response. It seems that the contract was a large one and went on for a number of weeks. During one site visit however, the clerk of works accepted a Polo mint when offered.

My father apparently returned to his car wreathed in smiles. 'I've cracked it!' he thought. He could not believe it, though, at his very next meeting when the first thing the clerk of works did was to offer him a reciprocal Polo! He just did not want to be compromised – even for a Polo mint.

My father also recounted the story when, owing to petrol rationing after the war, it was difficult for him to carry on visiting all his operational sites by car, even with the generous petrol ration allowance he received as an approved Government contractor. On one of the USAF bases he told his sorry story to an American in charge of the aircraft fuel bunkers and talked him into letting him fill the tank of his Riley $2\frac{1}{2}$ Litre sports saloon with aviation fuel. He nearly took off when he reached almost 100 mph in double quick time along the perimeter track.

One story I always loved to hear as a child was how decorators in the old days used to 'float a door'. At that time the foreman painter always wore a bowler hat and mixed the paints on site. This was before the days when paint came in sealed cans ready for use, and crucially, before driers were added in the manufacturing procedure to aid the drying process.

The foreman used to mix the required colour using oil and other ingredients. He would then station a painter on each corner of a horizontally laid door and proceed to gently pour his prepared mixture in the centre. Then, it seems, the foreman's instructions would begin – 'over your side a bit, Jim – bit more now your side, George – now back a bit to you, Jim – slightly more to you now, Fred' and so on until the whole door was covered. Apparently the resultant sheen was something to behold. An even surface on a flush door has long since been achieved with a fine quality bristle brush, but the final result could never match that accomplished by 'floating'. It could never be repeated today, thanks to the presence of driers and the manpower cost involved.

In the spring of 1946 I was living with my family at our house in

Hayes when I had my first practical experience of the decorating trade. My father had arranged for the outside of the house to be painted with the metal windows in cream and with mid green for the wooden frames and sills.

I fell in love with the evocative aromas of oil paint and white spirit. After the external painting had been completed, my father had arranged for his best sprayer, Bob Strange, to apply a sprayed multicolour finish to the plastered walls of the dining room. As a nine-year-old, I was totally fascinated to watch Bob at work. He taught me the rudiments of setting up a conventional spray-painting unit with a main air line running from a portable petrol-driven compressor to a two-gallon pressure pot containing the paint, from whence came a fluid line and a second air line to the spraygun itself.

The noise of a small compressor running, together with the periodic hiss of the mixture of air and paint being released under pressure by the spraygun's trigger, is with me to this day. The sheer joy of visiting contracts in later years where spraying was specified, together with the certain knowledge that all the time you could hear the sound of a compressor humming away you knew you were making money, has remained with me always.

Soon after the work on the house was completed, I discovered some green paint on a shelf in the garage and thought what a great colour it would be to use on my beloved bicycle. As mentioned previously, my elder brother Derek had a most terrible temper, which he was hardly ever able to control. I will never forget one particular occasion in 1946, just after I had completed painting my little bike (known at the time as a fairy cycle). For some reason, probably to enable me to paint the underside of the frame properly, I had lifted the bike on to the drive and left it there to dry.

In the early evening, on returning from work in the City, Derek tripped over it. The air was blue, and in his wrath he picked up the offending machine and threw it high in the air. It landed on the driveway with the chain broken and the forks badly bent, looking like a tangled wreck. I cried my eyes out, and never forgot or forgave Derek for that incident. I was nine years old at the time and my brother coming up for twenty.

I do not remember either of my parents remonstrating with Derek in any meaningful way and now, many years later, I believe they were both very frightened of him and struggled all the time not to provoke his dreadful temper. At that time, the whole family were keeping their fingers crossed that with his National Service about to start, Derek would be sent abroad, and as far away as possible. So we were all delighted when, after basic training, his unit was posted to Egypt for the best part of three years.

* * * * * * * * *

My backside was becoming a little numb after sitting for so long on the wooden bench, so I got up and started walking up an incline away from the lake. As I went past the new children's play area I thought what my brothers and I would have given for a wonderful facility like this, with swings and roundabouts. We had to make our own amusements.

One of our favourite pastimes was the construction of home-made soap box cars, which we always referred to as trolleys. Making home-made cars from old scraps of wood and secondhand wheels was a great way to engage our imaginations and give us a fun (and practically free) toy.

Once built, the 'racing' of these trolleys used to keep us occupied for hours. There was a steep hill not far from our house which met a T junction at the bottom. The trick was to race down the hill before skidding suddenly to a halt to avoid any vehicle that might be crossing at the bottom. Although we did fit handbrakes to our trolleys which operated on a rear wheel, they were pretty ineffective at the speeds we reached down that particular hill.

Sadly, there were one or two houses near us which had been bombed and others which, for whatever reason, the owners had left. Consequently the rear gardens of these properties had become overgrown, but in some cases the fruit trees continued to bear apples and pears, so we spent many an hour 'scrumping' in these disused gardens.

Other ways we amused ourselves included making music with paper and comb, collecting all manner of things, including stamps and butterflies, and of course my favourite hobby, which was building things with my Meccano set. I once built a model of Tower Bridge and designed it so that I could raise or lower the two sides of the bridge simultaneously by turning just one handle at the side. At such times a visiting aunt or other elderly relative would pass such comments as 'I expect he'll be an engineer when he grows up'.

Another prized possession which occupied me for hours on end between the ages of about five and ten was my toy farm.

After a while I began to feel sorry for myself over the things in my childhood that I had missed out on, but whenever my mind dwelt on such matters it invariably returned to the greatest injustice I felt I had ever suffered, as a result of which, to this day over 60 years later, I could never bring myself to vote for the Labour Party.

After the war, the Labour Party won the 1945 General Election and in 1948, in common with every other 11-year-old, I was required to sit for the Eleven Plus exam. I had no special qualms about this for, in a class of 38 boys and girls, I had always come within the top half dozen or so in almost all of the various tests that were set for us and usually excelling in my favourite subjects of English, Arithmetic and Geography. The following is a typical school report for three years earlier, aged 8.

BOROUGH OF BECKENHAM

Education Committee

School .... WICKHAM COMMON SCHOOL.

Dept :

Report for Year/Term ending **August 3rd 1945.**

Name **Colin Fairhurst**   Class **6**   Times Absent **Often.**

Position   Times Late

Subject.	Marks (Max.)	Remarks.
Arithmetic	18/20	Good.
Drawing (Brush.)	9/10	"
English (i) Reading	19/20	V. Good.
(ii) Composition	18/20	"
(iii) Spelling	10/10	"
(iv) ~~Literature~~ Dictation	8/10	
Religious Knowledge		
Geography		
History		
Other Subjects :—		
Recitation	10/10	
Handwork	10/10	
Cursive Writing	9½/10	
Script Writing	10/10	

General Report **Colin has done well. He is a little forgetful at times, but his work is always neat and tidy.**

Date **Aug. 3rd 1945**   M. Willis (Class Teacher)

Mb Kidwell (Head Teacher)

After the initial written tests my parents were told that I had passed this stage with ease, and on the strength of that my mother took me to the local shops to buy a small present to celebrate. It was a child's table lamp with rabbits on the shade, and I treasured it for many years. After the written IQ tests, all that remained was for me to attend for an interview at Beckenham Grammar School, the school of my parents' choice.

On the morning of the interview, my father, who was very proud of the fact that he was a qualified accountant and managing director of his own firm, had taken me to one side and said 'It is possible that they will ask you what your father does for a living, and if they do, just say that he is an accountant and company director'.

I duly went on the bus to Beckenham Grammar School with my mother, and while she waited for me in a small reception room near the main entrance, I entered a large room which had a long table behind which sat three persons with various papers in front of them.

'Good morning', they said in unison, and the one on my right said 'can you please tell us your name and address?' Having dispensed with the introduction, the one in the middle then made me smile slightly by saying 'Can you tell us, Colin, what your father does for a living?'

Very proudly, I replied, 'He's an accountant and a company director'.

'I see' he said. Then, without my realising its significance, all three of them turned, as if one person, to some papers on their right. The interviewer on my left, a lady with white hair, read out from the top sheet of paper and said 'We are now going to test your general knowledge; could you tell us first of all what, approximately, is the current price of coal per hundredweight'?

I didn't have a clue, and thought it was a very strange question, so I couldn't possibly give a sensible answer. However, being brought up to be very polite, all I could say was 'I'm very sorry, but I'm afraid I don't know'.

I waited for what I hoped would be a more sensible question, or at least one to which I would know the answer. Then the man in the centre said, 'Right, thank you very much, could you ask the next boy to come in please?'

That was my entire interview. A few days later my parents received a letter declining me a place at Beckenham Grammar.

The day after this interview, my mother had spoken to one of her neighbours in Hayes about my experience. This lady, who happened to be a teacher at a local girls' school, told her that this procedure was not unusual when there were too many pupils applying for the number of places available. It seemed that the authorities had to have some way of denying a place to those children whose parents, in their view, could afford private education. They knew it was highly unlikely that anyone, let alone a child, would know the answer to the question about the price of coal, as in those days, only a few years after the war had ended, it was fluctuating wildly on a daily basis. Presumably, in the unlikely event that a child did know the answer to that particular question, a further, even more difficult question would have been asked.

This diagnosis was later confirmed when I discovered that one of my primary school friends, who also generally fared very well with his school work and whose father, coincidentally, was also an accountant, was likewise denied a grammar school place. My parents learned that shortly afterwards the family in question had decided to emigrate to Canada.

My father then spent a lot of time in researching suitable preparatory schools, knowing that a change to this type of schooling would be difficult for me as most boys went to such schools as seven or eight-year-olds and, for example, had started to learn French at that age, so I would always be at least three years behind in that subject.

I understood many years later that at that time my father had a secretary whose cousin had, in the pre-war period, attended Cranleigh

Public School near Guildford in Surrey and had thought very highly of it. Accordingly my father contacted Cranleigh School to obtain a prospectus and to enquire if there were any particular preparatory schools who specialised in sending boys there. The name of Springfield Park School in Horsham was given to him.

So in September 1948, I was sent to Springfield Park School. My parents, who by then were quite disgusted with the eleven-plus system, had decided to send my two younger brothers to Springfield Park as well, so that in the future neither of them would be subjected to the same reprehensible treatment.

Getting to know my father better, as I did in later years, I do believe that he would not have been averse to asking for a 'discount for three' on the fees. Whether he did so, or whether the request was granted, I shall never know.

Despite any reservations about the state education system itself, the ability of the teachers in my primary school was never in doubt. In the three forms, Form IVC, Shell and the sixth form, which I attended during my two and a half years at Springfield Park, I won the annual form prize two years out of three. The teaching was very thorough, as one would have expected with classes of only 10 or so pupils, but I do remember having a very heated argument with one of the teachers regarding the spelling of the flower chrysanthemum. He insisted that the word was chrysantheum, leaving out the penultimate 'm' and pronounced and spelt as such. The rest of the class seemed to be thoroughly enjoying our bantering until eventually, I became extremely cross and told him I didn't think he should be giving spelling lessons if he himself was so poor at spelling what, after all, was not a particularly difficult word!

One or two aspects of life at this school were not too appealing, especially the washing facilities. Other than being limited to one weekly hot bath, the lack of hot water for daily washing was one grim reality.

The washroom we used after games consisted of two long rows of fitted iron basins, the type one would expect to encounter in a prison or similar establishment, with one cold tap to each basin. In the bedrooms there was no access to running water, either hot or cold, just a very large jug and bowl, the jug being filled by the matron each night.

On the plus side, however, the sports facilities at this school were fantastic. There was a large sports field and we had the opportunity of competing against other similar-sized preparatory schools. In my last term I captained the school football team, and we either won or drew most of our matches.

I believe one of the reasons I was given the captaincy of the football team, apart from my age, was that I enjoyed a high turn of speed for short distances, which enabled me to outstrip most of our opponents when in possession of the ball. It was something I had always taken for granted. I almost certainly inherited it from my father, who was a born sprinter. His speed was the main reason he was chosen to play on the wing for Preston schoolboys in his youth.

From the age of five until I left Wickham Common School at the age of 11, I never encountered any situation where I was in danger of being beaten in an informal running or sprinting event against other pupils. In those days there were no formal sports days or similar occasions where one's talent might be tested, but it was common knowledge that I was the fastest sprinter in the school.

When I went on to Springfield Park School I rather took it for granted that I would automatically win the 100 yards and 200 yards sprints on Sports Day. I was completely taken aback, therefore, when I came second. The winner every time was a young man from Guatemala called John Liddle.

Coincidentally, Liddle's parents had decided to send their son to the same public school, Cranleigh, so I didn't hold out too much hope when the first Sports Day arrived there and John and I lined up for the two short sprinting events. I needn't have worried however, as it seemed that John had burned himself out by the age of 14 and I managed to get my revenge.

David was only seven when he joined Springfield Park, so John and I were detailed to look after him. All boys were known by their surnames only, and any brothers at the school were known by the suffix 1 or 2. Our friends the Anderson twins, for instance, were Anderson 1 and Anderson 2 (although it was extremely difficult to tell them apart) and my brothers and I were always referred to as Fairhurst 1, Fairhurst 2 and Fairhurst 3.

The headmaster, Dr Veasey, a Cambridge-educated Latin scholar, was known for his very dry sense of humour. Possibly on account of the way all three of us Fairhursts would lunge head down at the tape in sprinting events, he would change our name to Hairfurst (hair first). It was then, at the age of eleven, that I learned of the legendary Dr Spooner after which such inversions are named. He lived in the nineteenth century and was educated at New College, Oxford. I thought it was quite fun to be called Hair First 1.

The most famous of the Springfield Park School alumni was Lord Sheppard, known for many years to the general public as the Reverend David Sheppard, Bishop of Liverpool, and to many thousands of cricket fans as the great England cricketer. Sheppard was an England batsman who became an ordained minister and rose to become Bishop of Liverpool. He died in 2005, just one day short of his 76th birthday. His obituary in the 7th March 2005 issue of The Independent stated:

'David Stuart Sheppard, Baron Sheppard of Liverpool (6 March 1929– 5 March 2005) was the high-profile Bishop of Liverpool in the Church of England who played cricket for Sussex and England in his youth. Sheppard remains the only ordained minister to have played Test cricket. He then went up to Trinity Hall, Cambridge, and played for Cambridge University

(blue 1950, 1951 and 1952; captain 1952), Sussex (captain 1953) and England. He toured as an undergraduate with Freddie Brown in 1950-51 without success. In 1952 he topped the English batting averages, scoring 2,262 runs at an average of 64.62.

David Stuart Sheppard, cricketer and priest: born Reigate, Surrey 6 March 1929; played cricket for Sussex 1947-62 (Captain 1953), England 1950-63 (Captain 1954); ordained deacon 1955, priest 1956; Assistant Curate, St Mary's, Islington 1955-57; Warden, Mayflower Centre, Canning Town 1957-69; Chairman, Evangelical Urban Training Project 1968-75; Bishop Suffragan of Woolwich 1969-75; Chairman, Peckham Settlement 1969-75; Chairman, Martin Luther King Foundation 1970-75; Chairman, Urban Ministry Project 1970-75; Bishop of Liverpool 1975-97; Vice-Chairman, Archbishop of Canterbury's Commission on Urban Priority Areas 1983-85; Chairman, Central Religious Advisory Committee for BBC and IBA 1989-93; Chairman, General Synod Board for Social Responsibility 1991-96; Chairman, Churches' Enquiry into Unemployment and the Future of Work 1995-97; created 1998 Baron Sheppard of Liverpool; President, Sussex County Cricket Club 2001-02; married 1957 Grace Isaac (one daughter); died West Kirby, Merseyside 5 March 2005.'

I had no problem passing the Common Entrance exam to my chosen public school, but having started late in life, as compared to my contemporaries, in learning Latin and French, I was placed in the lowest class, the third form. Consequently I lost a great deal of enthusiasm at Cranleigh and certainly did not excel academically, but I very much enjoyed all the sporting activities, especially athletics.

As an intermediate (i.e. 16 year old) I surprised myself and everyone else with a long jump of 19 feet 11 inches to create a new school record for the event while training for the annual Sports Day in the summer of 1953. Out of interest I checked on the situation in about 1980 and to that day my record remained unbeaten. Since then, of course, all such measurements are taken in metres, thus making precise comparisons very difficult.

One so called 'sport' which I most certainly did not enjoy one little bit, but which was compulsory during the first two years, was boxing. It turned out to be quite fortunate that, for some reason, there were only three boys in my weight category and that a few days before the competition one of them had been transferred to the sanatorium with an infectious disease. This left only me to fight against Stuart Stevenson in the final, without ever having entered the ring.

Stevenson and I both loathed boxing and hated the idea of either hurting anyone or being hurt ourselves, so we got together before the fight and made a pact not to inflict any pain on each other. As a result, we both went through two complete rounds without a serious punch being thrown, albeit with serious looks of intent on our faces and much enthusiastic dancing around each other and with a great deal of sparring and general acting going on.

The referee, a geography master, stopped the bout briefly to remonstrate with us and declare that we hadn't been taking this match seriously, so while in the umpteenth clinch we whispered to each other that it seemed we had no alternative but to put on some semblance of a fight. We decided to attempt to land gentle punches, but only to the upper body, and on no account anywhere on the head.

At the final bell it was decided that we were both wimps, but that I had apparently landed one more punch to the chest than my opponent and was therefore declared the winner. What neither of us knew was that there existed an unwritten rule that anyone winning his weight would not be required to enter any further compulsory fights while at the school. No one had thought to tell us this. Later on, Stevenson said that had he been aware of this ruling he would have made a greater effort!

Another compulsory activity at Cranleigh was for all boys to join the Combined Cadet Force, or CCF, which gave an insight into Army life and afforded opportunities to shoot a .22 rifle, discover how to strip and re-assemble a Bren gun and learn other military skills.

One side benefit of CCF training was that all participants were issued with army denims, and these were occasionally put to a use for which they had not been provided. On reflection, I realise that we must have been utterly crazy to have attempted some of the tasks we set ourselves, always at the instigation of one madcap boy called Christopher Dixon. Three or four of us would get up at about midnight, when everyone else in the dormitory was fast asleep, and don our khaki denims over our pyjamas. We would then creep outside and carry out some daredevil feat of roof climbing.

I will never forget one particular night when three of us had followed each other up a huge old Victorian drain pipe until we found ourselves straddling the apex of a pitched roof three floors from the ground. Down below we could see the dim outline of the Jims' quarters. 'Jims' was the name we all had for the dining hall waiters and other ancillary staff who, because of the isolation of the school, lived on the premises. During this specific roof-climbing session, we had been well on our way across the pitched roof to a lower building at the other end when one of my friends caught his foot on the edge of a tile and dislodged it. It slithered, not too noisily at first, down the side of the roof, but then, after being deflected outwards on reaching the guttering, it hit the corrugated iron roof of the Jims' cycle shed below.

There was an almighty clang, and almost immediately all the lights blazed out from the Jims' quarters and several windows banged open. Fortunately the occupants were all looking around at ground level to see what had caused the noise and did not immediately think of looking upwards. This gave us a valuable few seconds to hang down from the other side of the roof by the ridge tiles. Without a powerful torch, no one could see the row of fingers in the darkness.

We had to hang on like this for some minutes until the lights went out one by one and we knew that we had not been discovered. I was so frightened by this experience that I managed to persuade one of my friends into agreeing never to go roof climbing again, and we never did.

At 15 and 16, I was especially keen on tennis and fives. The school boasted four hard tennis courts and two Eton fives courts. I recollect that I must have been extremely keen on tennis at that age, because in the summer months, when the weather was reasonable, I would get up more than an hour before anyone else in the dormitory on a Sunday morning to go and practise, volleying a tennis ball against the outside brick wall of the fives courts.

Ever since my very first experience of playing with words in the 'baby go fair, not fair' episode, I had enjoyed making puns. Soon after I started at Cranleigh the punning began in earnest. One of the most amusing situations arose one afternoon in the East House changing room after a game of rugby. The conversation of some of the older boys at the other end of the room had dwelt briefly on the subject of the appearance of pubic hair on most of the younger boys. One of them noticed that, inexplicably, I had started to blush quite badly and, in Cranleigh School jargon, I was 'doing a beet' (presumably on account of a beetroot facial appearance).

'Why are you beeting, Fairhurst?' they said, and in a split second I replied 'I'm beeting about the bush'!

Another pun of which I was quite proud at the time arose during my first few days at Cranleigh. I was late for a geography lesson, as I had lost my way, and was stopped by a master who had just come out of his classroom.

'What are you doing here and where should you be?' he demanded. Without thinking, I glanced down at my itinerary for the day and said 'I'm not sure, sir, someone will have to geog. my memory!'

Although I was subjected to a small amount of bullying when I first went to Cranleigh, life for the most part was quite acceptable and I found the activities of some of my friends to be very amusing. It was clear from a very early age that one of them, Chris Gardam, was going to make a fine businessman when he left school. He was no sportsman whatsoever, and skived off almost everything energetic. Instead, he would invariably be found in the large school bicycle shed indulging in his pastime of engineering bikes from all the odd parts that had been left lying around for years. This was a very profitable hobby for him.

It was Chris who unwittingly held the record for the time taken to complete the junior cross-country run. He devised a clever route that doubled back through part of the school farm and cut out over half the course. He waited around a while in the milking shed until he felt he had got the timing about right, and remained undetected as he emerged through a hole in a hedge a few hundred yards from the finishing line. Unfortunately he had not waited long enough in the milking shed, hence the unlikely record.

Some of my friends at school were very talented musically, and when I had a spare moment I would often go to the music rooms where pupils practised with their chosen instruments. One boy was a brilliant pianist. I would greatly enjoy listening to him, especially when he played the 'rippling water' music of Debussy. This boy later won an organ scholarship to Cambridge.

The subjects I enjoyed most at school were English language, general mathematics, physics and chemistry, probably because the standard of teaching was quite high in those particular subjects. The teaching levels in other subjects ranged from poor to deplorable. It has to be remembered that in the immediate post-war period it was extremely difficult for schools to employ the right calibre of teaching staff and most people believed that if you went to an expensive Public

School then the standard of teaching would be fantastic but so far as I could see the main advantage was the much smaller class sizes. As examples, there was 'Effy' Tucker and 'Bibo' Loveday.

Effy Tucker had been a commissioned officer in a cavalry regiment during the First World War, and because much of his time had been spent in France during the conflict, he was allocated the job of Senior French Tutor. While the other masters had been content either to walk, cycle or drive to school in the mornings, Effy would invariably arrive on a horse and tether it to a drainpipe near his classroom. I never did discover why his nickname was 'Effy', though I could hazard a guess, given the amount of swearing in the Army. He had obviously been extremely well regarded, however, for on his death in 1984 I was surprised to see a long and very warming tribute to him in the *Daily Telegraph*.

It seemed 'Bibo' Loveday got his job as a teacher only because he was the brother of the Headmaster, the Reverend David Loveday. I doubt if anyone had ever known what Bibo's specialist subject was; he seemed to fill in as and when required. More often than not just before 9 am, he could be seen from the houseroom windows zig-zagging his way to school across the South Field from the general direction of the Headmaster's house, where he lived with his brother. He seemed constantly to suffer the effects of inebriation, which is why he was nicknamed 'Bibo' by the boys - as all good Latin scholars will know, this means 'I drink'.

Despite the inadequate standard of teaching in the French department, and although a very late starter in that subject, I had been interested in the language and tried very hard, especially in the period leading up to the French 'O' Level examination. It seemed my enthusiasm had paid off when I was told that I had exceeded the required pass mark for the written section. The oral section was, however, quite another matter. Shortly before entering the room where the oral was to be held, a rumour circulated that the person taking the exam was a woman. A woman? *Quel horreur*! None of us had ever heard a woman speaking French, so I entered the room with trepidation. I did manage to start off with a breezy *'Bonjour Mademoiselle'* and she seemed very pleasant, so what was I worried about?

After the customary *'asseyez vous'*, she asked me a question while looking out of the window to where a tractor was chugging up and down on the school farm. For some inexplicable reason I thought she was asking me about the *tracteur*, but she wasn't, and after that I completely lost the plot. After I left the room I realised that the word she had used was *trottoir* (pavement). I managed to work out that what she had actually said was *'pourquoi est-il pas de trottoir dans le village?'* (why isn't there a pavement in the village?). I thought she must have a screw loose asking me why there wasn't a tractor in the village when there was one in front of her plainly to be seen. Needless to say I failed the French oral, and hence the entire 'O' Level.

During my last year at school, one of the advantages of being in the sixth form was that we were allowed to keep a bicycle. The previous year, for my sixteenth birthday, my mother had bought me a racing bike. I used to cycle for miles in the holidays, and once I even managed to cover the 100 miles to Brighton and back in the day. The ride took from 9 am until 6 pm with only a stop of about half an hour on Brighton sea front. To cycle the 40 miles home at the end of term a couple of times was, by comparison, not too onerous.

On looking back, it does seem that the game of cricket must have been very high on the agenda for each of my schools, for after recording earlier the exploits of Rev. David Sheppard, an old boy of Springfield Park School, I find that the most famous of Cranleigh School's alumni was E W Swanton. *Wisden Cricketers'* Almanac recorded his passing as follows (this is an extract from the full obituary):

Ernest William Swanton, CBE, who died on January 22, 2000, aged

92, was the most influential and most durable cricket writer of the 20th century. In the columns of the Daily Telegraph, he was always E. W. Swanton; to his friends and enemies alike, he was 'Jim'. There were plenty of enemies and he was called many other names besides over the years, but he was never ignored. In the 30 years after World War II, as the Telegraph cricket correspondent, he carried an authority both in print and in person that perhaps no writer can have surpassed in any sport. And the glory never faded. In a quarter-century of nominal retirement, he continued to write columns that were read with eagerness and some trepidation in the game's committee-rooms. In an unusual moment of self-deprecation, Swanton cheerfully referred to himself as a dinosaur. In fact, he was the reverse: he hated many of the changes in cricket, but he adapted to them, and retained the ability to comment on them confidently, relevantly and pertinently without ever losing sight of cricket's eternal values - hence his enduring importance.

Swanton was a walking database, encompassing almost the whole of 20th-century cricket. He believed he had been taken in his pram to see W. G. Grace batting for London County, and vividly recalled having watched Surrey v Yorkshire in the two day Championship season of 1919, and the Oval Test of 1921. At his school, Cranleigh, he played just once for the First XI. Then - having decided not to follow his father on to the Stock Exchange - he went straight into journalism, aged 17, and graduated from a menial job at the Amalgamated Press to the Evening Standard in 1927. He soon found himself as the rugby correspondent, but wrote regularly on cricket and began reporting Tests in 1930.

Though he was imbued with the values of cricket's establishment, he was often a voice for change. He welcomed overseas players in the County Championship, and one-day cricket. ('This 'instant cricket' is very far from being a gimmick,' he wrote after the first Gillette Cup final in 1963, 'and there is a place in it for all the arts of cricket.') Swanton was appalled when Gloucestershire sacked Tom Graveney as their captain in 1960 in favour of the Old Etonian, Tom Pugh, and was an early convert to the idea of boycotting South Africa over apartheid. He had become uneasy on the

1956-57 tour, and his strong connection with the West Indies - he led two private tours there and had a holiday home on Barbados - helped propel him into the progressive camp. He abhorred sledging, coloured clothing and the four-day Championship.

It was his personal style that brought him the most detractors, and he did not always treat social inferiors graciously. The historian Rowland Bowen rechristened him Pomponius Ego. Ray Illingworth remarked that he was too snobbish to travel in the same car as his chauffeur. Swanton reported only rarely from the more down-market county grounds: he is believed to have visited Leicester and Northampton only once each, and these occasions had to be treated like state visits, with elaborate preparations so that both he and his amanuensis would not have to endure routine privations. He expected a gin and tonic on cue. Once, when told the bar had run out of ice, he responded irritably, 'Didn't you tell them who it was for?' This is a well-sourced story. The Telegraph sub-editors were not allowed to change a solitary comma of his copy, and they waited gleefully for his mistakes. These were, however, infrequent. His excesses were softened by both his belated marriage, in 1958 - to Ann Carbutt, a widow and an accomplished pianist and golfer - and the passing years. He was a much nicer man in old age. As Lord Runcie said at his funeral: 'The solemnity, prickliness and, yes, arrogance that were part of the serious perfectionist gave way to the gentle self-mockery and kindly wisdom which never seemed to fail us.'

After retirement from the Telegraph in 1975, he still seemed ubiquitous. He wrote regularly in the paper and for The Cricketer, where he was editorial director from 1967 to 1988, and eventually acquired the unlikely magazine title of president. He became president of Kent in 1981. He chaired the MCC committee that helped build the indoor school at Lord's, and was chairman of the arts and libraries committee, taking an abiding interest in the treasures of Lord's. Only the presidency of MCC and a knighthood eluded him, and he probably thought wistfully about both.

My main hobby at 14 and 15 was making model aircraft from specially-manufactured kits. These started with rubber-powered free flight models with wingspans ranging from three feet to five feet, but my pride and joy was a diesel-powered free flight Keil Kraft 'Ladybird' 44" wingspan model which I fitted with a 1.00 cc ED Bee diesel engine. When I emigrated to New Zealand three years later, this aircraft came with me, carefully packed in a sturdy plywood vacuum cleaner box.

It is therefore probably the only model aircraft of the 1950s that has circumnavigated the Earth. Some 40 years later the plane had lost all its original dope-strengthened tissue and for many years hung in pride of place in my study. In August 2011 I donated it to a large specialist model shop in Maidstone, where the manager was delighted to arrange for it to be displayed, together with a printout of its complete history.

Keil Kraft 'Ladybird' Free Flight Model Aircraft

Towards the end of my time at Cranleigh, I played wing three-quarter in the 2nd XV rugby team and enjoyed many games against other schools, including St Paul's and Mill Hill in London and Brighton College. This was brought to a halt during a game at home against Hurstpierpoint College when I received a serious injury while lying on the ground protecting the ball for my forwards to heel out to the rest of the three quarter line. An opposing forward, whether from an excess of zeal or pure vindictiveness, hacked away blindly in the general area of the ball but in fact kicked me so severely in the groin that I was whisked off the field to the sanatorium. This injury was to change the course of my life.

I left school in December 1954 with six good 'O' level passes, and it didn't take me too long to secure my first job, as a trainee quantity surveyor. I started work in January 1955 at the Fleet Street offices of Franklin & Andrews, a small firm of quantity surveyors with six partners and a staff of about 20. Today, more than half a century on they are still trading under that name, but now they are part of Mott McDonald with a total staff of 14,500 working in 120 countries. The group is one of the world's leading construction economists, but continues to retain its core skill of quantity surveying, operating across all economic sectors.

I started work at a very menial level, one of my tasks being to arrive at the office before any of the senior staff and replenish the drinking water jugs in the partners' offices and the toilet rolls in their toilets at the unbelievably low salary, even for those days, of £7 per month. 'Squaring dims' and 'taking off dimensions' soon became second nature to me, and with my 'O' levels making it unnecessary for me to sit for the preliminary quantity surveying examinations, it was not long before I sat for and passed the First Exam and was duly enrolled for the Intermediate Exam.

However, that injury on the rugby field soon put a spanner in the works. Within six months of joining Franklin & Andrews, I collapsed in agony and was rushed to Farnborough Hospital. After a fairly major operation I was told that I might never have children. On top of my injury I was suffering from jaundice. I had to remain in hospital for just over five weeks, followed by a week of convalescence in a hotel in Eastbourne. My parents discovered what had happened on returning to England from a six-month holiday in South Africa, and were aghast.

At that time the family home was Pelham Lodge, the Edwardian House in Bickley mentioned earlier in this book, where my father had arranged for a hard tennis court to be constructed at the bottom of the garden. I was very keen on tennis, as I mentioned earlier, and as I recovered I would practise serving for hours.

Mainly as a result of their own experiences of the recuperative powers of time spent on the ocean waves, my parents suggested that what I really needed was a long sea voyage. As it happened my tennis coach, Ernie Kelly, had just emigrated to New Zealand with his wife, Minnie. Ernie had decided to sell up and emigrate to take up the offer of a job coaching and working in a large sports store in Queen Street, Auckland. My father suggested I should jump on board a ship and join them. That way I could recover from my illness on the voyage and improve my tennis skills when I got to the other side of the world.

It so happened that I was expecting to receive my call-up papers for National Service any day, which may have had something to do with my decision to take him up on the offer. But that was not the main reason for my enthusiasm for this plan. Ever since I had been quite small, when I would enjoy many hours playing happily with my toy farm, there had lurked an ambition at the back of my mind to work on a sheep farm. It was hard to think of a better place to do this than New Zealand.

Although the ultimate intention was unspoken, it was quite clear to all concerned that I was actually proposing to leave the family behind and make a new life for myself in New Zealand.

CHAPTER TWO

To the other side of the world

So it was that on a bright early September morning in 1955, I was delivered by car to Tilbury Docks in London to board MS *Rangitata* of the New Zealand Shipping Line. The good ship *Rangitata* was bound for Wellington via Las Palmas in the Canary Islands, Kingston in Jamaica, the island of Curaçao, the Panama Canal and Pitcairn Island in the Pacific.

After bidding my parents farewell at the dockside, I leaned over the port rail as the *Rangitata* slipped its moorings and waved from the promenade deck until they were completely out of sight. I suddenly felt very alone in the world, much as I had seven years earlier when my father had driven away after depositing me for the first time at my new prep school. However I soon came down to earth and realised that I had everything to look forward to. I was at the start of a wonderful voyage to the other side of the world.

I was directed to a small but beautifully-appointed cabin, Number B2. A year later, I learned from a colleague in New Zealand who worked with the line, this cabin was occupied by the recently-resigned British Prime Minister Anthony Eden following the Suez Canal débâcle.

Looking back now, I recognize how very fortunate I was to be afforded the opportunity of such an incredible adventure at the age of only 18. In those days most ocean liners operated a two-class system, and the *Rangitata* was no exception. As a first-class passenger,

I was not permitted to venture into the second-class area of the ship, and likewise, they were not allowed into the first-class area. However, from the rear of the upper decks I was able watch the second-class passengers splashing happily in their pool below, and it seemed that they were all having a much more jolly time than the generally older and more staid first-class passengers.

New Zealand Shipping Company's Rangitata

For passengers fortunate enough to have been allocated principal cabins, it was the custom in those days to be invited to dine at the captain's table; it still is with some. I found myself each evening of the five-week voyage enjoying the privilege of dining with three other passengers, together with the captain and one of his senior officers.

The officers took turns at dinner depending on their responsibilities, and on occasion the captain's duties kept him on the bridge. My three fellow passengers were Mrs Rose Harcourt, Andy Broadbent and Tim Foss. Rose Harcourt was a very refined lady in her sixties who had recently lost her husband and was now bent on forging a new life for herself in New Zealand with her daughter, who

34

had emigrated about a year earlier under the assisted passage scheme.

She was a kindly soul, and despite what could have been a lonely situation for her, she was quite jolly and a great asset to the small party. Andy Broadbent had been 'something in the City' and was now heading for Christchurch, in the South Island, where he was to take up a senior post with the Bank of New Zealand.

Tim Foss was about my own age and had just celebrated his 18th birthday. Tim and I hit it off immediately, partly because we were from similar backgrounds. He had attended Clifton College, where he had fared pretty dismally with his 'A' level results. As a boy, he too had had aspirations about becoming a farmer like his father, but his father had become ill and unable to continue with the family farm in Dorset. As a result, his father had decided to sell the farm and send Tim to New Zealand, where his uncle managed a large sheep station.

It was very fortunate for me that Tim was keen on all types of games and sports. We were in our element on board ship and spent a great deal of time playing deck tennis, shuffleboard, table tennis and both deck quoits and bucket quoits. After a few days at sea one of us discovered a large, old and very battered pewter egg cup which evidently had been thrown out by the galley staff. We used this to great effect when staging our various competitions, and about once a week we would hold a mini-Olympics for a selection of games and one of us would carry off the title of Rangitata Victor Ludorum.

The voyage was fairly uneventful until we reached the Panama Canal, apart from an incident just after our first port of call at Las Palmas in the Canary Islands. Attracted by the very low cost of alcoholic drinks in Las Palmas, I purchased a bottle of local brandy, or 'firewater' as my colleagues on the ship called it. After dinner on the night we left Las Palmas I suppose I must have indulged in a few brandies too many, for my friends suggested I had drunk too much and advised me to go and lie down. However, as is often the case with people who have drunk to excess, I was adamant that I was perfectly sober. To prove the point I proceeded to climb up on to the ship's highly-varnished wooden rail and embarked on a very carefully balanced walk along it for about 20 feet.

To the onlookers, of course, this appeared to be much more dangerous than it really was; for one thing, the rail was about five inches wide and for another I was conscious all the time of leaning slightly in towards the ship so that, should I have fallen, I would almost certainly have landed on the deck and not gone over the side. The next day, of course, I fully appreciated what a foolhardy act I had committed.

Ports of call to take on fuel and provisions in the Caribbean included Kingston in Jamaica and the island of Curaçao, but what I was really looking forward to was the experience of sailing through the Panama Canal. In fact the excitement was tempered to some degree by a visit to Panama City. I will always remember it as the most disgustingly filthy place I have ever visited, and that includes a town in Tunisia where heads and parts of heads of dead animals slaughtered by a butcher had been left lying in the fly-ridden gutter.

After we had negotiated the Panama Canal there was always interesting wildlife to be seen. Of special fascination for me were the flying fish to be found in the South Pacific. I noted that their streamlined torpedo shape helped them to gather enough underwater speed to break the surface, and their large wing-like pectoral fins then enabled them to become airborne. Another passenger told me that flying fish are thought to have evolved their remarkable gliding ability in order to escape predators, and I saw many of them reaching heights of about three feet out of the water and then gliding for quite long distances, sometimes in excess of 200 yards. Other sights to be long remembered were the soaring albatrosses, and of course the ever-popular schools of dolphins.

Having stopped to refuel and take on provisions at Pitcairn Island in the Pacific, the Rangitata arrived at Wellington in mid-October 1955. Some friends of Ernie Kelly had arranged to meet me off the ship, and they kindly gave me a quick tour by car of the city of 'Windy Wellington' before continuing on to my final destination of Auckland.

My only luggage was a small suitcase for overnight use and a massive cabin trunk in which were stored all my worldly possessions (including my beloved Keil Kraft 'Ladybird' aeroplane – complete with small diesel engine – which I had built at home three years previously). I had been warned that the train journey from Wellington to Auckland, while covering some of the North Island's most attractive scenery, was quite a frightening experience, and that I should make the trip by plane with my cabin trunk being sent on in advance by rail. This was to be my very first experience of air travel.

The plane was a twin-engined De Havilland Dove with nine other passengers on board. I had not been told that it would fly over the thermal region of New Zealand's North Island. We were flying at only about 5000 feet, and some of the scenery was quite spectacular.

I was beginning to enjoy this first experience of air travel - until the thermal region was reached. Without any warning, the plane suddenly rose straight up in the sky about 20 feet and then, just as suddenly, dropped immediately by about the same amount. This frightening experience was repeated on at least two more occasions until the plane was clear of the area.

Auckland's airport at the time, Whenuapai (it means 'good land' in Maori) was quite capable of handling non-jet aircraft and did so all through the 1950s, but in the 1960s this particular airport reverted to military use only. Whenuapai Airport was only about ten miles from the city centre, so I took a taxi there and found a small hotel within my price range, where I decided to stay for two nights.

Soon after arrival I bought a copy of the Auckland Star, the local evening paper, and returned to my room to study the job advertisements. There were two possibilities that caught my eye, and I duly noted the telephone numbers. The next morning I walked to the railway station to collect my cabin trunk, but by the time I had sorted out the paperwork and emerged from the station there were no taxis to be seen anywhere. Resourceful as ever, I managed to hoist the trunk onto my back and trudge back to the hotel in the city centre.

The following morning, as pre-arranged in England, Ernie arrived to collect me and take me to his new home, a small bungalow on Auckland's North Shore. We had to take a car ferry across, for in those days there was no harbour bridge.

Ernie and Minnie made me very welcome, but they made it clear almost at once that their financial position was such that they would be unable to accommodate me for more than three nights. They were happy, however, to let me use their telephone, and I made an appointment for an interview the next day with one of the firms whose advertisements I had seen in the Auckland Star.

It was a small, old-established family firm of customs agents called Shirley W Hill & Co Ltd. To my surprise, it transpired that Shirley was a man. He had founded the firm many years before and was now in his late seventies. The managing director was his son, and he seemed to be very impressed with my educational qualifications. He offered me the job as an office junior on the spot. I was to assist William, who was a few years older and had joined the firm straight from Auckland Grammar School four years earlier.

I found the work quite interesting, as it took me out of the office a good deal. However much of it was of a mundane nature involving the presentation of bills of lading at the Customs House on behalf of various clients who employed the firm's services for the importation of a miscellany of goods, such as pianos for the Hamilton Piano Company. On occasion the work also involved going on board various ships, notably those of the Blue Star Line, to check goods against the bills of lading.

On one occasion, as I was passing a bonded dockside warehouse, I heard loud noises of merriment floating on the afternoon air and looked inside to find out what was going on. Apparently a large case containing 24 bottles of Drambuie had been slightly damaged in the unloading process, and a bottle in the corner of the container had cracked and was leaking out on the floor. A customs officer had spotted this and declared the whole container a write-off. This meant that the remaining 23 bottles were 'up for grabs', and several officers and customs agents' clerks were having an impromptu party on the proceeds. When I appeared I was offered a bottle, probably to keep me quiet. I thankfully accepted it and took it back to my lodgings where, taking a tiny sip every few days, I made it last several weeks.

After three nights as the guest of Ernie and Minnie, I managed to find accommodation in an old tenement building on the south side of the harbour, which made it much easier to get to work. The tram was the normal method of transport around Auckland for those without a car. The distance from the city centre was measured in sections, and buildings outside the centre were said to be so many sections out of town. I later found this use of the word 'section' to be quite confusing, for it was also employed in describing a plot of land, and a house or bungalow was said to have been constructed on a 'large section' or a 'small section'. If it was in a large rear garden where it was approached by a driveway between two houses, this was referred to as a 'panhandle section'.

My lodgings consisted of one room in this very large Victorian terraced property of about 12 bed-sitting rooms. Linen and towels were provided, but there were no cooking facilities other than a very old and dirty gas oven at the end of a corridor one floor down, shared by all the other tenants. At the other end of this corridor was a bathroom, also shared by all the building's occupants.

In response to the lack of suitable cooking facilities, I went out and purchased a Judge Brand electric jug. For some reason, conventional electric kettles were not very popular at that time in New Zealand and almost everyone used electric jugs. I used mine for almost everything, including boiling an egg, and on many occasions my evening meal consisted of cold meat or fish from a tin with potatoes and cauliflower or peas, all boiled up in my electric jug.

I was able to vary my diet with baked beans or sardines on toast, as my room boasted a small gas fire which also served as the only source of heat when the weather became chilly.

I could not afford to go out for any entertainment; anyway, other than the cinema there were only the milk bars to frequent. Even if I fancied the occasional beer, anyone with any sense would keep well clear of the drinking houses. In those days these establishments were very uninviting places, decorated for the most part in white tiles and resembling the décor of public conveniences.

One of the most unattractive aspects was the way the beer was served by the use of a pressurized hose pipe. The bartender was able to save time by lining up half a dozen glasses in a row and then simply spraying the nozzle along the line. Their licences did not permit the sale of alcohol later than early evening, as a result of which people (almost always men) would come out of work and down as many beers as they could before closing time. Drunks were often to be seen in the road between 6 pm and 8 pm.

My personal entertainment was provided by a second-hand portable gramophone player and a second-hand radio, both of which I had managed to acquire for less than £5. The radio stations were very strange to me. I had been used to the Home Service and the Light Programme at home, but the stations in New Zealand had names like 1ZB and 2YA.

I was quite unaccustomed to the continual interruption of programmes by advertisements. There was one particular advert which was played so often that it still comes readily to mind after more than half a century. It was for Four Square Stores, the equivalent of the Spar grocery stores in England at the time. The advertising jingle ran as follows (sung of course in a New Zealand accent):

Hi there, ho there, hop along to Four Square
Four Square, that's where you will get the best fare.
Buyers, savers, variety galore
When you go and get your shopping at the Four Square Store.

I stayed in this bedsit for about three months, and during the whole of that time I can only recall eating one conventionally-cooked hot meal with meat. This was when another tenant, a middle-aged woman, took pity on me and told me that on the forthcoming Sunday it was her turn to use the oven and she was going to have a roast joint. She said that if I went out and bought myself a small joint of meat she would put it in the oven with hers. This I duly did, but I forgot to get any vegetables, so I ate my roast lamb with baked beans.

My lodging house was in Ponsonby, the poorest and most run-down area of Auckland. However the rent was only £2 a week out of my £5 weekly salary, and it was only two sections to work by tram, so I was in no hurry to move somewhere else.

Unfortunately I was being woken up more and more often during the night by the scratching and scampering of rats and mice, and was losing more and more sleep. I felt I could put up with having mice for companions, but rats were something else. When they started appearing by the dustbins in the rear yard I reckoned it was time to move on.

Ironically, 50 years later in 2007, I learned from a New Zealander visiting England on holiday that Ponsonby had been fully gentrified and was now one of the most sought-after residential areas of Auckland.

I was being coached at tennis quite seriously by Ernie Kelly, and I was surprised how much my game had improved as a result. Ernie told me one day that a scout representing the New Zealand Davis Cup Squad had watched me in action one day and said that I had the sort of talent that could lead to my playing in this famous tournament within a few years. Although this sounded a bit far-fetched to me at the time, it must be remembered that there was a dearth of tennis talent in New Zealand at the time. In Australia, by contrast, Frank Sedgeman was at his best, and had reached the 1956 US final. The Aussies had a couple of particularly talented young players by the names of Lew Hoad and Ken Rosewall (Hoad beat Rosewall in the 1956 Wimbledon men's final).

Apart from tennis, I loved to relax with the fishing gear I had bought at Wiseman's Sports Store in Queen Street, where Ernie Kelly worked. I caught several snappers from the rocks in Auckland Harbour. These fish were so abundant that rumour had it you didn't even need bait to catch them – you just threw in a line with a hook on the end and pulled them out. It never happened to me.

Early one evening, as I was contemplating seeking fresh lodgings, I was walking down Queen Street in the city centre when I noticed a man approaching me wearing what appeared to be an Old Cranleighan tie. I thought he must be an impostor, so I tackled him. He said his name was Cosmo Davies and he was indeed an Old Cranleighan who had come to live in New Zealand with his family in 1950. He was 26 and married and lived on a dairy farm a few miles south of Auckland at a place called Manurewa, where he was the farm manager.

Also living with him and his wife was a very old friend of his from England who was an old Clifton College boy (after Tim on the Rangitata, this was the second Clifton old boy I had met in less than a year). The farm provided Cosmo with a reasonable-sized house, and as he had no children there would be room for me if I would like to come and stay. He said he knew his wife would be really pleased, not least because the farm manager's job was not particularly well paid and the extra cash would come in handy.

I went with him to visit the house and meet Cosmo's wife. She was delighted to have me as a house guest, and in fact to live as one of the family, so I moved in.

During my time at Cosmo's farm I enjoyed life immensely and found myself volunteering for various jobs, including using the brand new stainless steel milking system which entailed getting up at 4 am. I was able to assist with a major project involving the installation of an electric fencing system around a five-acre field. The four of us in the house got on really well, and despite the obvious lack of funds we managed several days out (where the petrol was about the only expense) in Cosmo's open tourer, a very old Auburn. I had never heard of this American car manufacturer before – apparently it had ceased trading before 1940 - but it served our purpose very well and on a couple of occasions, on deserted roads, I was allowed to drive for short distances despite not having a driving licence. I remember that one of our trips took us to the West Coast near Auckland, to a small seaside resort called Piha, where there was a beautiful beach. The sand was very soft and fine in texture but jet black in colour, another reminder of the time when, millions of years before, the whole island had been volcanic.

On another very memorable occasion we all went to the Ardmore motor racing circuit not far from Auckland, the site for the 1956 New Zealand Grand Prix. This race would, apparently, always be remembered as the Stirling Moss Benefit Meeting. Following the end-to-end win of Prince Bira of Thailand in the previous year, racing conditions had been revised for the 1956 race. No prizes were given for leading each lap, and as a result the final would be shorter.

Before the race even began, most people had already conceded victory to Stirling Moss, who would be driving his Maserati 250S fitted with Dunlop alloy wheels and the latest state-of-the-art Dunlop disc brakes in place of the original large Maserati drums. Already his fame was such that it had seemed all the car had to do was hold together and Moss would bring it home. He was of course the winner, and through a connection with of one of Cosmo's friends I was permitted to have my photograph taken after the race sitting in his car. Unfortunately that particular photograph has been mislaid during one of my many moves, but I do have a picture of Stirling in his Maserati.

Stirling Moss in his Maserati 250S during the 1956 N Z Grand Prix

However, the most exciting event for me that year was when I was privileged to watch an international rugby match which no one at home in England at the time could have dreamed of seeing. It was an unforgettable match between the home side, the All Blacks, against South Africa's Springboks. In the four-match test series of that year, New Zealand had led narrowly by two matches to one, and the final test at the Eden Park ground in Auckland would decide which of these two great sides was the superior.

After a very exciting game, the All Blacks came out as the winners 11-5 to take the series 3-1. It was their first-ever series victory against South Africa on New Zealand soil.

In October 2011 while on a Mediterranean cruise, I was able to see the final of the 2011 Rugby World Cup on the ship's large outdoor TV screen. I was very pleased to see that the venue for this epic match was the same historic ground at Eden Park where I had seen the All Blacks winning 55 years earlier. New Zealand beat France by the narrowest of margins (8-7).

I was entranced by the very intimidating Maori Haka performed before the match, and several months later, while completing my New Zealand National Service, I asked one of my Maori colleagues for the actual words used and the actions of the haka. I was told that the words used on the rugby pitch were:

Taringa whakarongo!
Kia rite! Kia rite! Kia mau! Hi!
Kia whakawhenua au i ahau!
Hi aue, hi!
Ko Aotearoa e ngunguru nei!
Au, au, aue ha!
Ko Kapa o Pango e ngunguru nei!
Au, au, aue ha!
I ahaha!
Ka tu te Ihiihi
Ka tu te Wanawana
Ki runga ki te rangi,
E tu iho nei, tu iho nei, hi!

CHAPTER TWO

Ponga ra!
Kapa o Pango, aue hi!
Ponga ra!
Kapa o Pango, aue hi, ha!

The words mean, in summary: *Let your ears listen, get ready, let me become one with the land. New Zealand is rumbling! The team in black is rumbling! Stand up to the fear, stand up to the terror. To the sky above! Fight up there, high up there! The shadows fall, darkness falls! Team in black, yeah!*

* * * * * * * * *

In the aftermath of the war Spraycraft, my father's little painting contracting business, had been going through a very difficult trading period. Almost all the work had been for various Government departments, mainly the Air Ministry and War Department, and by 1953 there was very little work about because of a moratorium on Government spending.

The Government had spent huge sums on building reconstruction work from 1946 to 1952, and the money was no longer available, nor would it be for the foreseeable future. Therefore my father had no choice but to complete his existing contracts and cease trading until conditions improved.

My letters home must have been full of enthusiasm about my new life, because in 1956 my parents decided to give up their life in the UK and join me in New Zealand. They would sell the house, take my two younger brothers, John and David, away from school, and come out to join me with the intention of staying for good. With so little work, it was not too difficult for my father to pay off the few employees still on the payroll and cease trading.

One day I received an air mail letter to say that my family were all setting sail on a sister ship of the *Rangitata* called the *Rangitoto*, and they would need accommodation on arrival. So I left Cosmo's farm in South Auckland and rented a four-bedroomed house on Auckland's North Shore in a district called Takapuna.

At this point my father had firmly decided to live in New Zealand for the rest of his life. I believe this decision was influenced to some extent by his old partner, Freddie Love, emigrating to South Africa ten years earlier, as he had been hankering after moving abroad ever since Freddie's departure. Before leaving England, therefore, my father had arranged to transfer all his savings, quite a considerable sum, to the Bank of New Zealand.

And then came a body blow. When my family had already set sail and were on the high seas, the New Zealand Government introduced a new law. It stated that, with immediate effect, anyone bringing funds into the country would be unable to repatriate this money, and if they remained in the country for longer than six months therefore would have to invest it in New Zealand.

My father was dumbfounded by this news. It meant that from the date when the *Rangitoto* docked in Auckland, he had only a few months to decide whether or not to stay for good, despite the fact that both John and David had been offered places at Auckland Grammar School. This was a dilemma he had not anticipated when he had set sail. Having discussed the problem with all of us, my parents decided that there really was no alternative but to go straight back to England.

My father gave two additional reasons for the change of plan which he said had finally tipped the balance. In my view they were both extremely petty. The first was that the succulent joints of New Zealand lamb he had enjoyed in England were not available to the general public in NZ, as all the best lamb was sent for export and the nearest available equivalent was hogget, or second-year sheep (before they became mutton). The second, even sillier, reason was the choice of cheese in the shops. Whereas in England there was a reasonable choice of this commodity (blue cheese, Stilton, Cheddar, etc.), in New Zealand there were only two types, known simply as mild and tasty.

Good-quality cars were very sought after in New Zealand at that time and my father was able to sell his beloved Armstrong Siddeley Sapphire and my mother her Austin A35, which they had brought with them on the ship, for a considerable profit, which helped to defray some of the costs of the voyage. We talked about my joining them on the return trip to England, but as I pointed out to my father, only three days earlier I had received my call-up papers for New Zealand National Service and had been given instructions on how to get to Papakura Camp for basic training in the Royal New Zealand Artillery. However, I did not see myself having a future in New Zealand after that.

'I've worked and lived here for some months now' I said. 'I know what I would really be suited to, and that's a career in business. What about this for an idea – if you agree to restart Spraycraft, I'll make arrangements to sail home as soon as I can after my National Service'.

So that plan was decided upon, and the family set sail for England knowing that I would be joining them in a few months.

The attractive three-bedroomed brick bungalow which my parents had purchased in Mission Bay now had to be sold, and I would have to seek fresh accommodation before joining up. Fortunately my parents had kept in touch with a lovely couple called Perrin who they had met on the outgoing voyage. Ken and Vi Perrin had a four-year-old son, Robbie, and lived in a pleasant modern timber-framed house on the outskirts of Auckland. When we approached them about the possibility of my living with them they were both very glad to oblige, not least as it would give them some welcome extra cash.

Although Ken had come out to New Zealand to take up a managerial position with the firm he had worked for since leaving school, London and Liverpool Insurance Company, I believe his remuneration package was not all that handsome and his lovely wife Vi had not been able to work for some years since the birth of their son.

I very much enjoyed my few months of living with Ken and Vi, and we had some really good times together. Robbie was a great little lad, and I vowed that if ever in the future I was lucky enough to have such a good-looking little boy with blond hair I would call him Robbie.

Eventually the day came for me to report at the designated camp to commence National Service. The Papakura Military Camp was, and remains to this day, an important New Zealand Army military camp located about an hour's drive South of Auckland in the suburb of Papakura North. Established on the outskirts of Papakura Town Centre in 1940, it is now the National Headquarters for the New Zealand Special Air Service.

When I arrived at the gatehouse on a very hot and humid day, it looked as if little had changed in the intervening 17 years. The facilities were quite basic and I was allocated a bed in a Nissen hut which housed nineteen other beds, one of which was a spare.

Despite my obvious 'Pom' accent, my immediate neighbours were very friendly. On one side was a young man who seemed to be a few years older than the rest of us, who were all about 18 years of age. It transpired that he was a teacher from Wellington who was 24 years old and he had agreed for his National Service to be postponed for some years while he completed his teacher training course.

On the other side of me was a Maori boy who had only recently left school, and it was he who taught me to strum the ukulele I had bought second hand a few weeks before joining up. He also taught me several Maori words and phrases, including the whole of the Maori Haka and the longest place name in the world (a village in southern Hawke's Bay north of Wellington), called

Taumatawhakatangihangakoauauotamateaturipukakapikimaungahoronuk upokaiwhenuakitanatahu. This is the name of a hill 1001 feet high, close to the small town of Porangahau. This proved to be too long a name for me, and apparently for most people, to remember, but I managed to learn by heart the abbreviated version, which is Taumatawhakatangihangakoauauotamateapokiwhenuakitenatahu.

This place name, he informed me, was the longest in the English-speaking world and several letters longer than the famous longest name in Wales, *Llanfairpwllgwyngyllgogerychwyrndrobwllllantysiliogogogoch.*

The very first day of training will always stick in my memory, for it was then that the sergeant in charge of weapon training brought out a Bren gun and explained how to strip it and put it all together again. He lined us all up and told us to copy what he had done and see if we could master it within a specified time limit.

In an earlier chapter of this book I mentioned that it was compulsory while at Cranleigh School to join the CCF (Combined Cadet Force), which gave the opportunity to learn how to strip and re-assemble a Bren gun, so when it came to my turn I was twice as fast as anyone else. I think it was on the strength of this that within two weeks I was promoted from Gunner to Lance Bombardier and put in charge of the hut of 18 young soldiers. Then after a further month I was promoted again to Bombardier (the equivalent of Corporal).

When basic training was completed I was given quite a responsibility by being put in charge of the three large guns overlooking Auckland's Waitemata Harbour, which entailed issuing orders to each gun in turn for the three main functions of Load, Make Ready and Fire. I was probably only given this job, at least in part, because of what they called my 'clear English accent'!

We had very little time for relaxation in the Army, as the National Service period was very short and we had much to learn in only a few months. One pastime I was able to enjoy, however, was when Tony the teacher, together with another lad and myself, regularly went down into a large empty concrete bunker we had discovered, which we found made an ideal echo chamber. We would sing in harmony various songs Tony knew and which suited our voices, but one song in particular was our speciality, and that was a top ten hit at the time – the Everly Brothers singing *All I have to do is dream*. I recollect that once, when one of our colleagues found out what we got up to when we disappeared, with raucous encouragement from several others, he made us sing to them in the hut, but the harmony and the sound we made bore little resemblance to what we had achieved in our 'echo chamber'.

One day when I was due to be demobilized from my stint in the Royal NZ Artillery, I was asked to go and see the Commanding Officer. I wondered what I had done wrong. He smiled at me when I entered his office, which surprised me as he had always looked so stern before. He bade me to sit down and asked if I had ever considered making the Army my career, because if I were to sign on for nine years he could pretty well guarantee that I would enter with a commission, as a second lieutenant, from the outset.

I replied that I felt very flattered that he thought so highly of me but that I had made my mind up that I would return to England very soon. He wished me good luck for the future and said he thought I would do well in whatever career I chose.

I returned to live with Ken and Vi and go back to my job in the Customs House until a berth became available on a ship bound for England. Then my travel agent in Queen Street told me that a ship called the Southern Cross had a free berth and would sail from Wellington in mid-January.

I had seen very little of New Zealand during my stay, the main reason being lack of funds. I did not fancy a return air flight to Wellington, but in any event my financial state precluded this option. Anyway, I knew I would love to see Rotorua and Lake Taupo before leaving, and of course this venue would be on the route taken by the train.

After saying my goodbyes to everyone I knew in Auckland, I took my cabin trunk and caught the train south, which stopped at Rotorua. This was truly an amazing experience. The first thing that surprised me, and for which I was unprepared, was the awful bad-egg stench of hydrogen sulphide pervading the air.

A boiling mud pool in Rotorua

A Rotorua geyser

I was only in Rotorua for two nights, but during that time I was able to see quite of lot of the Maori traditions, such as the ladies and girls performing a *poi* dance. I learned that a traditional Maori *poi* consists of two flax strings attached to weighted balls of moss and other materials, while modern *poi* are often made with synthetic materials, rather than natural ones. The strings are swung rhythmically while dancing or storytelling and I learned that the traditions surrounding Maori *poi* vary from tribe to tribe within New Zealand.

Maori ladies performing a poi dance

On the second day I joined a small group for a boat trip on Lake Taupo, world renowned for its trout fishing. But despite the millions of fish it was reputed to contain I never saw one, and nobody on our boat managed to catch anything.

During my last evening in the lakeside hotel I was having a drink in the bar when I was joined by an American tourist who had been travelling extensively in Australia and New Zealand. We were up talking until the bar closed, and I found him to be a most interesting man. It was during our long conversation, when I was telling him of my plans once I returned to England, that he did his best to persuade me to go and live in the USA. There, he assured me, with my education and ambition to succeed in business, I would have a fantastic opportunity to accomplish all I dreamed of.

I recall telling him that it was a nice thought, but I had promised my father I was going home to England to assist him in restarting his business, and I intended to keep that promise. But I never forgot that conversation and often wondered over the years if I could have enjoyed a more rewarding life in America.

In mid-January 1957 I set sail for England on a Shaw Savill & Albion line ship, the Southern Cross. We had a poignant farewell from the Wellington dockside, with a Maori choir singing Now is the Hour in their own language (Po Ataru), and I later learned that this ended up as New Zealand's first million-selling record. There were streamers everywhere and much shedding of tears. It was a scene never to be forgotten.

My father had kindly paid for the first-class ticket out in 1955, but this time the cost was down to me, so the best I could manage was to share a second-class cabin with three others. My cabin mates were a farmer from Yorkshire who was returning home after having failed to make a go of it in the South Island and a father with his 10-year-old son from the Nottingham area, who was returning home because his wife was homesick. She had to share another cabin with three other females. They were all pleasant enough companions, but understandably the conditions were extremely cramped in our little cabin with two lower and two upper bunks.

Shaw Savill's Southern Cross

The first port of call on the homeward voyage was Sydney, and I was able to go ashore and explore the north part of the city, having been able to walk over Sydney Harbour Bridge.

The next stop was at Melbourne, followed two days later by a 24-hour mooring at Adelaide. Both these cities were very clean and smart and in Melbourne I was able to remind myself of my visit to Australia by purchasing a boomerang, which still has pride of place on my study wall.

The passage to the last of our scheduled stops in Australia, the Port of Fremantle for the City of Perth in Western Australia, took us through the Great Australian Bight and some very heavy seas. Many passengers had never experienced anything like it, and there was much suffering from sea-sickness. In Perth several passengers from Wellington disembarked, and a crowd of young and very friendly Australians joined the ship for the journey to Southampton.

The ukulele which I had acquired in New Zealand now came into its own, and a crowd of us young ones would invariably gather on the high games deck in the balmy evenings after dinner and sing along to my playing.

We saw a great deal of wildlife on the 4800-mile journey across the South Indian Ocean, including whales, dolphins, flying fish and several species of rare sea birds. At one point on the long passage from Australia to South Africa I was told by one of the officers that our ship was over a thousand miles from the nearest point of land, and I suddenly became very frightened. The strangest thing of all was that in this part of the ocean, so far from any land mass, there were no waves to speak of – just a massive swell. For some strange reason the *Southern Cross* did not roll from side to side or pitch from end to end in the conventional manner, but actually 'pitch rolled' diagonally from off the port bow to the starboard stern for the entire five-week voyage.

While the ship was dealing with this huge swell, this movement was quite unnerving. When you were standing on the top deck in the massive swell the ship, albeit a 20,000-ton liner, seemed an insignificant speck on the sea's surface. I will never forget the experience of looking around at the top of the swell, when you could see for what seemed to be fifty miles or more. Then, after a period of about twenty seconds, you would sink lower and lower to the bottom of the swell and all you could see, about five miles away, was the near horizon encircling the ship at an angle of some twenty degrees above you.

After many days at sea, the ship eventually reached the Natal capital of Durban. This was in early February, the hottest time of year in South Africa, but in Durban in particular it was also extremely humid owing to the prevailing winds coming ashore from the Indian Ocean.

After disembarkation I took a short rickshaw ride, and then, with a few of my new-found Australian friends, we took a trip outside the city to see a typical native kraal with large families living together in modest-sized mud huts. One of our party was a very pretty Australian girl who was travelling to London to train as a ballet dancer, and I asked her to join me one night in visiting a night club in Durban. We had a lovely evening, but as the area looked a bit dodgy we took a taxi back to the ship. I kissed her on the cheek as I escorted her to her cabin. I later heard that she thought there was something the matter with me, as I did not ask her if I could join her in her cabin for the night!

After Durban we called for a short stop at Cape Town, but the weather was very cloudy so there was little point in arranging a trip up Table Mountain. The only other port of call on the way to Southampton was Las Palmas in the Canary Islands.

While we were on the ship, it had been arranged that about a dozen of us would meet up a week after arriving in the UK at the Prospect of Whitby, a very well known pub in London's East End – even the Australians had heard of it. Although it was pleasant enough to see again the crowd of young people who had been my companions for over a month, somehow there seemed to be something missing, and the conversation became quite stilted. We departed, wishing each other well for the future, but making no arrangements for a future gathering.

CHAPTER THREE

Joining the family business

When I arrived back in England from New Zealand in the middle of February 1957, I couldn't help but feel thoroughly depressed at the miserable sight of England in winter as the grim, grey buildings and rain-sodden fields slid by the misted-up window of the train on its way to Victoria Station. However, having lived in New Zealand for 16 months with its wooden houses, corrugated iron roofs and modern, but fairly poor-quality, public 'furniture' such as street lighting columns and road signs, it was strangely reassuring to see again the old-fashioned, grubby but solid structures of my homeland.

When I arrived at the family home, which was then a small rented house in Beckenham, my mother told me my father had been taken into hospital for a major operation. Added to that, my favourite uncle, Uncle Will (my mother's brother-in-law) had passed away during my five-week voyage and I had of course missed his funeral.

Realising that my ambition of starting up Spraycraft again with my father now had to be put on hold, I answered an advert in the *Daily Telegraph* for a junior sales negotiator with a West End firm of estate agents, Styles Whitlock & Peterson, who were based in the prestigious St. James' Square area.

Two weeks after returning home, my parents' short term lease on the Beckenham house expired and a detached house was purchased in Westmoreland Road, Bromley. With my father in hospital, I found myself helping my mother to furnish the new house which was not easy as neither of us had our own transport. My mother had sold her car, having taken it by ship to New Zealand a year earlier, and I had yet to pass my driving test.

I enjoyed my work as a sales negotiator and was very proud of the role I played in my firm disposing of a long lease of an extensive office building in Glasshouse Street in London's West End. One day my boss asked me if I would be prepared to work one evening by taking home the keys to this particular office block and then returning in the evening to show a prospective purchaser round. The following day I learned that the client had made an acceptable offer for the lease and I was congratulated for my efforts.

The firm had a reputation for selling country properties and estates, and I was involved in negotiating sales as diversified as the six-year lease of a mews property near Sloane Square and a large country house near Winchester.

I had already had six driving lessons before leaving for New Zealand in 1955, so it was not too difficult to take up the challenge once again. All I really needed was practice. There was a major problem with driving tests at the time, with an extremely long wait, and I had heard that in these circumstances it was permissible for a learner to drive without a qualified driver in attendance as long as 'L' plates were clearly displayed. I therefore bought myself a small Austin 7 tourer for £30 and drove it back from Orpington, where I had purchased it, with its tatty curtains flapping in the wind. My mother was astonished when she looked out of the window to see it on the drive.

The Austin drove quite well, provided I didn't go further than about 10 miles without a break, as the radiator would overheat. I took myself off to places such as Biggin Hill aerodrome to practice. Accordingly, when I did eventually take the test I was able to pass at the first attempt, although I was particularly fortunate on the day of the test because there was a bus strike which made the suburban roads much easier to negotiate.

By June my father had recuperated enough to be able to drive once again and had managed to rent a one-room office in the building he had been working in several years earlier, above a garage in Widmore Road, Bromley. The most amazing and fortunate thing was that he was able to get back his old telephone number, Ravensbourne 1100, one of the best telephone numbers in the area. Surprisingly, no one else had applied for it in the intervening period.

The time had finally come to say goodbye to the land of estate agency and, with luck, begin an exciting new life as a painting contractor. On Monday 24th June 1957 my father and I went to our new office, where all we had to start with was a shared desk, two chairs and a small Royal brand portable typewriter.

This is a photograph of the actual machine. It shows how far office equipment has come in 50 years or so.

Our original Royal portable typewriter

During that first week at the office, a couple of months after my 20th birthday and just before I was called up for National Service, my father told me that he had to decide what to do about an investment property he had bought in Bickley just after the war. It had been let to the War Department for several years and had been used for housing officers employed at RAF Station Biggin Hill. He explained that the tenants had given notice to quit as it was now surplus to their requirements.

I went with him to inspect the house, No. 49 Southborough Road, and found it in a sorry state of repair. I proceeded to draw up plans and realised that it would not be too difficult to convert the house into two flats. This was achieved by retaining the ground floor in its original state and then (a) sealing the staircase off, (b) building a new wall three feet inside the large living room, and (c) putting an external door in the wall by the living room, which left a corridor between the new and original living room walls leading to the staircase (which had been sealed off from the ground floor). I thought it was quite ingenious, for although the ground-floor flat was not very large, the new first-floor flat was of a reasonable size as it included a further two rooms on the second floor plus a large attic room.

Right at the back of this attic, well hidden behind a chimney breast, I discovered two large Victorian oil paintings. One depicted a pleasant Scottish landscape, while the other was an oval picture of a young girl wearing a kilt and holding a dove. My father said I could keep them as part payment for all the work involved, and several decades later my son Robbie sold them for me in Cambridge for a few hundred pounds.

During a short holiday to Northumberland in 2005, Ann and I made a visit to Cragside, which was a house William Armstrong (later Lord Armstrong of Bamburgh Castle) had built in the late 19th century amid Northumberland moorland near the village of Rothbury. As I looked at the various works of art on show, I was astounded to come across 'my' painting of the girl with the dove! Perhaps it had been valuable after all.

The company name in those days remained Spraycraft Co Ltd,

and the plan was to carry on with what my father knew best – the spray painting of industrial buildings such as aircraft hangars and factories. After a month of sending out sales letters on our new headed paper, with my father making telephone calls to some of his old contacts and suppliers, we at last received an enquiry to paint a corrugated iron Nissen hut at Birchangar Airfield near Bishop's Stortford in Essex.

My father's simple maxim was (1) get the enquiry, (2) land the contract and (3) make it pay. He knew exactly what he was doing when it came to estimating for such a project, and it duly transpired that our tender proved to be the lowest submitted. This, then, was the first order we had received since the Company's relaunch. The job was particularly apposite, as the hut was identical in structure to the one which had been the subject of the very first contract ever awarded to Spraycraft back in 1941.

The Nissen Hut at Birchanger

I was so pleased with landing this work that I set about designing and making a special sales board to be erected alongside the main road at Birchangar. It was robustly constructed of wood with a substantial wooden edging, and in order to make the words stand out on the sign each letter was carefully carved from linoleum and neatly tacked into place. The whole board was first painted over completely with aluminium to seal the surface and finally the letters were picked out in red on a bright yellow background.

It became apparent very soon after we had started work that the old days had gone and the opportunities were no longer available for my father to carry out the sorts of contracts that he had been used to. In order to save money on building maintenance work, the Government was intent upon importing from America a newly-devised system for maintaining the country's RAF and USAF bases.

Previously, each project had been treated individually as it arose. Estimates had been sought on a lump sum basis, the work carried out to an agreed specification and then paid for. The new idea was to seek quotations from suitably-qualified firms for all maintenance work on any one RAF Station, for example, to be undertaken on a previously agreed schedule of rates. The method of tendering involved quoting a percentage, either on or off that schedule.

The early contracts required percentage quotations for three distinct types of work, hangars, married quarters and all other buildings. Each of these three categories would then be split again between internal and external work, thus requiring six sets of percentages for each contract. To make the whole exercise worthwhile, it was proposed that each contract would be for a period of three years, with suitable penalties should either party wish to terminate a contract before the three years had expired.

Through one of my father's senior surveying contacts at the Air Ministry he was very fortunate in being offered the opportunity of submitting a competitive tender for RAF Biggin Hill. When the tender documents arrived they were in the new name for the Government Department now responsible for such works, the

Ministry of Works, or MoW, later to be called the Ministry of Public Building & Works (MPBW).

There was a huge advantage in being able to secure such a contract with a three-year period of guaranteed work. Accordingly, my father spent many hours poring over the percentages and how these would be reflected in the trading result. After much pondering as to whether or not his calculations had been correct, he submitted his price. He was duly awarded the contract. Although it was only for the trade of painting on this occasion, it turned out to be the very first contract for long-term maintenance ever to be let in the UK.

It was understood by all parties that this new method of contracting was only an experiment at this stage and would be closely monitored to determine what, if any, problems arose during actual execution. Subsequently my father discovered that his percentages off the schedule had been very competitive.

The contract had barely got under way when a tender was received for a similar contract at RAF Kenley in Surrey. My father, in true entrepreneurial spirit, shaved just a little off the Biggin Hill prices and duly landed that particular contract by a very narrow margin. Again, less than three months later, another related opportunity arose to submit a similar tender for RAF Kidbrooke in South East London (this site was used mainly for storage and was later bulldozed to make way for a 60s concrete housing estate).

It seems strange now to realise that these three contracts were the forerunners of all the many thousands of building maintenance contracts (all trades) that have since been carried out in the UK.

The Biggin Hill contract was not without its problems, and I was personally involved with a change in the wording of all the later term contracts. This arose from a works order that was raised shortly after the contract commenced. The order was for the painting of a high-level water tower; such a structure was well known by painting contractors at the time as being one of the most difficult to paint, owing to the awkwardness of access, as the tank was wider that the supporting steelwork.

The order had been raised on the basis of the tower coming under the heading of 'other buildings', which carried very competitive rates in the schedule, but it would have been impossible to carry it out without losing a small fortune. I contended that this was an exceptional situation and should be classified as a special item attracting what were called 'starred rates'.

On reading carefully through the main contract it suddenly occurred to me that a water tower was not a building as such but a structure, and the contract made no allowance for structures and gave no specific rates. At first the clerk of works on site disagreed with me on this, but I took this to a high level in London and eventually it was agreed that I was right. I noticed with some satisfaction that all future painting term contracts had a new section termed 'steel structures' in addition to the original sections of hangars, married quarters and other buildings.

Over the next two months we landed two or three further small contracts, and then came a bolt from the blue. At a time when I was just beginning to get to grips with the business, I received my calling up papers for National Service. Almost two years was to be stolen from me, at the worst possible time.

Several letters went back and forth to an address in London's Red Lion Square contesting the two-year period, since I had already completed National Service in New Zealand. Eventually, because what New Zealand called the Compulsory Military Training Act only involved 14 weeks of intensive full-time training, the authorities permitted me a reduction of three months from my UK National Service.

In September 1957 I therefore bade farewell once again to my family, and duly presented myself for initial registration at RAF Cardington, Bedfordshire to do National Service all over again.

After ten days of being fitted out and some basic training, I was put on a train with a number of other recruits to RAF West Kirby in the Wirral in Cheshire, just across the River Mersey from Liverpool. During our first evening in the hut several of us got talking about what part of the country we had come from; there were three or four of us from the London region. I happened to let slip that I had only recently returned to England from New Zealand, where I had already served a form of National Service. From that moment on, and for the rest of my National Service, I don't believe anyone ever knew my first name. I was just called 'Kiwi', even by the officers.

During the first morning at West Kirby the officer in charge advised us all that for anyone who might be interested, a special room was being set aside that afternoon for an initial test to see if any of us was suitable to be granted a commission.

What an opportunity! Here I was, only 20 years old. I had been all round the world and already completed basic training in the Royal NZ Artillery, where I had risen to the equivalent of Corporal. Surely I must be in contention for such a promotion?

A dozen of us were selected to take the test, so we sat at desks while a very young officer, not much older than ourselves, handed out pens and asked us to start off by giving a synopsis of what we had been doing and what we had achieved before being called up. I thought this was fantastic, and just the chance I wanted. So I set about my task. First I recalled some advice from my schooldays, when the English teachers had always emphasized the importance of a succinct title. After a moment's hesitation I wrote down my title, My Life Thus Far. I was just considering how to start when the young officer strutted by my desk, glanced over my shoulder, and started to tap my pad with his baton.

'What's this?' he said. 'What does it mean? It doesn't even make sense. You're wasting our time! You'd better leave the room now'.

With that, I was ushered out. That was the end of my application for a commission in the Royal Air Force. It was just as well that I hadn't been selected, as I would have found it extremely difficult to deal with such ignorance and stupidity.

I found the eight weeks of basic training and general 'square bashing' very boring, having done all the drill before, both in New Zealand and in the school corps. When it came to my old favourite of stripping and re-assembling the bren gun, I really came into my own, and the sergeant found it hard to believe the speed with which I could carry out this task.

After basic training I was posted to RAF Credenhill near Hereford for Trade Training and passed out as a Clerk General Duties. Shortly after that, I was drafted to RAF Benson for further Trade Training. This was the station, it may be recalled, where my father's firm had painted the Queen's Flight hangar five years earlier.

We were given a list of various 'advanced' trades on offer, ranging from motor mechanics to typing, and I opted for the latter. After a few weeks of bashing away on a typewriter I passed the final test at 40 words per minute. Those of us who had reached this standard of touch typing, and who had shown aptitude, were encouraged to expand on our clerical prowess by learning Pitman's shorthand. I eventually passed the shorthand course at 100 words per minute. Although I have rarely found the ability to use shorthand a great advantage in later life, I had no idea, with the advent of personal computers, how handy it would be to learn how to 'touch type'.

I quite enjoyed my time at Benson Camp and was able, on occasion, to get a bus into Oxford to see a bit of life. Even the shorthand and typing classes were quite appealing, as there were a number of WRAFs (Women's Royal Air Force personnel) on our course.

One afternoon, soon after arriving at Benson, we were told that, as new recruits, if we thought we would enjoy the experience, the pilot of a Chipmunk training plane would be able to take us up one at a time for a short training flight, just to give us a taste of what flying was all about. I volunteered immediately, for as an avid aero modeller in my teens I had always wondered what it would be like in the air in a plane which seemed little bigger than the models I had made.

I was quite excited as we sped along the runway until we had lift off, and found it exhilarating to look down and see the Thames winding beneath us. The little single-engined plane took only two people, with me strapped in behind the pilot. There was an intercom between us and the pilot asked me if I minded if he did a roll. As I seemed to be well strapped into my seat I said OK, but immediately wished I hadn't. It was the most unnerving experience I have ever had, and I would never want to repeat it. It occurred to me that perhaps flying was not for me. First there had been my experience flying over the thermal region of New Zealand's North Island a few years earlier, and now this.

After qualifying as a shorthand typist and accordingly being promoted from LAC (Leading Aircraftman) to SAC (Senior Aircraftman), I was posted to what was to become my permanent camp, RAF Colerne, on the outskirts of Bath in Wiltshire. Just before the move to Colerne I was asked if I would like the opportunity of working overseas, but declined as I felt that, having already lived abroad for some time, I would prefer to serve out my time in England. They then said this was a pity, because an opportunity had arisen for a shorthand typist at SHAPE in Paris. SHAPE was the acronym for the Supreme Headquarters Allied Powers Europe, and from 1951 to 1967, before their move to Belgium, it was an important sector of NATO. This would have been a most prestigious posting, but I had already declined without knowing what the RAF was offering me! Ah well.

At Colerne we still had to drill on a regular basis, but my main day job after a few weeks of settling in was working as a shorthand typist (as opposed to a mere typist), and being placed in charge of the typing pool in the HQ building.

This position also had other responsibilities. As the only typist with shorthand ability, I was required on occasion to report to the Commanding Officer's suite to take down shorthand and type his confidential RAF, and sometimes private, correspondence. This was at a time when it was known that National Service was likely to end in the not-too-distant future, and with that in mind the authorities had started to employ civilian staff for certain functions, including typing.

Thus I found myself in charge of a typing pool of eight, of which four were girls from the Bath area. For the last six months of my service I was acting as the CO's personal assistant. He was a middle aged Group Captain, and a more amiable and charming man you could not wish to meet.

I was more fortunate financially than many of my friends, for in addition to my RAF pay I was also in receipt of a continuing small salary from Spraycraft. This enabled me to trade in my rickety little Austin 7 tourer and acquire a much more sophisticated vehicle, a ubiquitous Morris Minor convertible. The Morris was very advanced for me after struggling to get around in the Austin 7 and having to stop every few miles or so for the engine to cool down.

One of the many benefits of the Morris was its reliability. I was able on several occasions to visit certain contract sites within about an hour's drive from camp, and this helped to keep me in touch with the firm. I was also able to cover the cost of coming home at weekends by giving lifts to my friends who lived in the London area. By charging them half the going rate for the coach trip, I was still able to turn a profit even if I only took one passenger.

One particular trip back to camp in 1958 I shall never forget. As

I was on my own for that journey, I had left it a lot later than usual before setting off. In those days during the winter months it was not unusual to have a thick 'pea souper' fog descend, especially in the Greater London area, as the Government's Clean Air Act of 1956, passed in the wake of London's Great Smog of 1952, took a few years to be effective.

I was of course very concerned by the lack of visibility, but it was imperative that I got back to camp in time for the 8 am Monday parade. The continual use of windscreen wipers was a help and there was some assistance from the street lighting columns, but once I had cleared the West of London suburbs I could barely see a yard in front of me and was forced to drop my speed to no more than walking pace on the derestricted A4 main road. I was thinking that, at that rate of progress, there was no chance of arriving back at camp on time.

Then I had a brainwave. If I didn't have the interference of the windscreen to look through I was sure I would see a lot better, so I stopped in a layby and took the canvas hood back a couple of feet to enable me to see over the top. I realised the dangers of breathing in such foul air so, having donned a woollen hat, I wrapped a large yellow and white school scarf round my mouth and nose and then adjusted the driver's seat so that, once I had started the engine and got going in second gear, I could just reach the accelerator and brake pedals while still in a position to see over the top of the windscreen.

I was absolutely frozen, but managed to reach a speed of about 15 mph, still in second gear. Luckily, because of the deplorable fog and the late hour, there was virtually nothing else on the road that night, and I managed to get back by 7 am after a horrendous 8 hour journey. When I returned to my hut and went into the bathroom, I glanced at myself in the mirror and could not believe my eyes.

I unwrapped the scarf to find that the area I had been breathing through was totally blackened. My face was really comical, with a pink area around my mouth and nose, while the rest of my face and ears was quite black except for small circles of pink around my eyes. I looked like an actor in a comedy film who had been down a coal mine and had coal dust blown in his face before coming out.

At Colerne, one of the worst camp chores we had to perform was to take it in turn, in groups of six, to do Guard Duty. Sometimes, in the depths of winter, this could be really miserable, especially with a strong easterly wind blowing. We always patrolled in pairs, and I can remember more than one occasion when I asked my fellow guard to cover for me while I crept into the garage where I kept my car and huddled down into a travelling rug on the back seat for half an hour or so to keep warm.

There was one night when we thought we must be dreaming. My fellow guard and I set off patrolling our designated area at 2 am and came across a newly-erected marquee. It had obviously been the site of a great banquet not long before we arrived, but it was now deserted, with what had been attractive floral displays hanging at odd angles from the central wooden poles.

When we saw what was on the two long tables – wow! We had never seen anything like it before in our lives. There were several bottles which were perhaps a quarter full of various wines, plates of salmon, chicken and other delectable sandwiches, cakes that were only half eaten, crisps, and all manner of canapés and vol-au-vents. There was a touch of the Mary Celeste about the place.

Having checked the two exits and finding nobody in sight, we tucked in until we could not possibly have consumed another thing. That was by far the best guard duty I was ever asked to carry out.

CHAPTER FOUR

Family matters

It was November 1959 when I first saw Ann across a crowded dance floor at the Bromley Traditional Jazz Club, which met regularly in the White Hart Inn, Bromley, an old coaching house near the Market Square, now sadly demolished as a victim of the 'regeneration' of that part of the High Street.

Ann was by far the prettiest girl there, and it seems I was fortunate to have met her at this particular venue as it was the first time she had been there, and even then it was only because she had been persuaded to come out for the evening by one of her nursing colleagues at Farnborough Hospital.

When the Ken Colyer Jazz Band had finished for the evening, I led Ann outside to where my little black MG sports car was parked in the pub's car park; it was a J2 model with cycle wings and an original MG engine (by then many of that particular model had been fitted with Ford 10 engines). I asked her if she would like to come for a coffee at a place in Beckenham called the Prompt Corner, where the young people of the day hung out.

She was slightly concerned when she first saw the car, as it still bore the name 'Delia' painted in script on the driver's side following a few outings with a previous girlfriend, Delia Smith.

Yes, it was that Delia Smith. She was only seventeen when I knew her in 1958, and I believe she only went out with me 'on the rebound' following a break-up with her previous boyfriend. The only thing I remember about her is that she considered my clothing not very trendy and persuaded me to update my image by purchasing a pair of the 'winklepicker' shoes which had become very fashionable at the time. I thought they made me look ridiculous, as the points protruded out at least three inches from the end of my big toes. I believe I only wore them once in her company before she decided to get back with her original boyfriend. I was amazed to see Delia appear on television around 15 years later (it was around 1973) with her first cookery programme.

On our first date I took Ann to a pub on the road to Croydon called The Cricketers. Only I could have done this - I spilt my drink all over her dress. She was obviously a glutton for punishment, for despite this inauspicious start to our relationship, she agreed to a second date, and we went for a drive in the MG.

We were travelling at between 40 and 50 mph down what was then a country road, again making for The Cricketers, when suddenly the car screeched to a halt, far quicker than could have been achieved by application of the cable brakes fitted to the car, stopping so abruptly that the two large headlamps, which were fixed on a strong rod across the radiator grill, buckled forward with the force of the stop and were both looking very sad indeed with one tilted half down and the other completely down.

From a later inspection by a garage it seems that a connecting rod in the engine had gone through the side of the engine casing, apparently not an uncommon experience with that particular model of MG, hence the number which by then had been fitted with Ford engines.

'What are you going to do?' said Ann. I replied 'We'll walk to the pub – it's not very far, and I can telephone my younger brother David and arrange for him to come and collect us and tow the car back home'.

She then said 'What will you do about the car once you've got it home?' Full of bravura, I uttered the memorable words: 'Oh, well, I'll just have to go and buy another one!'

Colin's 1932 MG J2 sports car, 'Delia'

It was a very sorry sight to see the garage tow my little car away, but it did cross my mind that I had probably brought on its demise by my treatment of the engine. There had been an occurrence a few weeks earlier, for example, when I had been a little short of cash for petrol, so I had filled the tank with white spirit from a large drum kept in the yard at work which was used for thinning out paint. When the engine finally burst into life, the ensuing white cloud of smoke that followed me was quite unbelievable.

During our courting days, one memory that will always stay with both of us is repeatedly getting ourselves locked out of the nurses' home on returning from an evening out. With a great deal of effort on my part and energy and agility on hers, I would lift her up to an open ground-floor window for her to gain access to her sleeping quarters.

The evening I proposed to her was certainly not a formal down-on-one-knee affair. Although I had thought long and hard about such a commitment, in the event it was a spur-of-the-moment situation. Out of the blue, I simply asked 'Will you marry me?' to which her unforgettable reply was 'Yes – when?'

We got engaged in October 1960 and married the following September. The weather was very kind to us on our wedding day, 16th

September 1961, and we arranged absolutely everything ourselves, even including booking rooms for Ann's mother and certain other family members at the hotel where the reception was held, the Bromley Court.

In those days Ann did not drive, so I spent the morning of our wedding day racing around collecting buttonholes for the men from a Bromley florist and the two-tier cake, previously ordered by Ann, from a baker's shop in Orpington. It was not exactly a grand affair, as we had to pay for the whole event ourselves.

My brother John was in Aden at the time doing National Service, so he could not be my best man. Over the previous couple of years I had become very friendly with a young man who was a near neighbour and against whom I used to race my MG around the streets of Bromley very early on Sunday mornings. He confirmed that he would be honoured to act as my best man. He had been born in Holland, although, having been educated at Imperial College in London, he spoke perfect English. I was impressed by his Dutch title; his name was Baron Eric von Schmidt auf Altenstadt.

'Spritey'

After the reception, which several of Ann's nursing colleagues attended, the two of us drove off in 'Spritey', the bright yellow Austin Healey 'Frogeye' Sprite which I had bought a few months previously. This was not a name that required a great deal of thought to muster up. First we went to the bungalow in Sidcup, which I had previously decorated, to change out of our formal clothes, and then we drove off to have an evening meal at the Grasshopper Restaurant just outside Westerham before returning home for our first night of married life.

Our bungalow in Merrilees Road, Sidcup, was my pride and joy. We had acquired it with a generous deposit from my father about three months before our wedding. It was quite dilapidated when purchased and there was evidence of major damage, we assumed by a wartime bomb, as two of the four doors leading off the small narrow hallway were of completely different heights.

I had spent several evenings and weekends decorating the entire inside and exterior to make it as perfect as I could for my new bride. Our finances were very tight indeed, and we had a strict budget to adhere to. This required laying a linoleum surround to our bedroom floor rather than having the expense of covering the whole area, and a very pretty, but very thin, carpet for the central area.

In the living room, I had sanded and stained the floorboards and we had bought two inexpensive six foot by three rush mats. The biggest disappointment for Ann was the kitchen, which at some stage had been added on to the main square structure. Although just over 11 feet long, it was only four feet wide. The house was fairly close to the road, but it did boast a 60-foot frontage, a short driveway to a small detached garage and a nice-sized rear garden with a huge, very old and quite dilapidated greenhouse.

Neither of us fancied secondhand bedroom furniture, so this had been bought on hire purchase, with two wardrobes from a large furniture store in Bromley the most expensive items. We also bought a new food storage cabinet for the kitchen. The only help available to Ann for washing clothes was an old-fashioned hand-operated wringer, which cost us the princely sum of £7.

Owing to our financial situation, our dream of a week's honeymoon in Italy had to be abandoned. Instead we hired a 30-foot motor cruiser on the Thames. This was something I knew I could handle, as during the last summer at school one of my friends, Robin Lee, said his father would generously agree to allow him and two friends of his choosing to take the family's new luxury motor cruiser up the Thames from Thames Ditton for a week to celebrate the end of our schooling. Neither Robin nor I, nor for that matter the other boy involved, Peter Greenhill, had had any intention of going on to any form of higher education, so this had been a holiday to celebrate our freedom to earn a living.

Having had this experience, it was quite a shock to see our honeymoon cruiser, the *Maid Melora*, awaiting us at Thames Ditton. It had been chosen from the Maid Line brochure, but evidently the picture in the brochure had been taken many years earlier as an initial inspection indicated that every aspect of the boat was old and tatty. The only alternative was turning round and heading back home, so we looked at each other and agreed to give it a go.

Apart from some very attractive scenery en route to Oxford, the holiday was not a great success, not least because I had no idea that Ann would find it so difficult to assist in handling the boat, and especially that she would not be able to leap nimbly from the lock side on to the boat as my friends and I had done seven years earlier!

I was shocked to find, on returning home from our honeymoon, that I was about £100 overdrawn at the bank. Immediate action had to be taken to repay this as quickly as possible, which meant that spending on anything other than essentials was out of the question for a while.

Once she had agreed to get married, Ann gave her notice in at Farnborough Hospital, where she was quite advanced in her SRN (State Registered Nurse) course. I thought it would be a terrible waste of effort to give up at this stage, so I persuaded her to continue until she qualified. She approached Sidcup Hospital and was able to continue until she eventually qualified in 1962. I was immensely proud of her. By continuing to nurse, she was able to contribute generously to our standard of living, notably by buying an expensive and beautifully-made radiogram with twin speakers which, for its day, was very advanced technology.

Fortunately, with our firm's financial year ending in August, I was able to foresee by early October of that year that we were heading for a trading profit of about £3000, so I sought my father's agreement to distribute 10% of this in time for Christmas, with me taking the lion's share of £150. This meant that after taxation, I was able to clear my debt with the bank and have a little over for Christmas.

From accepting a lot of nightwork contracts, even during one of the UK's regular economic downturns, we had two more successive profitable trading years, which enabled us to move from our £3600 Sidcup bungalow (which we sold in 1964 for £3850) to a much nicer £4300 three bedroom semi-detached house in Orpington. By now Ann had qualified and secured a part time nursing job at Bromley Hospital. Although she found it quite stressful at times, as much of the work was in the A&E department, she made some good friends there.

In 1964 I was getting on well with a new Estimating Director, Albert 'Pip' Pippard, who my father had appointed two years earlier. One day he told me about a caravan site a few miles inland from Hastings where he and some friends had caravans. He said the site was in a really pretty location, and set in woodlands with a lake. 'Why don't you come down with Ann and visit us one weekend?' he enquired. 'I'm sure you will both really love it'.

So off we went one Sunday, following Pip's directions to Coghurst Caravan Park. We had to agree it was a very attractive site and it would be fun to have somewhere to go for weekend breaks. The lake was quite large, and when I saw it I thought it would be an ideal spot to bring the boat and learn to sail. We came down another weekend to see what was available, but none of the caravans in prime positions were for sale. Instead we were shown an older type caravan which, although situated on the edge of the site, had the advantage of a wonderful view of cattle grazing in a field behind.

We decided to buy this particular caravan, and in due course I towed the boat down and taught myself to sail. We kept it for about a year, but Ann, especially, became very unhappy with the toilet arrangements. There was a modern toilet and shower block near the centre of the complex, but with our caravan being so far away, we had a long walk over long wet grass, which was not much fun if you had to go in the middle of the night!

Although the monthly site rental was not, on the face of it, very expensive at £15, the site was only open and usable for six months of the year. As in practice we did not make use of it more than one week in four, it worked out (with depreciation) that it cost the equivalent of £150 per visit, which in those days was more than the cost of staying in a five-star hotel!

One day, about a year after our move to Orpington, I was discussing cars with one of our neighbours, Ron Jones, when he told me that he had a lot of fun as a member of the Sevenoaks & District Car Club. He was what one would call these days a bit of a petrolhead, and he related the various activities the club organized, including saloon car racing on a grass track in the country, hill climbs and driving tests. I was intrigued, so when he suggested that Ann and I bought two tickets for their annual dinner dance, we went along. It was a really enjoyable occasion, heightened further by our meeting another couple, Anne and Trevor, who remained friends for many years.

In those days my car, officially owned by the company, was a Triumph Herald estate to which I had fitted slightly wider tyres for a better grip, especially with hill climbs. I never won any of these events, although I usually finished somewhere in the top third. This car really came into its own when it came to the special driving tests the club laid on, because of its incredibly tight turning circle, much like that of a London taxi.

I shall never forget the time when we all went up to Brentford

Market, eight miles to the west of London. The market had been completely cleared for the day and dozens of cones had been strategically placed to represent garages and narrow roadways. The idea was to complete a complicated designated course in as little time as possible, with three attempts for each driver in each class.

I was competing for the Lorraine Barrow Trophy and managed the course in the fastest time, thus giving me a splendid cup to take home in celebration. One of the competitors was also a keen photographer, and when I had completed my record round he came up to me and said 'I'm really looking forward to having these shots exposed. I know I've got one of you coming round a corner with only two wheels on the ground at one point, but the most amazing thing is that, for a split second, the rear tyre of one of those two wheels lifted fractionally off the ground as you braked, so I think I may have one of you on one wheel!'

I became very excited when I was given the opportunity one Saturday to compete in a saloon car race at the famous Brands Hatch circuit. The only modification I made, which all the competitors were required to make, was to affix a large empty oil can under the engine to prevent any oil getting on to the track from an engine blowout. Additionally, I had to buy a suitable helmet. I was in a class for cars up to 1200cc, which included Ford Anglias and Vauxhall Vivas. So far as I could see I was the only one with a Triumph Herald.

When I arrived at the pit area I considered backing out, because I saw that all the other cars had modified engines and specially lightened bodies, and many of the mechanics were in smart overalls. I felt completely outclassed before the race had begun.

As we set off for our practice lap, I needn't have worried too much as I seemed to be holding my own, especially on the corners. I was very relieved when we were all then informed that, for safety reasons and because some of us had never before raced at Brands, we would not after all be racing round together. Instead the competition would be on a timed basis for a full lap. When it was my turn, I really gave it my all. Although my top speed down the main straight was inadequate and I could really have coped with a lot more power, I certainly made up the time on the bends, particularly through Druids. I was pleased with the final results board, which indicated that my time was the seventh fastest out of the 21 drivers competing.

Just after Christmas in 1966, our first child, Penny, was born. Like many young couples in those days, we had decided on a home birth. There was a fleeting moment, however, when we bitterly regretted this decision, as the weather on the day of Penny's birth was very bad with a good deal of ice on the roads, on top of which had fallen a three-inch layer of snow.

When I called the doctor he said he would attend as soon as he could, but in the event he was too late to deal with the birth. It was therefore up to me to assist the midwife who, it appeared, had no difficulty arriving on time.

Attendance at the birth of your own baby is something I think all fathers should experience, if only to witness the tremendous discomfort, pain and suffering that has to be endured by the womenfolk.

I was so very proud of our new baby, and my main priority at this time was for Ann to get some well-earned sleep. So I took Penny, wrapped in a blanket, downstairs into the living room. To ensure I did not doze off in a dangerous position while holding her, I sat on the floor, propped myself up against the wall, and cradled her in my lap until we both fell asleep together until morning.

I loved being a dad, and was really proud of my small family. Ann had to leave her job to look after Penny and I continued working long hours to provide for us. However I always tried to keep the weekends free.

By this time I was certain that there was a huge market for the service our firm offered. While not exactly booming, business was progressing satisfactorily by the late 1960s, and early in 1968 I was able to change the Triumph Herald for a much more sophisticated and more powerful car, a royal blue Triumph 2000 saloon. I was unable to get this into the garage until I took the garage doors off, extended the walls outwards by six inches, and then replaced the doors.

1968 saw the introduction of the forerunner of today's mobile phones. A firm called Pye of Cambridge introduced to the market a compact, amplitude-modulated, mobile radio-telephone which provided two-way speech communication between the units of a mobile fleet and a base station. The equipment consisted of a conventional full-sized black telephone handset which was fixed between the two front seats of a vehicle, an aerial in the centre of the roof and a receiver the size of a small suitcase which was fixed to the floor of the boot. When you had the equipment installed, or whenever you changed your car, it had to be taken to a special Pye depot in Croydon to be wired up. The system was generally known as the London Radiophone Service and it enabled the user to communicate with another vehicle, provided of course they had the same equipment installed, or to a base unit, or more importantly to any telephone worldwide, if the vehicle was in the Greater London area and in a fairly high position for decent reception.

At the time this was a technical wonder, and Alan Ward and I could see huge benefits from being in constant contact whenever we were needed. We had them installed in our cars at a cost of £2500 each – a massive amount at the time, although during the first week I did receive a call which otherwise I would not have had and calculated that the financial benefit from that one call covered the cost of the equipment.

One superficial side benefit of having a radio-telephone was that in a dark blue Triumph 2000, which was one of the cars the police used, and with the aerial located in the centre of the roof, if you were following another car and wanted to get by in a hurry, you simply had to lift up the handset and pretend to talk into it. If the driver in front was using his rear view mirror he would immediately move over, more often than not!

It was about this time that Ann decided she wanted to learn how to drive, as this would be much more convenient when our next child was born, for she had discovered that she was pregnant again. We went to look at a lovely three-bedroom detached house with a double garage on the Bickley Hall Estate near Bromley, which, coincidentally, was one of the many houses we had painted when the estate had been built only two years before. At the time we had carried out the work I had never dreamed that only two years later we would be in a position to purchase one of these lovely properties, albeit one of the smallest designs.

By scraping the barrel I worked out that we could just about afford it. My offer of £11,200 was accepted and the vendor even introduced me to a good solicitor friend of his who would act for us both to save costs, and also an up-and-coming building society called the Hastings & Thanet (which later changed its name to Anglia and finally, after many years, to the Nationwide).

The result of my meeting with the building society manager was his agreement for me to increase my mortgage of £2800 to an incredible £6750. To both Ann and me this seemed such a massive percentage of the purchase price that as soon as we moved in we gave the new house a name – The Millstone.

Ann passed her driving test at the first attempt and our friend from the motor club, Trevor, sold us a small minivan which he had 'done up'. It didn't take either of us long to realise that this van was inappropriate and far too dangerous for Ann to drive, so we changed it for a second-hand Ford Escort which had become available when the manager of one of our subsidiaries had been fired for incompetence. At about the same time I part-exchanged the Triumph 2000 for a brand new Jaguar that had just come out, the XJ6. I ordered one in bright red with beige interior, but it was subject to a long delivery and the only garage where I could get one was in Streatham.

The day finally arrived when I received a telephone call to arrange for its collection. I duly arrived on the morning of the appointed day and was told by the receptionist that the manager would like to see me in his office. Wondering what on earth could be the problem, I went in to meet him. 'I don't know how to tell you this' he said, almost in tears. 'Just before you arrived, we had an accident with your car. The young engineer working on it was unused to the automatic gear system and for some reason, which we are at present investigating, the car leapt forward while being serviced straight into a metal clamp secured to a workbench. It has gouged a 'V' shaped slice out of the front of the bonnet. Obviously we'll repair it as quickly as possible so that the damage will never show'.

I was dumbfounded, and had to drive back home in a courtesy car they loaned me. When my Jaguar had been repaired a couple of weeks later, I went to collect it. Although it seemed OK at the time, when I got it home in a better light the 'V' shape was still just about discernable.

When the car was ordered, I was so overwhelmed by its design and other attributes that I did not think of the drawbacks of having an engine of only 2.8 litres in such a large vehicle. After three years, therefore, this car was traded in for a beautiful 4.2 litre Jaguar Daimler.

In June 1968 Ann was expecting our second child, so we thought it inadvisable to holiday abroad that year. Instead we had a holiday at Westgate-on-Sea on the East Kent coast, staying at a hotel called the Ingleton, where we became very friendly with another couple who also had a small daughter.

As we knew that the Ingleton was right by the beach, I had towed down my sailing dinghy on a trailer. While preparing it for a sail, another guest at the hotel, David Musset, came over to chat to me about it as he was also a sailor and usually sailed with friends who kept a boat on the Isle of Sheppey. I got on especially well with David, mainly because apart from his interest in sailing he also ran a business. We discovered that we were in a similar financial situation, because at that time I owned about a third of our company, whereas although his company was only about a third of the size of ours, he owned 100% of it.

Ann got on extremely well with David's wife, Joan, and it helped that she was a similar age and they lived in Petts Wood, not far from us. We remained friends until David suddenly died at a very young age of a brain haemorrhage about 20 years later.

Before the holiday finished, David came to see me, obviously very excited by something he wanted to tell me. 'You'll never guess what I've found today' he exclaimed. 'In a back street in Margate this afternoon I came across a hobby shop and the owner and I started chatting about sailing. He showed me two complete kits for building your own sailing dinghy. It's really suitable for two people maximum, and it's called a Puffin.

'I thought what a splendid idea it would be if we each bought one – they are not very expensive – and we could take the kits home and build them in our garages'.

So that's what we did. A few weeks later I got out the plans, together with all the various shapes of plywood and other bits and pieces, and started to build my boat. It took a lot longer than I had imagined, but I was very pleased and proud with the result.

When some years later I asked David how he was getting on with his kit, he just grimaced and said that when he had first opened the box it looked far too complicated, so he closed it up again. He never did build his boat.

It was about this time that, for a bit of fun, I decided to gamble a few pounds on the Grand National. Everyone was talking about it and a sweepstake was organized at our office. I noticed an advertisement in the paper by national bookmakers William Hill stating in large print that they paid out on the 4th horse (unusual in those days). I considered the number of horses involved, and the day before the race I studied the form of each and noted their preferences for hard or soft going. Finally, from an appraisal of the weather forecast for Aintree, I made my choice of three horses which I fancied, thinking that surely at least one of them must come home in the first four.

Sure enough, one of my selections came in third and I collected a reasonable payout. This is good, I thought, and carried out the same procedure the following year. This time I collected a tidy sum when one of my horses came in 4th at 66 to 1.

I'll do this every year, I thought to myself – it's an easy way to earn a few extra pounds. I duly made my selections on the third occasion and submitted the completed form to William Hill in exactly the same way as I had done the previous two years. I was very excited when one of my horses came in 2nd and another 4th by a short head. This is going to be a better payout than before, I told myself.

When no winning cheque was received as was customary, I wrote them a letter complaining that I had heard nothing from them despite having two horses in the first four. William Hill replied that my bet was invalid because it was 'an ante post bet'. I did not understand this, and still find it incomprehensible over 40 years later. I had followed exactly the same procedure as in the other two years but instead of paying out they called it an ante post bet. I assumed that, as I had been so successful on prior occasions, they had to think of an excuse not to pay out. Being as facetious then as I am now, I replied 'how can this possibly be an 'ante post bet' – it doesn't make any sort of sense as 'ante' in Latin means of course 'before', and post means 'after' so how on earth could it have been a 'before after' bet?

Naturally I never received a reply, but the incident certainly taught me a lesson and I have never laid a bet on a horse since.

Our second child, Robbie, came along on 16th September 1968, the day we were celebrating our seventh wedding anniversary. Following our successful holiday at the Ingleton Hotel in Westgate, we had another holiday at the same seaside location, but this time chose a hotel that had been recommended to us called the Ivyside. We had such a lovely time there that in 1970, with Ann expecting our third child, we decided to buy a holiday home there, just a few hundred yards from the beach.

It was hard work and sparsely furnished to begin with, but the family always enjoyed the many holidays we had by the sea at Westgate. When we first went there, they had donkey rides on the beach and we always thought of it as a place where time had stood still for decades, with the weekend hordes passing by within half a mile and clamouring for the bright lights of Margate and Dreamland about four miles away.

We kept this holiday home on for 25 years, finally selling it in 1995. It was not without a tear or two of genuine sadness that the family parted from No. 33 Norman Road, Westgate-on-Sea. Although I sailed my little homemade Puffin dinghy many times from Westgate beach, sometimes with the children but mostly alone because of its size (only 6' 6" long), I was always very aware of the dangers of the sea, especially after a particular incident in 1974.

Because of my inexperience as a self-taught dinghy sailor, I was always concerned about the wind direction when taking the boat out to sea and would never venture out when there was any possibility of encountering an offshore breeze. But because I originally taught myself to sail on a lake, it never occurred to me how influential the tides could be. So I set sail on this lovely sunny calm day in the summer of 1974 and was really enjoying the ideal sailing conditions. As the sea was so calm, I went out a lot further than usual, probably about four miles from the shore. I then thought, reluctantly, that I should perhaps consider turning back, as I had been out for over an hour.

I duly 'went about' and started to head back for home, but after about ten minutes or so of sailing what appeared to me to be fairly fast with the single sail hauled in quite tight, I noticed that I still seemed to be level with the same point on the shore. In fact if anything I was further out than when I had started!

I thought 'Oh dear' - or words to that effect. Here I was, about four or five miles out to sea off Margate and not making any headway at all. There were no other boats in the area and I was quite alone, sailing as fast as my little boat would go and yet still heading slowly out into the estuary.

It was only then that I realised I had been caught by a strong current, and even with this strong breeze I would never make it back without some drastic action. First of all, instead of sitting near the rear holding the rudder, I held on to the sail rope while at the same time positioning myself on the central thwart (the structural crosspiece forming a seat for a rower in a boat).

I tied the rope to the thwart between my legs to leave both hands free, then took up the oars and rowed for all I was worth. As I rowed, I could well have imagined some old sea-salt on the shore with his telescope wondering what on earth I was playing at. There was this tiny vessel, appearing to sail at full speed and with the oars being applied like mad.

After half an hour or so my arms were really aching, but I was encouraged to see by my reference point on shore that at least I was holding my own and had not progressed any further towards Holland. After another half hour my rowing rate had slowed down a bit from sheer fatigue, but fortunately I had by then managed to come inshore far enough for the strength of the tide to have waned a little. Slowly but surely I edged closer and closer to the shoreline, though of course I was a long way east of my setting-out point. Once safely ashore, totally exhausted, I had to leave the boat and walk back to get my car to return and tow it home.

1971 started with a serious problem. It came to light when our two children, Penny and Robbie were ill and Ann went to our local doctor's practice in Bickley to register. It so happened that the senior partner, Dr Renton, had dealt with my parents' family over a number of years from the time when our family home was also in Bickley, and there had been several occasions when he and other members of his practice had been treated very badly by Derek, my elder brother. At first Dr Renton refused to have anything to do with Ann, assuming that as a Mrs Fairhurst she was either married to, or connected with, Derek.

Later on the same week I went to make an appointment to see the bank manager on a matter concerning our company. The lady at the reception desk physically recoiled when I used the name Fairhurst, and said she didn't think he would see me.

I insisted on an explanation. It transpired that because they had been told by my father that his son would be running the family business while he was away, and had assumed he meant his eldest son, they had assumed I was Derek. The girl was distressed because it was she who had been in the manager's office fronting the main road when, a week or two earlier, Derek had become incensed about some action or other that the bank had taken and had thrown a brick through the window. He had been arrested by the police, but only cautioned.

With these experiences happening so close together, and with a third child due any time, I decided to do something about it, so I went to see my new solicitor, Chris, the man who had dealt so admirably with our recent house purchase, to ask his advice. I said 'I can't have my children growing up with this sort of thing hanging over us – I want to legally disown Derek'.

Chris told me that it was not possible to disown a sibling. Parents could disown their children, but you could not disown a brother.

'Evidently the problem you have is with your surname, Fairhurst' he said. The only thing you can do realistically is change it.'

'But I like my surname' I told him. 'Why should I have to change it?'

He suggested I should do as another of his clients had done in similar circumstances – insert a hyphen between my second Christian name and my surname. That way my surname would become Douglas-Fairhurst and I would never again be confused with my brother.

I asked if it would have to be changed by Deed Poll. He explained that it was just called a Special Deed, but would include my immediate family, which means my wife and children would also adopt the new surname.

On hearing this, my first reaction was 'That's good, and having a double-barrelled surname sounds very grand, I really like this idea'. So I went ahead, and in April 1971 a Special Deed was drawn up to change our surname from Fairhurst to Douglas-Fairhurst.

I must say that ever since that day I have rued having to change my name, because of the sheer inconvenience of signing cheques and other documents (at one time I was signing at least 200 business cheques each month), added to which the education system doesn't always provide school leavers with the knowledge of what a hyphen is and very often it is rendered as an apostrophe!

When Lucy, our third child, was born in July 1971 we knew that we had to find a larger house, which would not be easy as the country was going through a dramatic housing boom. As an example, The Millstone, which we had bought for £11,200 only three years earlier, was now valued at more than double this. During our two previous property sales, Ann had proved to be a brilliant saleswoman, and on this occasion she excelled once again by securing a sale in the sum of £23,450. With only a small increase in the mortgage and cashing in some savings, we purchased a five-bedroom detached house just off Chislehurst Common. We moved in in May 1973 and lived there for four years.

CHAPTER FIVE

Travelling for business and pleasure

After settling down in England and getting married in 1961, there was no further travel abroad until 1964, when Ann and I flew to Jersey for a short holiday. Unfortunately this was only memorable because it rained for much of the time, but we did meet a lovely old couple from Sweden, Bo and Inga Malmberg, with whom we

Fig. 13 Colin and Ann on tandem

remained friends for over twenty years. They were a well-connected couple from the city of Norrköping and I believe Bo was related to Johan Lundström, a famous Swedish industrialist and inventor who pioneered the production of safety matches.

One memory that has always stayed with me from the Jersey holiday was hiring a tandem to see more of the island. We caused a few raised eyebrows when we set off from the hotel, and we were certain they never expected to see us alive again as we wobbled off down the driveway, narrowly missing a car coming down the road towards us.

Two years later we holidayed in Igls, a small village in the Austrian Tyrol not far from Innsbrück. The outward journey was quite eventful, as the last 15 minutes of the flight from Gatwick to Innsbrück took us over some very mountainous terrain. I was astonished, on looking out of the cabin window, to see the plane's landing wheels miss the top of a craggy mountain by not much more than the overall height of the aircraft, some 30 feet!

My extreme concern was justified, as a few months later we learned that another aircraft, having negotiated the same mountain peak, had insufficient room to land in the Innsbrück valley and all those aboard lost their lives in the ensuing crash. It was after this that all international flights into Innsbrück ceased, and subsequent flights to this part of Austria had to make use of Münich Airport.

Having landed safely at Innsbrück, there was a major problem with the coach which was taking us along the winding mountain road to our hotel in Igls. It was Ann who first noticed it and raised the alarm with the driver. We were seated towards the rear of the coach and, on looking out of the window, she noticed smoke coming from under the rear wheel arch. This got worse until flames began to appear.

Once the driver had been alerted he immediately stopped the coach, to discover that the rear offside tyre was on fire. We all got out of the vehicle very smartly and the fire was put out, but we had to wait a long while for another coach to be sent for us. What would have happened to us if Ann hadn't been so observant?

The holiday at the Sport Hotel in Igls was a great success (despite

Ann being badly bitten by a horsefly which had come over from the stables next door), and we vowed to return one day. This was when we first learned that it is almost always a mistake to return anywhere that you have really enjoyed yourself. In 1980, with our three children in tow, we took another holiday in Austria, this time in Seefeld. Again we had a lovely holiday which the children enjoyed immensely, but one evening we decided to push the boat out and went across the square from the hotel to a very smart-looking restaurant. After the meal, I asked for the bill and to my surprise the waiter wouldn't accept my nice new American Express Gold Card (this was in fact the very first one to be issued in England, ending with the digits 0001) and alleged it wasn't gold but brown. When the manager was called to the till he said 'Haven't you got a nice green one like everyone else? We can't take this brown one - we have never seen one before'.

Apart from that, and Ann having her purse stolen in a local souvenir shop, a great holiday was had by all.

Before we left, however, we could not resist the temptation to make a short return trip to Innsbrück and then up the hill to Igls to make a brief visit to the hotel where we had enjoyed such a wonderful holiday 14 years previously. It now looked very different and fairly run down. We looked at each other and saw what a mistake it had been to make a return visit.

We were fortunate to have enjoyed many wonderful holidays abroad when the children were small, although it was often very hard work and not always helped by the fact that my idea of somewhere to stay sometimes differed from that of Ann. The question of the actual destination was never a problem, it was simply that, having worked so hard for our family holidays, I felt we all deserved the best and accordingly preferred to stay at high-quality hotels, whereas Ann would rather stay in rented accommodation of some sort. I knew that if we rented a house or cottage then the person who really deserved a holiday from looking after the children day in and day out, Ann, would have merely been swapping one kitchen sink for another. We often argued about this.

Although very enjoyable, our trips abroad were not always without incident. One of the most frightening times was when we went to the Algarve in Portugal. Penny was four years old and Robbie two. The four of us had been walking out in the local town when, without any warning, Robbie suddenly stepped off the pavement and ran into the path of the traffic approaching from behind. I darted after him and caught his arm just as a very alert driver screeched to a halt.

There was another occasion when I thought we had lost Robbie, a year later when we were enjoying our first seaside break at our new holiday home at Westgate-on-Sea on the Kent coast. Ann was paddling with Penny and I had been designated to look after our son. I was sitting in a deckchair watching him as he played with his bucket and spade. Although he was getting further away, I was still continuing to watch him assiduously as he wandered down towards the sea, trailing his spade behind him.

And then I realised with horror that the boy I was watching was not Robbie at all. I went into a cold sweat.

I jumped up and tore across the sand to the place where I had last seen the real Robbie and ran up and down the beach, each traverse getting further from my starting point. After more than ten minutes of being frightened out of my wits I eventually found my son playing happily by himself in a small rock pool at the far end of the beach. Later, when I explained to Ann what had happened, she wasn't very happy!

During the school summer holidays of 1979 we decided to take our three children to Disneyworld in Florida. Our travel agent was known to us, being the father of one of the girls at Penny's school. We were none too pleased with his recommended airline, which flew us to Miami. It was Air Florida, a small US carrier based at Miami International Airport which had only started operations in 1972 after being formed in 1971. Our aircraft was an early model Boeing 707, and as we queued up to reach our allocated seats I could see from some distance away that my luck was out. Sitting in the seat next to mine was the largest, fattest, man I had ever seen. I cannot imagine how he had managed to squeeze himself in between the two arms. The rest of him was spilling out on each side so far that the only way I could sit was facing towards him at an angle of almost 45 degrees. I had to sit like this throughout the nine-hour flight, and trying to eat a meal was an absolute nightmare.

Being late July, it was very humid when we landed at Miami. Soon after our arrival at the hotel in Fort Lauderdale we went out for a short walk, thinking it might be a little cooler in the night air – it wasn't. We walked for only about ten minutes, looking for somewhere suitable for the five of us to sit down and have a meal, and opted for an Italian-style restaurant. After studying the menu and not understanding a lot of it, the children all thought a pizza would be a safe bet, so Ann and I agreed to join them and called the waitress over.

'We would like five Margherita pizzas, please' I said, to which the reply was 'You want five? Coming right up, sir'. We could not believe our eyes when ten minutes later five of the biggest pizzas we had ever set eyes on were brought to our table. They were absolutely huge, each measuring twelve inches square and about two inches deep. One pizza of this size would really have been enough for all five of us to share.

To add to the experience, Ann and the children had all sensibly ordered bottles of still water, whereas I had ordered root beer, without having any idea how revolting it was. I found it difficult to come to terms with the types of food on offer in Florida, the vast choice of how it could be cooked and the amount one was expected to consume. I considered the choices on offer to be utterly ridiculous, and in fact on the first morning in the café area at breakfast I walked out after the waitress spent what seemed like a full five minutes listing the various ways an egg could be presented.

This holiday was not all doom and gloom, however, and the highlight was the trip to Disneyworld I had promised the children. As Orlando was over 200 miles to the north of Fort Lauderdale, I decided to push the boat out and arranged to hire a six-seater light aircraft to take us from the local airfield to just outside the entrance to Disneyworld, with a limousine to pick us up from our hotel and whisking us to the airfield for the 90-minute flight.

The flight alone was quite exciting, as it took us over the Everglades and gave us a wonderful view of Lake Okeechobee. Although I had been up in a small light aircraft before, during my National Service in the RAF, I had no idea how to control the plane and found myself looking over the pilot's shoulder at the instruments to glean the rudiments of flying. After taking off and realising there was of course no co-pilot, I wondered what would happen if the pilot were to be suddenly taken ill with a heart attack, for example. Fortunately there were no difficulties regarding the pilot's health and we all had a wonderful day in Disneyworld.

Austria has been the destination for two further holidays for me, without the family. These were both skiing trips, where I went as a guest of the Chislehurst Round Table. This came about when one day in the autumn of 1983 Ann was talking to one of our neighbours in Bromley, Alan de Maid, a leading local estate agent. He told her of the great times he had enjoyed over the past few winters going skiing with some business friends. Ann thought this was something I might be interested in, so she asked me to go to Alan's house to see if there was room for me on the next trip.

Alan said he would be most pleased, as the more the merrier. He told me that, on account of his age, he no longer did any downhill skiing, but enjoyed '*langlaufing*', which he explained was the name they used for cross-country skiing.

The first trip, with a group of 12 businessmen from the Chislehurst area, was to Ellmau in the Austrian Tyrol. While all the others were experienced skiers, having been before and become fully accustomed to coping with red and black runs, I joined an absolute beginners' class.

After the first day I was starting to get the hang of it, and on more than one occasion was grateful for my good natural sense of balance. This sense of balance, however, did not help me the following day. After about an hour's lesson, the instructor had begun to lead the class up a slight incline when one of my skis came out of its binding. By the time I had sorted it out, they had reached a junction and turned left, and I could see they were making for an entrance to the chair lifts.

It occurred to me that I could catch them all up much more quickly by cutting across to the point where they were heading. As it was up an incline, I took my skis off, slung them over my shoulder and set off walking at a brisk pace across this area, which I noticed was virgin snow - an area, I was informed later, called 'off piste'.

How utterly stupid can one be? I had only gone about five yards when, without warning, I went straight down into the soft snow up to my chest.

'Oh my God!' I cried to myself 'How the hell do I get out of this?'

I had stopped sinking and sensed my feet had arrived on something firm, possibly ground or a rock. Fortunately I was still clinging on to my skis. I kept thinking that if only I could find some way of distributing my weight on the skis I could perhaps lever myself up, so I arranged them one on either side of me. By using all the shoulder strength I could muster, I managed to wriggle up high enough on the skis so that I was more than half way out of the snow. Then, slowly but surely, I got back to the section of hard piste that I had left some time earlier by using my arms alternately to move forward about six inches at a time.

When I finally caught up with the class, the ski instructor seemed not the least perturbed. He had assumed I had gone back to the hotel!

My second skiing trip, two years later, was fraught with problems. For a start, I should probably never have gone on this particular trip, for Ann had slipped on the ice on the driveway to our house and broken an arm a few days earlier. She said at the time that as it had all been arranged and paid for I should still go, but after I returned home she said she was surprised I had still gone and left her with a broken arm and three children to look after.

The resort for that holiday was St Anton in the Arlberg region of the Tyrol. The resort was very classy and the hotel was much more comfortable than the one where we had stayed in Ellmau. I was sharing a room with Arthur Hart, an insurance adviser whom I had known for many years. In my late forties, I was quite a late starter for skiing, but Arthur was at least ten years my senior and he hadn't started skiing until he was in his mid fifties.

I really admired him for his fitness and his skill as a downhill skier. However, on the second day of our trip, he must have bitten off more than he could chew, because he lost his footing on an icy slope and slid into a rock causing the most dreadful bruising. The next morning he could barely move and for the rest of the holiday I found myself regularly having to help him in and out of a hot bath to relieve the pain. Poor Arthur had no more skiing that holiday, and he has never touched skis since.

By the fourth day I felt much more confident and managed, along with the other members of my ski school, to get down a red run without too much difficulty. After lunch up the mountain, when the school had finished for the day, the instructor asked if anyone wished to stay up there for a while longer for practice. I said I would like to continue for a little longer, although it was beginning to snow again.

I donned my goggles and set off on a short practice run, but within a few minutes the snow had increased to the point where visibility was greatly impaired. I remembered the instructor's advice when he had told us earlier that if ever we lost our bearings on the mountain - look out for the lines of plastic orange markers. I strained my eyes through the snow and could just make out some orange markers in the distance, so I set off, very cautiously.

Just as well, for after a short distance I stopped abruptly. I have no idea what made me stop in my tracks at that point but I discovered that I was only six feet from the edge of a precipice! The snow was beginning to ease off a little, so I stepped forward, to see below me a narrow ledge about ten feet wide, 25 feet down. I realised that if I had not stopped when I had and had gone over the edge, there was only a slim possibility that my fall would have been arrested by the ledge. I stood there shaking for about a minute and thinking that someone must have been 'up there' watching over me.

Something far worse happened on the afternoon before we were due to leave for home. I heard that night that two very experienced skiers in our group had been skiing off piste with a local female guide, again a very experienced skier. It seems that she had been leading the other two and had been caught out by a small avalanche ahead of them. She was swept away and died of her injuries.

The whole party was mourning her that evening, and after that experience I never wanted to go skiing again. Even the journey home was disastrous, as Münich Airport was closed because of the extreme weather conditions and we had to hang around for several hours before the organizers could arrange a coach to take us to Zürich.

In the autumn of 1982, realising I was going to be spending a great deal of time with our new subsidiary in Gibraltar, I decided to invest in a house along the coast in Spain. This was a newly-constructed three-bedroom, two-bathroom town house on three levels, with an extended section on the top level over the adjacent property, which offered a superb balcony with a white marble floor. The house was between Marbella and San Pedro de Alcantara in a condominium called Villacana, and the extensive grounds were well maintained, with an abundance of beautiful semi-tropical plants and flowers. An added attraction was a lovely view from the balcony of the mountains to the right and sea in the distance to the left.

There were various reasons for this purchase. It would provide holidays for the family, it was only about an hour's drive to Gibraltar and it would save a great deal of money on holidays, because we would no longer have to pay for expensive hotel accommodation. In theory it would also prove to be a good investment in the longer term.

With the occasional slight downturn, property prices generally on the south Spanish coast had seen a consistent upward trend for 30 years. One of the problems faced by British owners in the past had been that of capital gains, and the hefty amount of tax that had to be paid in respect of them. In order to avoid such a problem I hit upon the idea of purchasing the property through a Gibraltar-registered company, as there is no capital gains tax on Gibraltar-owned assets.

I therefore made an appointment to see the firm of solicitors which had dealt with our acquisition of the majority stake in our Gibraltar subsidiary, Fairhurst Guncrete (Gibraltar) Ltd. He agreed with me about the effectiveness of such a move, and I duly came up with a suitable name based upon the address of the house in Villacana, which was No 38 Calle de Don Pietro, and called the new Company Pietro Properties Ltd. Who knows, this could prove to be the forerunner of other property purchases in the future.

It turned out to be great fun owning a property abroad. On the strength of it Ann went to adult education classes to learn Spanish and I also picked up some of the language, although my grammar left something to be desired as it consisted almost entirely of nouns.

Soon after the *escritura* (deeds) had been signed, I went out to Villacana for a week to furnish the place. Any language barrier was largely overcome by old-fashioned sign language although, in practice, many suppliers of furniture etc. spoke English.

Ann and I remember one very amusing situation at a time when I thought I was getting to grips with the Spanish language. Very often, instead of flying out to Malaga Airport, we would enter Spain by landing at Gibraltar and going through the border. The delays at the border control were notorious, and I thought it would hurry things along if I confirmed with the border guard that we had only clothes and nothing else. When it came to our turn for inspection I wound down the car window and said in my best Spanish accent '*Las ropas solamente*', meaning, or at least I thought it meant, clothes only. I wondered why the guard gave me a huge grin and waved us through.

'Do you realise what you just told him?' said Ann. 'You used a double plural. You should have said 'la ropa, solamente' but you used the plural of clothes, which doesn't exist, so the rough translation of what you actually said was 'clotheses only'!'

An even more embarrassing episode arose several years after we had bought the house when we were entertaining my brother John and his wife Margaret for a week, mainly so that John and I could play a few rounds of golf. The first day we decided to tackle a local course at El Paraiso, near Estepona.

By now I was beginning to manage quite a few words and phrases in Spanish, so I was keen to show off my knowledge to John. We parked the car and went to the clubhouse to enquire about teeing-off times and to pay the green fees. We were directed to the professional's shop, where the pro was seated in a corner replacing a grip on a club. For some strange reason which I will never understand, I opened my mouth and said '*Habla usted Español?*' (do you speak Spanish?). Of course what I had intended to say was '*Habla usted*

Ingles?'. I will never forget the incredulous look on his face as he nodded very slowly and with a slow, long drawl, replied 'sss... i'.

John and I played a number of rounds of golf that holiday. Although we had totally different styles, it was amazing how close the scores always were. Although John was a more experienced and accomplished golfer than I was, I was often saved by one of the many lakes and other water hazards that were a feature of Spanish golf courses. Poor John was so often in the water that I renamed him 'agua Johnny'.

I had some strange experiences when playing golf in Spain. One time, when enjoying a round with Alan Ward at the Los Naranjos course near Marbella, one of my tee shots went horribly astray. It was quite a long drive for me, but I hooked it in the direction of a clearing in the trees way off to the left of the fairway. There followed the muffled noise of what sounded like a ball going through the pane of a greenhouse.

As Alan and I walked up the fairway I could see, in a small clearing, a large lorry which had been parked facing the fairway, sporting an external blue sun visor which stretched the width of the screen. The near side of this visor, being the passenger's side, was very badly cracked, with a big hole in it. Beside the lorry stood a man, pointing at his head with one hand and rubbing it in exaggerated fashion with the other.

As we got nearer he started gesticulating wildly, and Alan suggested that I should go over to see if he was all right. He calmed down a little as I approached and talked away rapidly in his native tongue, of which I did not understand a single word. The language difficulty was overcome, however, when I got out my wallet and produced a 5000-peseta note. He gave me a wide semi-toothless smile and waved me on my way.

When on holiday in Spain, I often used to play a round at a small but very pretty nine-hole course near our house. On one occasion, I was hit on the back of the head by another player's wayward shot. Luckily I was wearing a well-made sun hat, which cushioned the blow, but I was very wary on that particular course after that experience.

I had a further strange experience when playing on my own at the very difficult La Duquesa course near Estepona. After the first few holes, the course climbed gradually higher until, at its summit, there was a 470-metre par five hole with a magnificent view of Puerto de la Duquesa and the blue sea beyond. The most interesting aspect of this particular hole was that the green was way down below the teeing-off area and at an angle of about 15 degrees. The fairway was quite narrow and there were rough boulders and heather on either side – very intimidating. It had been constructed using a three-tiered system so that the ground was pretty level for the first 150 yards, then went down quite steeply for a short distance, then another 150 yards or so on the level followed by a similar decline, and then finally a remaining 150-yard section before leading downhill towards the green.

Having started to play golf quite late in life, I was never a big hitter of the ball, always favouring accuracy over distance. Where many of my playing partners were capable of driving the ball 250 yards or so, the furthest I could ever manage was about 180 yards. On this specific occasion I managed to hit the ball absolutely straight, and with the undulating ground in front of me I lost sight of the finish. I was fairly certain, however, that I had been accurate enough to reach the first slope.

I walked down pulling my trolley, but no ball was to be seen, so I continued to the next slope, but still no luck. Then, at the top of the third slope, I could not believe what I saw. In the far distance, only about 30 yards from the green, I could see what looked like my golf ball. It seemed that I must have driven the ball over 450 yards!

I realised what must have happened; I had driven the ball hard enough to reach the first slope and, because it was straight down the middle, it had enough impetus to carry it forward to the next slope, and had done the same thing again at the final section.

Needless to say, with only 30 yards to go, I brought all my powers of concentration to bear at this point and managed to chip the ball to within ten feet of the hole and sink the putt for an incredible 'eagle' three shots.

The following story is one I have told to many people, and all of them have expressed surprise, saying they have never experienced a similar incident. In the early days of working for maybe three or four days at a stretch in Gibraltar, I would stay overnight in Villacana and drive along the coastal road to the Rock. This was long before the motorway was constructed and the traffic was fairly light, as the border had not been officially opened at that time and I had to be in possession of a special pass to gain access.

I was driving happily along in my little hired car and keeping a safe distance behind the car in front when I noticed an 'Obras' sign ahead, which I knew signified roadworks coming up. As I got nearer, I saw a man standing by the side of the road holding a STOP sign upside down. Any second now he's going to hold it up, I thought, and then seeing two or three cars going through I accelerated to catch up the car in front in order not to get caught but to go through with the other vehicles.

By now there was no one behind me. I was just about to follow the others through when the man with the sign suddenly leaped out in front of me holding up the stop sign. I couldn't believe what he had done and I was forced to screech to a halt. 'You stupid ****!' I hissed to myself. 'You nearly got yourself killed!'. He then approached the windscreen waving a large wooden baton. I thought 'My God, he's going to do me in' and swiftly wound up the driver's side window. He approached the side window, still waving the stick.

I had no idea what his game was, but then I noticed on the other side of the road a policeman who was lolling on a railing and smoking a cigarette, as Spanish policemen are prone to do. With the policeman there, perhaps I'll be all right after all, I thought.

As the man continued to gesticulate with his stick, I lowered the window a few inches and said '*Ich verstehe Sie nicht*', which I knew from my limited German meant 'I don't understand you'.

My immediate thought had been that whatever was going on, I would not let him think I was English and would persuade him to blame the Germans. After several cars had passed coming the other way, he eventually waved me on and I was very relieved. I hadn't driven very far, however, when I happened to glance in the rear view mirror and saw, to my astonishment, the man with the sign handing his baton to another driver several cars behind me and the driver sticking out his arm and taking it into his car!

When I related this story to someone in my Gibraltar office, I was told that this was not unusual on Spanish country roads. To save the time and cost of erecting conventional traffic lights, they had devised this system of stopping the last car in a queue and handing a baton to the driver, whereupon, on reaching the end of the roadworks section, the baton would signify to oncoming drivers that the road was clear. The baton would then be handed to the other traffic-control man, who would then pass it to the last car on his side.

Ann and I had never been to Hungary, but in April 1991 we were tempted. It wasn't the advertisement for the delights of Eastern Europe we saw in the *Daily Telegraph* that did it so much as a picture of the iconic supersonic Concorde, which would take us to Budapest as part of the deal.

On contacting the sponsors of the trip we discovered that the flight would depart from Heathrow and fly north over the North Sea, breaking the sound barrier. After this 'champagne & exquisite meal' flight, Concorde would land at Budapest airport and we would be transported by coach to a hotel on Lake Balaton for three nights before returning to Heathrow on a plane operated by Malev, the Hungarian State Airline. As an added attraction, this short holiday would include 'a luncheon cruise down the blue Danube'.

This was too good an opportunity to miss, particularly as there was talk at the time of Concorde's days being numbered owing to the exceptionally high running costs.

We duly booked, and found ourselves staying the night at a Heathrow hotel, where we arranged to park our car for four days before climbing aboard this exciting aircraft. The flight was everything that had been promised and more, although going faster than sound proved an anticlimax when the pilot explained that the sonic boom would not be heard by the passengers, only those on the ground, or rather the sea. The most extraordinary aspect, I discovered, about flying at 55,000 feet (over 10 miles high) was that when I looked out of the window and then surveyed the sky above us, there was no blue sky as one would have expected, just the total blackness of outer space.

The British Airways Concord

Concord's luxurious interior, 1991

We were not told that this particular flight was the very first one that had ever been made by Concorde to Budapest, and there was much excitement on the ground, where a number of dignitaries were waiting to welcome us. The next day in the local newspaper there were a number of pictures showing the plane landing and some of the passengers disembarking.

Modern Hungary no longer has a coastline, but it does have the Hungarian Sea, otherwise known as Lake Balaton, and a rather ancient coach took us through the suburbs of Budapest to the Hotel Aurora on its shores.

The buildings and countryside on the one-hour journey to the hotel gave us some idea of the poor standard of living of the Hungarians compared with the UK, but we weren't prepared for what greeted us on arrival. First of all, while we were still in the lobby after checking in, our guide explained where we were to go for all our meals, as this 'hotel' had no facilities for the guests to eat. Instead, for each of the three main meals of the day, we were to walk 200 metres down the road and present ourselves at prescribed times in a large communal hall.

In our allocated room we found that there were two single beds, but instead of them being placed in the customary side-by-side position, they had been positioned end to end. The reason for this strange arrangement was revealed to us later. Apparently, with so many mouths to feed and so little food, it was to help in maintaining the birth rate to reasonable levels!

When we looked at the beds themselves, a very strange sight met our eyes. Upon each bed was a camel-coloured blanket, and in the centre of each blanket a huge oval hole, two feet long and a foot wide, had been cut and the edges neatly trimmed. For the life of me I had no idea of the reason for this except, perhaps, that a blanket with a large hole in it was cheaper to produce.

Our guide later explained that the reason for this hole was that very few Hungarians could afford bed linen as well as blankets and the hole was to 'show off' the fact that these beds had sheets in addition to blankets!

The general appearance of the room reminded me of what it was like in a poor-quality boarding house in England in the 1940s. An example was the flooring. Having digested the appearance and state of the hotel's décor while in the lobby area, it would have been too much to expect a carpet. There was, of course, no such luxury, the floor being covered by linoleum that had seen better days. Neither of us had seen 'lino' since our first home in 1961, and even then it was considered to be very outmoded.

On our first full day, we were collected by our 1930s style coach and taken into the heart of Budapest City, where we embarked on a river cruiser for our journey on the 'Blue Danube'. This was an interesting trip, and we learned about one side of the river being Buda and the other side Pest, the former rather hilly while the latter lay on the flat terrain of the Great Plain. None of us could fathom where they got the idea of calling the river blue.

We had a different guide for the actual river trip, and it was most interesting to talk to her as her English was excellent and we learned a great deal from her about life in Hungary now that the Russians were in the throes of pulling out their troops. She told us that because wages were so low, many of her compatriots had to hold down several jobs to earn a living. She herself had three jobs, a cleaning job early in the morning, the main one during the day of escorting river boats or acting as an interpreter, and a third working in a restaurant in the evenings.

We were free to look around the local village and lakeside on our own during the afternoon of our last full day. As we walked down to the water's edge, we noticed an area had been cordoned off and looked out to the end of a jetty where we saw a couple in 18th century English costumes. There were more of them, similarly attired, on the shore. It soon became clear that they were being filmed for a British TV drama. Apparently this particular spot was often used as a backdrop for film crews. Although we kept an eye open, we never did see the film when it was finally televised.

We were both so disgusted with the standard of food in the community centre that when we discovered what seemed to be a good-class restaurant, we threw caution to the wind and booked a table there for our last evening. We fervently wished we had done this on other nights as well, for not only was the quality of the food, wine and service superb, but I could not believe the cost when the bill was presented. Paid in Hungarian forints, it totalled the equivalent of just over £7. This was at a time when a similar meal in England would have cost us at least £40.

After the fantastic flight out with Concorde, what a difference we experienced on the return journey. The organization at Budapest airport was shambolic. After much pushing and shoving we finally received our boarding passes and sat down in the allotted seats, which were alongside each other in row 6 on the port side. When most of the passengers were on board, a strapping six-foot-plus Russian air stewardess came up to us and said 'you cannot sit there, you will have to move'.

'Why?' we asked. 'These are our seats, look', and we showed her our boarding passes.

'These seats are reserved for Russians' she insisted. 'You must move to the back'. A couple we knew from our Concorde flight who were sitting directly in front of us turned round and said 'those are your seats, so don't move'.

The woman's huge bulk had not gone unnoticed, and Ann realised that this altercation could have continued for some while, so rather than cause any trouble we agreed to do as she asked and were shown to two very cramped seats right at the back of the aircraft.

After the flight had taken off, the big stewardess came down the aisle to where we were seated carrying two small glasses of some sort of spirits, probably vodka, and very firmly banged them down on the table in front of us. She did this with a very stern look and without the hint of a smile, saying in a strong Russian accent 'these are for you'. Then she turned on her heel and marched back to the front of the aircraft.

We were of course astonished at the time, but in retrospect we found that particular incident most amusing. To crown it all, it was a bumpy and generally rotten flight back to Heathrow in a Malev aircraft and we swore that, whatever the future held, never to fly with Malev airlines again.

All in all 1991, being a palindrome year as it were, was quite eventful, for this was the year our first grandson, Ben, was born. It was also the year Ann and I celebrated our 30th wedding anniversary. In addition to our flight on Concord we flew to New York to see Robbie and hired a car to tour round New England.

Robbie had won a special academic award as Procter Visiting Fellow to study at Princeton University for a year, and we thought it would be rather nice to go and pay him a visit. He duly came to meet us in our New York hotel and showed us around the sights for three days, including the Metropolitan Museum of Art. We went to the top of the Empire State Building and dined one night at the revolving restaurant of the Marriott Hotel.

We also had time for a splendid lunch at the Tavern on the Green restaurant in Central Park. We had pre-booked a hire car from the centre of Manhattan, but I was very fearful of driving out of the centre of New York to get on the main freeway to Boston. I was dreading even more the drive back through the busy streets of New York to the garage once we had seen some of New England 10 days later; remember there was no satellite navigation system available at that time. However, I needn't have concerned myself as no problems were encountered when returning the car.

The people of New England were really friendly and some of the scenery was quite wonderful. We were on a fairly tight budget, so some of the places where we stopped over for the night were not exactly what one would have called salubrious.

We set off first of all travelling west through Connecticut and stopped the second night at Providence in Rhode Island, then on to see the famous Martha's Vineyard in Massachusetts. After that it was through Plymouth and Boston in Massachusetts and then following the coast to Portland in Maine and across the State of Vermont, where, at one point in the far distance, we could just make out the mountains of Canada. Finally it was back down south towards New York City via Springfield.

We knew before going to the States that many more Americans have never left their country than those who have travelled abroad, but we did find it humorous on our visit to Portland when, at breakfast in the hotel, a gentleman sitting with his wife called across from the next table asking 'say, I love your accent, where you from?' to which I replied ' We're from a town about 15 miles outside of London' to which he then said 'Gee, London, is that near Paris, France?'

On our return to New York we met up once again with Robbie, and one evening we went for dinner to the revolving restaurant at the top of one of the World Trade Centre towers. Robbie brought along a young lady friend of his who was the daughter of a Senator. The meal was fabulous and the view was amazing. That particular evening was definitely one of the highlights of our holiday.

Over the years we have had some lovely holidays all over Europe, including Cyprus, Malta, Spain, Italy, Majorca, Menorca, Portugal, Germany, France, Italy, Belgium, Holland, Denmark, Austria and Switzerland, plus of course Madeira and the Canary Islands of Grand Canary and Tenerife. It was while we were holidaying in Switzerland in September 2001 that we were shocked to see the news unfolding on the television in our room about the terrorist atrocity to the twin towers of the World Trade Centre in New York where we had enjoyed a wonderful meal in the revolving restaurant almost exactly ten years previously.

One of our most successful and enjoyable breaks was a two-centre holiday in Italy, where we stayed for a few nights in Bologna and then took the train to Florence for a few further days. Very tiring but most interesting.

In addition to conventional vacations, we have enjoyed about 20 cruises, starting with a Mediterranean cruise on Shaw Saville's *Northern Star* in 1974, with Penny, Robbie and Lucy, who were then aged respectively seven, five and three. Coincidentally, the *Northern Star* was an exact replica and sister ship of the *Southern Cross* on which I had returned from New Zealand 17 years previously. We couldn't afford luxurious accommodation, so the five of us shared a cabin with four berths down in the bowels of the ship, with Lucy in a cot.

The weather was fabulous for the whole fortnight and the crèche for the children during large periods of the day was a tremendous help. Most cruises have a 'highlight' port, and in this instance the main attraction was calling at Venice, where we stayed overnight on board the ship.

Another memorable cruise was traversing the Baltic to St Petersburg in Russia, calling at Helsinki and Tallin in Estonia, among several other interesting ports. We had pre-booked a tour which included the fabulous Hermitage Museum, but had not expected the total inflexibility of the Russian tour guide. As we entered the museum, Ann, together with a few other ladies, needed to visit the powder room. As they made their way there they were immediately prevented by the guide who said, very sternly, 'that is not allowed just now' and when, later on, they were allowed to go, she looked at her watch saying 'you have exactly seven minutes'.

Just for a laugh, while on the coach back to the ship, when the guide told us we were about to pass the headquarters building of the KGB I stuck two fingers in the air but I was fervently hoping that the surveillance cameras were not at that moment trained in our direction!

We went on one of our many cruise holidays with Fred Olsen in September 2009 aboard the *Braemar*, calling at several of the Mediterranean ports which by now were well known to us, including Cagliari in Sardinia and Lisbon, but also taking in one or two Greek islands and a day at the little volcanic island of Santorini, with its cliff-top town of Fira. As with many small ports of call, even with a relatively small ship the size of the Braemar, there was no possibility of the ship being able to moor other than by dropping anchor in the bay and ferrying passengers ashore using the ship's tenders. Even when observed from the ship, we could imagine the stunning views that awaited us if and when we were able to reach the town of Fira at the top. This then raised the question of how could we get to the summit.

On disembarking from the tender we found ourselves at the tail end of a huge queue waiting for the funicular railway. Guess what? We had completely forgotten the consequences of what happens when four other cruise ships arrive at Santorini on the same day. I quickly calculated that with the number of people waiting, we would have at least an hour's delay.

Then I remembered the previous evening that the lecturer giving the port talk on Santorini had mentioned that there were two other ways of getting to the top other than the funicular. One was to physically climb the 535 steps, and the other was to take a donkey ride.

We saw a small group of passengers from our ship making their way around a building at the end of the quayside, and after following them and climbing a short flight of stone steps we found ourselves in another queue, but this time a very much shorter one. About a dozen people were taking it in turns to clamber on to the backs of what the man in charge called donkeys but which we could see straight away, owing to their size, were in fact large mules.

Ann was given assistance to mount and I tried immediately to follow her in case she had any difficulties on the ride, but there was much jostling of people and mules and I found myself with four other people between us. It seemed to us that the mules knew exactly what they were doing, which was why, I suppose, our group of about 20 were left to progress up the 500-odd steps without anyone being in charge. If my mule, for example, found it was overtaking Ann it would immediately drop back to what it knew to be its correct position by stopping to nibble some vegetation growing from the rocks.

Eventually we reached the top without falling off, and ahead of me I saw there was nobody available to assist Ann to dismount. I slid off the side of my mule as quickly as I could. As I bent to the ground to pick up my hat, which had been dropped in the process, my mule gave me a mighty kick on the legs. But any qualms either of us had at the start of this incredible climb were quickly dispelled on walking up the final 20 steps to take in the fabulous views from the top.

View of Santorini's 500 Donkey Steps

Santorini from the sea, showing the capital, Fira, at the top

Colin, reaching the top

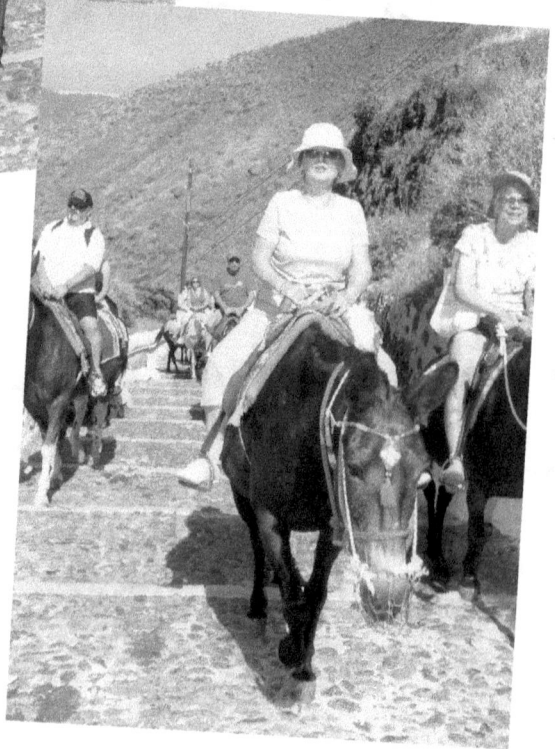

Ann, reaching the top

CHAPTER SIX

Achievement and innovation

It was while we were living in Chislehurst in 1975 that we had our most eventful year. Out of interest, I made a note at the end of my diary for that year of some of the highlights. The following is an extract from that list:

1975 - family and personal achievements

- Beaver Decorating Company record trading year
- Bought a new car for Ann
- Bought a new car for myself
- Bought larger sailing dinghy and motor
- Bulfords Builders make a profit in 1st year of trading
- Company's first full page write-up in *National Magazine*
- Company's first national exhibition at Earl's Court
- Established Cowfold office in Sussex
- Formed Group Twelve Advertising Ltd
- Formed Group Twelve Decorations Ltd
- Got prize for winning Brownies' fathers' race
- Had the best holiday to date
- Learned to play the piano
- Lucy won the little visitors' race at Penny's school
- Lucy's eye operation successful
- Overdraft at NatWest Bank paid off
- Penny highly commended at ballet

- Penny won 3 rosettes on sports day
- Personal number plate 800 CD purchased for car
- Robbie got a gold medal for poetry in London
- Robbie won the 'Tarzan' competition on holiday
- Total group sales exceed £1m for the first time
- Turned Southampton office loss into profit
- West Drayton Branch record year
- Won the 'town crier' competition at Pontins' Holiday Camp
- Won mothers & fathers' wheelbarrow race with Penny.

I had a meeting in the spring of 1976 with the Area Surveyor for the GLC (Greater London Council) at their Area 4 Regional Office in Rangers House, Blackheath. At that meeting I discussed with him the Easter programme for three school painting jobs which we had been awarded. He was evidently very pleased that we had been successful, as the previous year he had suffered problems with a contractor who had let him down badly, mainly through underpricing the work, while, on the other hand, our firm had always enjoyed an excellent relationship with all the staff at Area 4.

He then said 'When your firm does work for us, we never get any serious problems. We all know you have a reputation for doing a good job and I know I can rely on you because you've got your good name to maintain'.

Driving home from Blackheath, I thought about what he had said, Suddenly, it occurred to me what a wonderful slogan it would make for our firm, with its double meaning - 'A Name to Maintain'. So from that moment on, all our letterheads, business cards and other promotional items bore the slogan 'A Name to Maintain'.

In the spring of 1976, my long-awaited Jaguar XJ12 arrived, my first car bearing my new personalized number plate 800 CD. I had seen this number advertised in a Sunday paper. It was the original number on a very old moped and had to be collected from an address in Yorkshire. As luck would have it, Alan Ward was due to make a trip up there that weekend and he kindly arranged to collect the moped, complete with number plate and documentation, and bring it back to me. I then arranged for the new number to be affixed to the brand new XJ12.

The main Bromley Jaguar garage on Mason's Hill, KJ Motors, rang to say that the car had been prepared for the road and was ready for collection. I was sitting in the car in the service area having a demonstration of the instruments when the manager of the service department came up to the car and asked if he could take a look under the bonnet, as this was the very first model of its kind to pass through his workshop.

The bonnet catch was duly released to display the magnificent V12 engine with bunches of wires and all the other ancillary parts gleaming new. I shall never forget the expression of disbelief on his face as he took a step backwards and slowly shook his head from side to side. As if responding to an unasked question, he said 'I was just looking at all the things that can go wrong'!

It seems he had the right idea, because within a few days I was back with a serious glitch; two of the electric windows had already stopped working. This was not the only disappointment. The car had two very large lockable petrol tanks, one on each side of the boot, and I soon realised why the capacity had to be so great. This model, while very comfortable and extremely fast, could only manage an average of 9 miles per gallon (for comparison purposes, my present Jaguar, a 3-litre diesel XF model, averages 43 miles per gallon!)

We moved into Mullaway, our Sundridge Park house, in 1977 and about a year later, I was intrigued by an advertisement from a firm called Commodore in the paper giving details of a piece of technological wizardry which they termed a 'personal computer'.

About a week later, I was on the way home from a meeting in London and had about half an hour to kill before my train left from London Bridge. One of the shops at the station had small computers displayed in the window, so I went inside to see what this was all about as a sign in the window referred to one of the computers as being a Commodore Pet, the same model I had seen in the advertisement a week earlier.

The salesman showed me the equipment, which included a screen and built-in 'qwerty' keyboard. There were 'programs' as he called them, using American spelling, which were produced on C60 cassette tapes. One then placed the tape in a special tape deck which was wired in to the computer.

I thanked him for the demonstration and left to catch my train and to think about buying one. I was swayed, of course, by the fact that with my typing expertise, this equipment would be simple for me to operate, and I could see the advantages when it came to certain office functions.

Within a few days, I was back at the London Bridge shop purchasing my very first personal computer. Once I got it home and read the instructions I saw that with practice and perseverance, I could write my own simple programs in the Basic computer language. I then discovered that I could break into programs that had been professionally written and adjust them to what I wanted. Later on, however, it seems that the manufacturers of this and other computers caught on to this wheeze and started to distribute programs that were 'machine read' only, so this put paid to any alterations to programs. At the time, I do remember thinking that this computer idea could catch on.

One of the programs I bought was called the Gem software system and used little picture 'icons' to indicate which section you wanted to access. This, I believe, was probably the original of the system the Microsoft Corporation later called Windows.

The Commodore Pet was the first commercially-produced Commodore computer. It was originally introduced in January 1977, ahead of what were to become the other two ready-to-use computers, the Apple II and the TRS-80 Model 1. A moderately-priced, modern desktop computer might have 4 gigabytes of memory - 1 million times more than the original PET!

Commodore Pet computer

At a management meeting in 1984, a colleague mentioned the growing importance of PC in the workplace as local authorities, in particular, were paying much more attention to it. Ever one to use a pun, I remember saying, 'What, personal computers? I wasn't aware that many people had them, or by PC did they mean painting contractors?' An older member then joined in by saying that in his youth when people used the abbreviation PC they either meant a postcard or, more likely, a police constable.

Since that moment, and at various times over the ensuing years, I have made notes of the various uses for the initials PC, and these are listed at Appendix A.

Personal computers, being a new idea in the late 1970s and early 1980s, were the subject of a number of jokes. Without any intention of either joking or punning, my own father seriously thought that when I was talking about computers he assumed I was referring to people who travelled regularly by train to London for their jobs!

The best computer joke I came across at the time concerned a language instructor who was explaining to her class that in French, nouns are grammatically designated as masculine or feminine. One student then asked what sex was a computer. As the word wasn't in her French dictionary, for fun she split the class into two groups by gender and asked them to decide whether 'computer' should be a masculine or feminine noun.

The men decided it should take the feminine 'la computer' because:

- No-one but their creator understands their internal logic.
- The native language they use is incomprehensible to everyone else.
- Even the smallest mistakes are stored in the long-term memory for possible retrieval later.
- As soon as you make a commitment to one, you find yourself spending half your salary on accessories for it

The women, however, decided that it should be the masculine 'le computer' because:

- In order to get their attention you have to turn them on.
- They have a lot of data but are still clueless.
- They are supposed to help you solve problems, but half the time they are the problem.
- As soon as you make a commitment to one, you realise that if you had waited a little you could have got a better model.

Recalling the above joke has reminded me of another amusing incident in the 1970s. I was visiting a colleague in a North West London hospital and, having finally managed to find a space to park the car, was about to enter the main entrance when I saw a sign stating 'Beware – thieves operate in this area'. I thought this was very amusing in a hospital, although it was obviously not intended to be, but from that day I started to collect similar ambiguously-worded signs. Some of these are hearsay and doubtless apocryphal, but many

I have seen with my own eyes and they are all listed in Appendix D.

By 1978 I was monitoring on a daily basis the financial performance of several companies and branch offices and, prior to disposing of my personal interest in both Beaver Decorating Company and Beaver Office Cleaning Services, a typical working day for me after leaving home would be to call first of all at our Head Office in Palace Road, Bromley, after which I would then visit Bulfords Builders at Penge and then on to Beaver Decorating at Streatham. By about midday I would then be faced with a one-hour journey to our West Drayton office, where I would have lunch with Richard Pippard, the manager. After lunch there would be a one-hour drive to Chandler's Ford between Winchester and Southampton where, typically, I would spend about two hours before making the return two-hour journey to arrive home by about 8 pm.

The drive from Bromley through to Streatham and West Drayton was by far the worst section for me, as although it was not much more than 70 miles, this was before the M25 motorway had opened and sometimes the traffic congestion was horrific.

This exceptionally busy period coincided with an extremely traumatic time at home. Ann was having to cope with difficulties Lucy was having at school but, more critically, with Penny's anorexia. Robbie compensated to some degree at this time by excelling at every aspect of his school life at Eltham. Other than his academic successes, which eventually led to fantastic 'A' Level results and a place at Pembroke College, Cambridge, he generally took the leading role in school plays and in particular was blessed with the most beautiful treble singing voice. It was so rewarding to be present at his school's musical evenings, where he sang many solos as a junior. As if that wasn't enough, he was progressing very well with the cello, and Ann had to change her car for an estate version to carry it around.

It was about this time that Ann and I sat down one evening and agreed that our present life was becoming ridiculous, with the sheer number of activities in which the three children were involved, including piano, cello, drama, ballet, Guides, Brownies, singing, poetry and tap dancing. We vowed from that moment that the number of such extracurricular activities would henceforth be drastically reduced.

The mention of Brownies reminds me of the funny things children come out with. It was Lucy who took the biscuit in that direction. Before becoming Brownies, the very young girls were allocated the title of 'sprite' and I shall never forget the time when Lucy came home excitedly one evening exclaiming 'Mummy, mummy, I'm a sprout!'

She will also be remembered for the time when we were all in the car driving past a Chislehurst Church when one of us made a remark about the adjacent graveyard.

'Does anyone know what a graveyard is?' Ann enquired, while looking meaningfully at Lucy.

'It's where dead people live' said Lucy.

A few months after moving into our new house at Sundridge Park, I decided to change my car again. Many of the contracts being gained were of a much higher quality than hitherto, and a typical day's work for me would be to visit all of our offices as mentioned, so I thought it would be appropriate to get a car which (a) told the world of our success, (b) demonstrated to the staff that they were working for a flourishing firm, (c) was an insurance against my sustaining a serious accident while motorway driving, and (d) not least, had a history of little or no depreciation.

With the Jaguar XJ12 able to boast fuel consumption of no more than 9 mpg plus a very high depreciation cost, I was drawn to the idea of the firm providing me with a second-hand Rolls Royce Silver Shadow. I paid a visit to the local Rolls showroom and was attracted by a five-year-old model finished in two-tone silver and blue. I decided to buy it.

While the car was fantastic to look at and great to drive, it was not so successful in transporting passengers without making them feel carsick. I knew nothing about the technical side of the Silver Shadow when I bought it, but soon found out. It seemed that all models prior to about 1978 were constructed with what the trade called 'non-compliant' suspension. It made little difference so far as the driver was concerned, but the passengers hated the slow rolling motion.

Somewhat fortunately for me, this car came to grief after only about ten months of ownership as a result of a serious accident in a back street in Sidcup. I had been driving slowly up this short back street as it approached the High Street, keeping well to the left, when without any warning, an old van came hurtling round a right hand bend right over on to my side of the road. I stood no chance. It plunged into the Rolls, writing off the van and causing several thousand pounds' worth of damage to my car. We exchanged details and the driver gave me an address in Star Lane, Orpington.

This location meant nothing to me, but when I reported it to the police, the Duty Officer said simply 'Oh dear.' Star Lane was apparently well known to the locals as a gypsy encampment, and needless to say, the driver was uninsured.

Once the Rolls had been repaired I lost confidence in driving it again and passed in on to Alan Ward, who had expressed a wish to have such an eye-catching vehicle. I then went down to the Rolls showroom and was smitten by a much later model, confirmed as having the all-important compliant suspension. It was a joy to drive but a trifle flashy, being finished in pale gold metallic with cream leather upholstery and a brown leather roof. However, so impressed was I with this car that bearing in mind the very positive financial state of the company at that time in 1979, I enquired about ordering a brand new Silver Shadow.

It does seem extraordinary now, but in those days, mainly because the residual values of second hand 'Rollers' was so high, the waiting list for a new car was at least two years. Not only that, but the Silver Shadow model was to be phased out and replaced by a new model, the Silver Spirit. Finally, and quite incredibly, it was not of course possible to see the new model until it had been produced, so it meant ordering completely blind.

Eventually, after a wait of well over two years, the great day arrived and I received a telephone call from the garage to say my new car awaited me. With great excitement I went to see it. As it was the only Silver Spirit available to the garage, they had polished it up and there it was gleaming in prime position in the showroom.

At first it appeared to be slightly larger than the Silver Shadow it had replaced, but I thought I could come to terms with that. While waiting for the salesman to get the key, I looked through the rear window and could not believe the sight that met my eyes. There, in place of the familiar rear bench seat that I had been used to, was a pair of very deep and beautifully scalloped leather armchairs with a wide leather armrest between them. When the salesman arrived, I let fly.

'What on earth have they done to the rear seating arrangement?' I said. 'However comfortable they look, there are only two seats. I have three children, so who do you think will want to be the one to go in the middle? I'm sorry but I can't possibly accept this!'

I asked him what else they had in stock and was shown another brand new car, one of the very last Silver Shadow models to come off the production line. Coincidentally, it was in the showroom as the result of a cancelled order.

I fell for the colour straight away as it was finished in a very attractive powder-blue metallic paint with a dark blue 'Everflex' roof. Above all it still sported the rear bench seat for the children. I agreed to purchase it, but vowed on the spot never to order another car unseen.

At the time of moving to our new house, 'Mullaway' in Lodge

Road, Sundridge Park, I noticed that one of the attractions of the immediate area was that Lodge Road ran adjacent to Sundridge Park Golf Club. Inviting as it seemed, I had never touched a golf club and never intended ever to take up this sport. I recall saying as much to Ann as we looked across at the course one day as we drove by.

'You won't ever catch me playing golf, it takes up so much time' I said. But within four years of moving, I was having a drink one lunchtime with David Tyce, the landlord of the Anglesea, our firm's local pub in Palace Road, and we were discussing the merits of my taking up some kind of sporting activity. I was expressing a preference for bowls, as my grandfather had been a county player for Lancashire and my own father had played regularly and often came home with prizes.

'There's no difficulty choosing between bowls and golf' I remember David saying. 'Although there are some indoor rinks around, bowls is essentially a summer sport, whereas golf can be played all the year round.'

A few weeks after this discussion I was chatting to Kathy, my PA, and she said 'These golf days the firm organizes from time to time – you're paying for them, so why don't you play?'

The next time a company golf day was arranged, on this occasion at Ilford Golf Club in Essex, I invited myself along. I distinguished myself by going round at an average of over eight shots per hole in 147, a club record high, and on my return home booked some lessons with the golf pro at Sundridge Park Golf Club. After a few weeks I progressed sufficiently to successfully apply for a five-day membership of the club. They told me I wasn't good enough to play at weekends, but said I should keep practising and try to get an official handicap.

I started with the highest handicap of all at 28, and it took three years to lop one shot off this to 27. Then one day in 1988 I was invited by NatWest Bank to play in a competition at Chislehurst Golf Club. The course was quite a short one, which suited my game perfectly, and I amazed myself and my bank manager by going round in a gross score of 88 and winning the NatWest prize for the most improved golfer. On handing my card in at Sundridge Park the next day, I had my handicap cut from 27 to 23 overnight!

Every golfer has stories to tell of extraordinary feats and happenings while out on the course, and I'm sure my experiences were no different to many others, but I will never forget one experience, soon after I had joined the Sundridge Park club. I was about to tee off on a long downhill par-five hole where the correct line to take when driving off was slightly left of centre. Knowing that I had a tendency to hit the ball with a small but discernable fade from left to right, I needed to aim a little more to the left than most other players.

I noticed that there was a tall, thin poplar tree about a hundred yards away, standing guard in the direction of where I wished to aim. I pointed this out to my playing partner and he said 'Don't worry, I've never heard of anyone hitting that particular tree, but if you're concerned the best advice is to actually aim for it and then you will be sure to miss it'.

I took his advice and drove off, aiming for the trunk of the tree. My ball flew low and hard and hit the tree trunk smack in the middle. The strange thing was that the ball came straight back like a rocket towards me and finished just six inches behind the tee.

My partner could not stop laughing at what had happened, but he truly could not believe my luck at what came next. As the ball was on the teeing area I had to use a long iron to tee off again. When I did so, once again actually taking aim again at the same tree, the ball hit the trunk again, this time only coming back about half way. I often wondered what the chances were of such an occurrence.

During the following three years I twice won the Fairhurst Group Golf Society cup, and still proudly retain the small replicas. My most satisfying achievement on the golf course, however, was one spring morning in 1995 when I was playing with father-and-son pension consultants Arthur and John Hart. On the short 137 yard par three fourth hole of the Sundridge Park West Course, a tricky downhole hole where most competent golfers would have used a seven or eight iron, I always found it difficult to reach the green even with the use of a five iron. On this particular occasion I used my five iron as usual and the ball went to the right, but just reached the near right-hand corner of the left sloping green and started the long roll towards the flag.

When the ball went in for a hole in one I was ecstatic! The age old tradition of buying a drink for everyone in the bar at the end of the round proved to be no problem at all, as the three of us were the only players not out on the course at the time.

In April 1997, Ann went to a lot of work to organise a 60th birthday party for me, which was held at home with about 40 relatives and friends attending. The main present she had lined up for me were two flying lessons at Biggin Hill Airfield. The weather was not especially good, so it was arranged that the two lessons would be taken 'back to back'.

Having been a passenger on two previous occasions in small light single-engined aircraft, I was very excited by the prospect of being able to take full control under expert supervision. Despite the low cloud cover it was a truly exhilarating experience and I came away thinking that, in an emergency, I could actually get a small plane airborne and bring it (fairly safely) down again.

CHAPTER SEVEN

A flourishing business

During the last 12 months or so of life in the Royal Air Force, when I had a small Morris and was based at RAF Colerne just outside Bath, I was able in my free time to make visits to contracts my father was carrying out, such as the painting of a high-level water tank at RAF Greenham Common and an aircraft hangar at RAF Weston-on-the-Green in Oxfordshire.

While in the RAF, my brother John had been persuaded to leave his job in London as a trainee stockjobber to help my father out. They had managed to keep things going very well, but I was amused on one occasion when I came home for a long weekend's leave and my father showed me a small advertisement he had placed every night for a week in the London Evening News. It was headed 'Factory Painting without Dislocation'. It was intended of course to appeal to works engineers and the like who wished to have their factory painted without any interruption to production; this could be achieved either by working nightwork and weekends, or during normal hours by use of the specialist technique of boarding out the roof trusses and double sheeting with tarpaulins. But of course the wording of the advert also seemed to be saying that the work could be done without serious injury to the persons involved.

One of the first things I did when my life in the RAF had finished was to sell my Morris Minor and acquire a beautiful little MG J2 sports car. It was my pride and joy.

Although it was great fun to drive, it had what a car salesman would call 'very loose steering'. Because of the age of the vehicle, the police accepted a certain amount of 'tolerance' of the steering wheel but this had about four inches of play in the wheel. Another matter I had to come to terms with was the very poor braking system. These were cable brakes, and they were only capable of halting the car from 50 mph in about 30 yards.

Over the years, having driven more than 70 different cars and travelled a distance approaching 1.5 million miles, I have had many amusing and sometimes scary situations, but what happened to me one afternoon in the summer of 1959 will remain with me always.

I was driving south down Bromley High Street, and very occasionally, in warm weather, I would release the nuts on either side of the windscreen and fold it down flat on the bonnet. The car could not then be driven safely without wearing suitable goggles. So picture it – there I was in a very small black sports car with the windscreen folded down in 'racing mode' and wearing a flat Bentley 'Driver's Cap' together with racing goggles.

Then imagine what it must have looked like to pedestrians. As I came within 50 yards of a zebra crossing, a car 20 yards in front of me suddenly, and without any warning, decided to brake and let some pedestrians across. Immediately I could see that there was no possibility of my being able to brake in time, so on the spur of the moment I mounted the nearside pavement, at a speed which by now was down to about 10 mph, and steered between the glass shop fronts and a queue of about a dozen people waiting at a bus stop. As I drove by the bus queue I saw, out of the corner of my eye, a sight which one hears about but doesn't believe ever happens in reality – a lady's hair, just for a split second, actually stood on end!

I stopped the car a few hundred yards on, well out of sight of anyone who had witnessed this appalling spectacle, and shook like a leaf until I felt able to put the windscreen up and drive home.

After returning to work full time from National Service as a 22-year-old in June 1959, I took it upon myself to arrange for a small wooden hut to be erected on the site of the Royal Naval College at Greenwich where our firm had just been awarded the contract to redecorate the entire exteriors of all four main blocks, including all railings and regilding the domes. The purpose of this exercise was to study every aspect of the work, including time taken to paint each window sash etc, so that first-hand knowledge could be acquired for estimating purposes. Because I was on site permanently for a few weeks I became an obvious target for the wrath of the local Union convener, who, at regular intervals, would insist on calling all our men to my site hut for a Union Meeting.

On only the second day of my vigil, I walked to the block where our men had last been working to see how they were getting on. To my absolute astonishment, as I rounded a corner I happened to look up and saw what was probably the most frightening thing I had ever seen in my life. High up and about 15 feet from the underside of one of the domes was a narrow ledge, approximately 2 feet wide. On this ledge had been placed an empty 5 gallon metal drum. On this drum had been placed another, similar, drum and upon this last drum stood, or rather wobbled precariously, Tim Moynihan, one of the chargehands.

He was stretching up as high as he possibly could with a striker (a long wooden-handled brush made specifically for industrial painting in awkward areas) and attempting to paint an overhang about 15 feet above the ledge. Any second now, I thought, he was going to come tumbling down. My first instinct was to shout up a warning, but I didn't dare say anything for if he lost his concentration for even a split second that would surely have been the end of him.

When he did eventually complete the task and come down, I was furious with him for risking his life in such a manner. There were no further serious incidents. The Ministry of Works hierarchy who were responsible for the work were delighted with the result, and the final certificate for completion of the contract was signed in March 1960.

Two of the four blocks of the Royal Naval College
A Greenwich, as seen from the River Thames

Most of the other contracts at this time were fairly modest in size. Typical contracts were for the maintenance painting of post offices, various Government offices, such as labour exchanges, and schools.

One contract at about this time was, however, a real source of pride. It was known that the Duke of Kent wished to marry Catherine Worsley in 1959 but was told that this would have to be delayed for two years because of the impending marriage of Princess Margaret. In June 1961, therefore, the Duke and Catherine were married in York Minster, but later the main celebrations were held at Windsor Castle.

As this was reckoned to be the 'wedding of the year', it was decided to redecorate the Grand Corridor at Windsor Castle. Our firm was appointed to carry out this important work.

Everyone was so delighted with the result that shortly afterwards the first enquiry was received for painting the quadrangle at Buckingham Palace.

The Grand Corridor at Windsor Castle

As a young man of 24, I was left in charge for three months at a time while my parents went on an extended holiday to South Africa. Having a light-hearted approach to dealing with staff matters, I can well recall the day the book-keeper advised me that a small wage envelope had gone missing for a while with about £5 in it. After a brief search, it was eventually found caught up under an invoice on her desk. Jokingly, I said 'Oh, you crafty Clara it was there all the time!' and walked back into my office chuckling.

Then, after about half an hour, I went out to visit an office at the other end of the building and noticed that the book-keeper had left her desk. Without saying anything to anyone, she had apparently taken the hump and walked out. Two days later I received an incredibly irate letter from her saying, among other things, that she wasn't a thief, and certainly wasn't staying and working in an office where she was constantly being accused as such!

In the early 1960s the usual ten-yearly recession was upon us. I say 'usual' because history before and since has shown us that, in the building and associated trades at least, there have been extreme difficulties in obtaining work during the first few years of each decade. This was most unfortunate and inconvenient so far as I was concerned, for I was married to Ann in September 1961 and very soon afterwards, the more usual painting contracts that we were used to seemed to be fewer. This was a time when conventional factory painting contracts became more difficult to obtain as old factories were torn down and replaced with buildings using a lot more plastic and other surfaces that did not require regular maintenance painting.

Also, it occurred to the MPBW (Ministry of Public Building & Works) that savings could be made by carrying out the redecoration of an entire office block in London (and there were dozens of them) outside normal office hours. It was about this time, then, that 75% of our entire workload was required to be undertaken between the hours of 7 pm and 7 am. This gave the painters a 60-hour working week, but of course it was difficult to monitor the 'sleepers', of which there were two types. The most common type of sleeper was fairly obvious - the man who very often would have a part-time job, perhaps even a full-time one, elsewhere. When he arrived at one of our sites he would clock in with the foreman and be assigned an area to work in. Then, several hours later, he would be found fast asleep in some quiet corner.

The other, more fraudulent, sleeper, was when the foreman or chargehand added a friend's or relative's name to the list of employees on site. No one ever saw him or knew of his existence, but he was added to the payroll and a pay packet would be produced for him for the foreman to add to his own earnings. Fortunately, by strict supervision, many of these abuses were avoided.

Until we were able to afford to employ full-time supervisors it was one of my many tasks to supervise the nightwork contracts, so there were numerous times when I worked an 18 or even a 20-hour day. Typically, I would arrive at the office at 9 am and work through to 6 pm with a sandwich for lunch. After an evening meal at home at about 7 pm I would be off again in the car visiting various night jobs, not getting home until 3 am or even later.

In 1962, while my parents were on one of their regular winter holidays to their flat in Cape Town, one of our regular paint reps, Eddie Workman of Sherwood Paints, called in to see me. He thought I might be interested in a freehold yard with offices that was about to come on the market in Palace Road, Bromley. Up until then, we had expanded by taking on a further rented room next to the original one in Widmore Road and getting by with equipment and paint storage in a large rented garage the other side of Bromley, so the prospect of owning our own premises really excited me.

I went straight round to view the yard and offices before the sellers put it on the market, and after a brief haggle we agreed a price of £3650. Although I was only 24 at the time, I was quite conversant with property matters from my experience with the London estate agents for whom I had worked a few years previously. In those days the only method of communication with another country (other than telephone) was by telex, so I contacted a local telex agency to send an urgent message to my father in South Africa asking permission to proceed with the purchase.

He replied very promptly and was evidently delighted with the prospect of the firm owning its own premises, especially when he knew that the address was Palace Road – very appropriate for the type of work we were now embarking upon! The move of offices went very smoothly, and we were able to add a further telephone number which we reserved for outgoing calls.

At about this time, after my parents had returned home that year, it became apparent from discussions with potential clients that, while the name of Spraycraft was still appropriate for industrial painting, particularly where spray painting was permitted, it certainly was not suitable when dealing with the increasing volume of work on government offices, schools, post offices, etc that was now being executed. We set about thinking of a new, more suitable, name for the company. I assumed the task of coming up with something acceptable and approached Companies House to see if any of the names we had chosen were permissible. I tried several possibilities which seemed appropriate, but at first I did not realise the difficulties with the rules and regulations involved.

Obviously it could not be too similar to an existing name, but neither could it be a name which gave the impression that the company was much larger than it really was. It could not include words such as 'British' or 'International' for example, and for commercial reasons we would not want a name that limited our geographical area of operations, so one good name which could not be confused with any other 'The London Brush & Spray Company Ltd', for instance, was no use if we wanted to work in Southampton.

Eventually, as we were a family business comprising my father and three of his sons, I decided that a suitable name would be John Fairhurst & Sons Ltd. Naturally, my father thought it was a fantastic idea to have his name at the forefront. Little did I envisage the problems I would have in later years, when it became evident that I was the only son with the ambition and business acumen to run the business. As one of the sons (my younger brother) was called John, it was often assumed that he was in charge of the company whenever my father was absent. However this change of name was one of the best decisions we made. It made it much easier for Alan Ward to obtain enquiries when he joined the company on the sales side two years later.

Soon after getting married in September 1961, I saw that my beloved sports car 'Spritey' was not suitable for going on site with the requirement to carry paint, sundries and stepladders, etc. so I sold it privately and had a company car for the first time. This was a brand new Austin A40 hatchback in metallic silver-grey with a white roof and a red interior – very smart indeed, but not for long. I took delivery on a Friday afternoon in October and went home to our bungalow in Sidcup that evening to show it proudly off to Ann. After dinner I received an urgent phone call from Tom Higgins, the foreman painter in charge of our Kolster-Brandes (KB) factory painting contract a mile or so down the road at Footscray. He was in urgent need of five gallons of black bitumen to paint the guttering and downpipes.

I drove to our Bromley store, collected a five-gallon drum of 'black bitch' as we called it, and put it in the back of the A40. I was approaching the traffic lights at Footscray, only a couple of hundred yards from the factory gates, when another vehicle jumped the lights and I was forced to slam on the brakes. It seems that I had omitted to secure the back seat properly and the drum in the rear compartment shot forwards, splashing my clothes quite badly. More seriously, a quarter of the drum's contents landed in the driver's footwell, leaving the red carpet under about two inches of black bitumen.

I carried on to see Tom and he and his men did their best to clean me and the car, but although I could throw away my clothes, the carpet never recovered from this ordeal. The whole car stank of bitumen until it was traded in less than two years later. Ann was not amused!

Tom Higgins was one of the nicest and kindest people who ever worked for us, and it was a great shock and terrible loss when, a year or so later and while still only in his 50s, Tom died suddenly of a heart attack. I will never forget that is was he, while on his summer holiday that year, who had sent me a 'card' which was actually made from light plywood. Painted on it was a picture of what was plainly intended to be a tramp with his legs apart and arms stretched out on either side. Both of his trouser pockets were hanging out to indicate that he had no money whatsoever and the caption was 'sure - I always quoted the lowest prices!'

It was in the spring of 1962 that we carried out the repair and redecoration of two very large greenhouses in the grounds of Windsor Castle. One morning on a regular site visit I was sitting in my car with the clerk of works discussing the specification when, in the centre of a grassed area, I noticed a somewhat dishevelled man climbing out of what appeared to be an underground shelter (I later discovered it was a boiler house). The figure was wearing a dark blue boiler suit and carrying a large shifting spanner. As he emerged and stalked off to our left we could see that he was cursing away to himself.

'You know who that is, don't you ?' the clerk of works said. I replied 'no, but now you mention it he does seem vaguely familiar'. 'It was Prince Philip' said the clerk. Apparently he had been down in the external boiler room endeavouring to effect a temporary repair to the central heating system.

By June 1963 I had traded in the Austin A40 for a more practical vehicle, a Morris Minor Traveller, a classic medium-sized estate car examples of which are still in evidence on England's roads over 50 years later. With its ladder rack screwed well down it was able to take considerable loads, and on several occasions this was the way I started many new jobs with the vehicle's ability to take up to four trestles, four pairs of steps and several scaffold boards on the rack.

It was in this vehicle and during the summer of that year that Ann and I decided to tour Scotland for our annual holiday. This we did for almost a fortnight, staying in various bed and breakfast establishments for an average of little more that £1 per night each. I was quite anxious to get back home, as we had commenced our most prestigious contract to date, the painting and gilding of all gates and railings around Buckingham Palace. On the way down south it occurred to me that it would be only a little out of our way to call in to see how they were getting on with this work, so we headed into London and straight down The Mall to Buckingham Palace.

Main Gates of Buckingham Palace

In those days you could merely nod to the policeman on duty at the main gates, explain briefly the reason for your visit, and just drive in and park on the large area in front of the Palace and behind all the railings. Many tourists were peering through, wondering who this couple was who could drive in with such impunity and park in the forecourt.

I left Ann in the car and went up to where our men were working, under a protective tarpaulin to avoid any rain spoiling their efforts. After a brief discussion with the foreman and after watching two of the gilders at work, I left the site with some serious thinking to do as it was apparent that costs were escalating fast. If progress continued at the same rate, we were in for a considerable loss on the contract.

The painting of the railings was an ordeal in itself, as the precise colour and the degree of 'eggshell sheen' had to be produced as a special one-off order by Goodlass Wall & Co, who at the time were one of the country's leading quality paint manufacturers. The gilding of the spear heads and coats of arms was an exacting task. The actual process of gilding involved books of pure 24-carat gold leaf supplied by the leading specialists, Messrs. George M Whiley. This firm was one of the oldest in the country having been founded in 1783, and we had estimated that 7000 books of their gold leaf would be required to complete this work.

The gilders I had been watching had been brought up specially for this contract from Brighton and were four of only about a dozen tradesmen in Southern England with the experience and ability to undertake this type of work. They were using what had been known in the trade for hundreds of years as the 'tip & cush' method of applying gold leaf.

There are certain tools that make gilding easier, but I reckoned it would be possible to do leafing without any fancy tools. A gilder's cushion (or cush) was a piece of wood about 5 by 7 inches, with a cotton or wool bat on the top covered with a smooth non-oil tanned soft leather. A small loop of leather was tacked to the bottom for a handle to hold the cush while working. A thin piece of parchment was attached with tacks to the cush around half of the long dimension and up four or five 5 inches. This provided a windbreak for the delicate leaf, as of course the slightest breeze would blow it away.

A dull flat knife was needed to 'cut' the leaf into the desired shape. A small blade attached to a finger could also be used, and was handier than always picking up the knife for every required cut. The blades needed to be very smooth, but not necessarily sharp. Any irregularities would tear the leaf rather than score or cut it.

Gilder's Cushion   Gilder's Tip

A gilder's tip, made of a few badger hairs glued between two pieces of veneer, was used to handle the thin pieces of leaf. It was rubbed back and forth for the hair to create a static charge which attracted the leaf, allowing it to be handled more easily. It was almost impossible to handle leaf by hand, so a gilder's tip or dry paintbrush was used to move the leaf from its book to the cush and on to the work.

Gold leaf comes in books of 25 sheets with intervening pieces of tissue paper to separate the leaves. Some craftsmen cut the leaf in the book and do not use a cush. I observed that, for all the gilders' technical jargon, the only item essential to the application was a suitable brush with fairly strong hairs for working the leaf as it is applied. However, the most difficult task facing a gilder with the task of applying several books of gold leaf is the skill required in the sizing operation.

All DIY decorators are aware of the need to apply a suitable size on a plastered wall before hanging wallpaper to prevent loss of adhesion by the absorbing of water from the paste. It also makes the wall slippery, which helps when positioning each length. In the case of gilding, though, a special material, similar in appearance to a thin varnish, must be applied in order to ensure adhesion of the leaf, and this is known as 2-to-4-hour size. A skilled tradesman has to apply the size in front of the gilder and make certain that it has been applied at least two hours before the gilder arrives on the scene in order to achieve the right amount of tackiness. Then the gilder has a two-hour slot to carry out his delicate work before the size has dried and made his task impossible.

Of course at this point I should be relating the story of the wife of a decorator who told her husband not to worry as size wasn't important – but I shall resist!

With the problem of speeding up the process in mind, I straightaway went to a local Woolworth's store and bought half a dozen different grades of toothbrush of the type I considered suitable for the job in hand. The next day I returned with these to the Palace and asked the foreman to try them all out to see which, if any, would prove to be adequate to give a satisfactory job. After a short trial and error period, the brush with the softest bristles was shown to be adequate for the task.

This innovative approach proved to be highly successful in speeding up the gilding process and the remainder of the contract was carried out using toothbrushes. Fortunately the Queen was out of London on holiday at the time. I'm not sure what she would have thought if on looking out from one of her windows, she had noticed what was going on!

Buckingham Palace main gates, 1962

Buckingham Palace side railings, 1962

Gilder applying gold leaf, Buckingham Palace main gates 1962

With our more mundane contracts at the time in undertaking minor repairs and redecorations to all manner of government buildings, the general specification for the application of paint and emulsion to walls and ceilings was 'prepare and apply....' without stipulating how, specifically, the material was to be applied, it being assumed of course that this would be by brush. I had noticed that a new type of applicator, a paint roller with a tray, was coming on the market for use by the DIY enthusiast. I went to a store, bought the most robust one I could find and took it to a school we were painting during the summer holidays of 1963. I explained to the site foreman how it was to be used, but he was not at all keen on the idea, saying that it was amateurish and not suitable for a professional decorator. I persuaded him and another decorator just to give it a fair trial and returned the following day to see how they were getting on.

They had already been given a target to paint each classroom in three days in order to get a respectable bonus. What this meant in effect was that they would have to paint the wall surfaces, for

145

example, with 4" wide brushes at the average rate for a decorator, which is eight square yards per hour. After a little practice, these two men had discovered that with paint rollers a similar area could now be covered at between 18 and 20 square yards per hour. They were absolutely delighted.

Soon we had introduced the use of paint rollers on all our contracts and, as far as we were aware we were the very first painting contractors to do so. We found that some clients did not like the 'orange peel' effect of applying full gloss or semi-gloss paints with rollers, and duly amended their specifications to insist that the use of rollers would not be permitted.

On nightwork contracts, they were never aware that we still continued to use rollers for the sheer speed of application, but then to 'lay off' the area as we went along with 4" brushes.

Although it took a little longer to go quickly over the area again with a brush, this was still infinitely quicker than using only a brush. We even used power rollers for very large areas such as oil storage tanks. Many other contractors took to using rollers for large wall areas, so the rates we could obtain for this type of work came steadily down.

Our firm had been weaned on using spray guns for large areas such as aircraft hangars, but most clients by the end of the 1960s forbade their use as some contractors employed men as sprayers when they had received little or no training and had no idea of sheeting up or masking adequately. Consequently that aspect of the trade got a very bad name. Then along came a new invention from America – the airless spray. As described earlier in this book, conventional spray-painting equipment consisted of an air compressor, sometimes petrol driven and sometimes electric. This provided compressed air through a main air line at a pressure of about 60 lb per square inch to a two-gallon paint pot. From this pot there was attached a fluid line and a second air line to the spray gun. The gun was then used to apply the paint under pressure as a spray of fine mist.

Airless spraying was quite different. The compressor was electrically driven and produced a pressure, through a special high-pressure line, of about 3000 lb per square inch to the gun. The main benefit of such a system was that, without any air being involved, the resultant spray was just paint and there was little or no 'overspray' of minute paint droplets floating in the air.

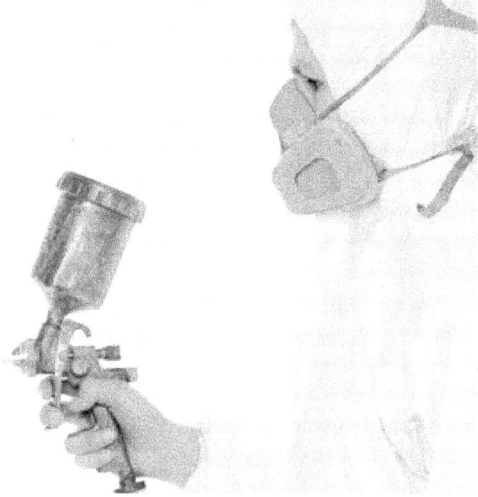

An airless sprayer at work

Although the spraying of paint was forbidden on many of the Government contracts we undertook in the 1960s, we did come across an invention which proved to be of considerable help. The painting of old-fashioned iron radiators, used extensively in government buildings, was always very difficult and time consuming until the 'Tuffy' became available; until then these radiators had always been painted by hand using a special bent tool called a radiator brush. The Tuffy was a fantastic little portable spraying machine designed specifically for radiators and similar hard-to-get-at small areas. Quite apart from the saving in time, because the use of a Tuffy was at least ten times faster than conventional brush application, it produced a much more professional finish, and we used these little machines to great effect for many years.

The main turning point in the firm's fortunes occurred when a young man of 25 called at our Bromley yard seeking orders for the paint manufacturer he represented, Murray & Jones. I learned that his name was Alan Ward.

Coincidentally I had been musing earlier that week that although the trade was awash with sales representatives from paint manufacturers, the contracting side of the industry was not being promoted in the same way. At the time I knew of no competitor who employed the use of a sales representative, and I was so impressed with this young man that I offered him a job on the spot.

Alan said he would be very interested and started with us shortly afterwards. After only a few weeks, though, he was persuaded by his old employers to rejoin them. Then, after only a further couple of months, he telephoned me to say he had made a terrible mistake and could he please come back.

His official restarting date was 31st March 1964 and within six weeks he had been responsible for generating several really interesting enquiries. He gradually became more and more successful, so much so that we were finding it difficult to cope with the volume of work generated; it was evident that a person of his calibre would inevitably be drawn into assisting to manage much of this additional work and he was quickly promoted to Contracts Manager, responsible for his own jobs.

In the autumn of 1964 we received an enquiry for the entire internal redecoration of Old Park Barracks at Dover. All very large contracts from the MPBW (Ministry of Public Building & Works) were sent out on a Bill of Quantities, and this was no exception. It was particularly welcome owing to the time of year, as it would mean several months of inside work all through the winter for a dozen men and also, unusually, the complex was unoccupied, making the task even easier. I really sharpened my pencil on this one, and we were duly awarded the contract.

Then, a few days after commencement, I received a call from the foreman requesting me to visit the site urgently as there was a problem with the preparation of the wall surfaces. These had been coated previously with a type of soft distemper over the underlying surface which was an oil-bound washable distemper (similar to today's emulsion). The specification called for 'wash back to original surface and apply one mist coat and two full coats of emulsion'. Our men, as instructed, had washed back the soft and peeling distemper and, as was usual in the trade at that time, allowed a period for the underlying surface to dry out, repaired any holes or blemishes with filler, and applied a thin coat of emulsion before finishing off with two full coats.

The Area Quantity Surveyor, a Mr Shambrook, had stopped the work and insisted that not only should we be washing off the soft distemper but the washable distemper underneath. Apart from being undesirable this was totally unnecessary, and almost impossible to carry out. I contended that once the washable distemper had dried it was a perfectly sound surface to paint on.

Mr Shambrook, however, was adamant and wanted it washed off right back to the plaster. I said this was impossible, but he replied immediately by getting out his handkerchief, wrapping it round his forefinger and spitting on it. He then proceeded to rub very hard on the wall, occasionally removing his finger to add more saliva, and carried on like this for about two minutes, eventually revealing an area of plaster about twice the size of his finger nail.

'There!' he exclaimed triumphantly.

I said 'You can't do that, there's acid in saliva and anyway if we employed this method it would take one man ten minutes to clean a square inch, equivalent to 24 hours for a square foot or four men for a month to clean four square yards. In any event, strictly speaking the original surface as specified is not necessarily the plaster but the brickwork'.

He then responded with those never to be forgotten words 'Yes, and I'll have it back to the brickwork if I decide'!

After this, we were hitting our heads against a brick wall, as it were. I was advised by a senior manager at the MPBW to ensure that the contract was completed and then, if we still felt we had a legitimate grievance, to make an official claim. So with mechanical scrubbing brushes and, where necessary, steam strippers, we eventually completed the work.

As advised, at the end of the contract, which took three times as long as anticipated and lost us almost £10,000, we made a claim, eventually settling for an ex gratia payment of £7,000.

During the period 1964 to 1965 we were dismayed to find that we kept coming second on some of the largest nightwork contracts to redecorate certain Government office blocks in London. We were always beaten by the same firm, a very large and well-known cut-price outfit. They were almost 20 times our size, with a reputed workforce of over 2000.

Every time we thought we had cut the price to smithereens, this firm just seemed to pip us with a lower offer. This was happening on such a regular basis that I was quite convinced that someone in our own organization had been passing our pricing details to this particular competitor, and those of us in the estimating department began looking over our shoulders to see who the culprit was.

At that time the tendering arrangement was that all offers on prescribed tender forms had to be received at the tender opening address by 11 am on the designated day, so it got to the stage when, instead of our usual practice of sending in the tenders by guaranteed first class post on the previous evening, I took to delivering them by hand and only completing the space for the price immediately before sealing the envelope and taking into the office a few minutes before 11 am. This seemed to make no difference. Only after a very long and frustrating period did we start to land one or two contracts again.

Some months later I was talking about this experience to a district surveyor of the MPBW and he explained what had been happening. The MD of the rival firm would take the tender documents, completed except the space for the price, into a phone box in the foyer of the tender office building and ring up his girlfriend, who worked in the contracts section on the floor above. She would let him know by some sort of code the lowest price immediately the tenders were opened, on the dot of 11 am. He would then quickly insert a slightly lower price and run up the stairs and into the office out of breath and less than 2 minutes late saying, 'So sorry I'm a bit late again – hope it's OK'. As they all knew him and he was the MD of their biggest contractor, they could hardly say no for the sake of a couple of minutes, so he got away with it time and time again. It only stopped when his girlfriend was promoted to another department.

Over the years we have had our fair share of strange people working for us. There was one occasion in 1965 when a painter turned up at our yard without an appointment, looking for employment. I said that he could try his luck with the foreman at a local GLC school we were painting, and he said that before he started he would need an advance of one week's wages to pay his rent. I said that if he was that desperate we could bend our normal rules regarding a 'sub' payment on account, and if he worked for a day we could pay him that very day to help out. He replied that that was not enough and ran out into the street calling out 'I didn't think your firm was any good and anyway I can see into the future and predict you will go bust in the next few weeks'. This incident really upset me for a long time, and wondered if he knew something I didn't.

In the spring of 1965 one of my young brother David's regular sojourns in the local pub produced an absolute gem, this time in the person of one David McLetchie. David had got talking to 'Ketch' as he became known, and it transpired that he had qualified as a marine engineer in Glasgow a year earlier but could find no suitable employment in Scotland, so had come down south for employment. He said he was willing to do anything. I believe David saw his opportunity to hand over to someone else the hard work of driving the firm's drop-side truck and the constant loading and unloading of all the plant and equipment necessary in our business.

In addition to being very bright and possessing a pleasant manner (although his Glaswegian accent was sometimes difficult to decipher), Ketch was very strong, and many times he succeeded in undertaking tasks that should normally have required two men. In short he was a fantastic addition to the wage roll and went on to serve over 45 years full time with the firm, only dropping back to part-time in 2010.

In 1965 we were asked to complete some refurbishment work to an office suite in London that was to be occupied by Barbara Castle, the newly appointed Cabinet Minister in Harold Wilson's Government. He had first of all appointed her as Minister of Overseas Development (1964-65) and then Minister of Transport (1965-68). It was in this post that she was responsible for introducing the 70 mph speed limit, breathalyzer tests for suspected drunken drivers and compulsory wearing of seat belts.

No one seemed to worry about the incredibly high cost of this refurbishment, of which the main expense was an area within the suite which was converted into a hair dressing salon. The public noticed how immaculate her hair was for each of her numerous appearances on television, but they would have been aghast if they had known how much public money had been spent on her office suite to make her pristine look possible.

We had a very difficult problem on our hands in the autumn of 1965, when we landed a contract to paint what we understood at the time to be a tunnel used by the Post Office sorting staff in the main London sorting centre at Mount Pleasant.

In fact, when the acceptance documents arrived there was reference to two tunnels. On investigation, I discovered that our chief estimator, Albert Pippard, known as 'Pip', had not read the tender documents properly. On his visit to the site he had seen only one tunnel, whereas halfway down this tunnel was another, very small, junction tunnel which led to a second large tunnel. Little wonder, then, that our tender offer had been considered to be very low!

This was only the start of our problems, as the specification for general preparation before painting included the phrase 'strip all previous coatings as necessary'. Pip had assumed that this meant scraping back all the loose paint to a hard surface as is generally acceptable in industrial situations, but soon after commencement the clerk of works made it clear that he was expecting all previous coatings to be stripped back to bare metal. We found that this was impossible to achieve with standard scraping tools. Then someone told us of the existence of specialist pneumatic stripping tools called Jason Needle Guns.

We discovered that a needle gun was an air tool that relied on a supply of compressed air that forced a piston backwards and forwards. This piston was connected to a number of very fine chisels that resembled needles. By pushing the needles forward at a very high speed - up to around 5000 times per second - the needle gun was able to rapidly chip away at any debris in an area and clear it back to bare clean metal in a matter of seconds without the need for any expensive and messy solvents or other cleaning products.

This tool could be held in a similar manner to a large pen, and we were told that it was capable of cleaning effectively enough to greatly reduce the amount of time a job takes.

Unfortunately we were unable to find a supplier of these guns with a mouth wider than about two inches, and with thousands of square yards to strip it was inevitable that the contract was going to lose us a great deal of money. I calculated that we could possibly have come out at cost had there been only one tunnel, but doubling the area left us with a loss of about £5,000 on a £10,000 contract.

Just after the Mount Pleasant contract was completed, and to lighten the mood a little, there was a very humorous episode concerning our Bromley yard, which we had purchased three years earlier. We had been concerned about a rickety stretch of fencing along one boundary and talked about the possibility of building a substantial six-foot-high brick wall.

Occasionally there were benefits from my brother David's habit of spending a great deal of time in the local pub, and this time he came up trumps when he returned to the yard from his usual liquid lunch accompanied by two sturdy men claiming to be bricklayers. They certainly seemed to know what they were talking about, so I gave the job to David to organize. They gave him a list of requirements with precise quantities of sand and cement together with 3000 bricks, all to be obtained from Roberts Adlard, a local builders' merchant. It seems that when David went to the store they asked him what kind of bricks he needed. David dutifully returned to our yard to ask the men what sort of bricks they wanted and they told him Flettons, one of the most common types of brick. Back at the builders' merchants they asked if he now knew the type of bricks to be ordered and David replied 'flat ones'!

In the spring of 1966, while living at Orpington, I was chatting to a neighbour. When I mentioned what I did for a living he asked if there was any chance of having some cans of paint at cost in order that they might redecorate the church hall at the end of our road. I agreed to go and take a look to see how much paint to order, and met the vicar. I think we must have been enjoying a profitable period at work, for I found myself offering our firm's services for free.

We sent in some men who redecorated the hall within a couple of weeks, and the vicar was delighted and sent me a lovely letter afterwards. Because it was church property I simply could not bring myself to charge them anything – silly really, because there have been a number of reputable decorating contractors over the years who have made a very good living by making a speciality of redecorating churches.

Also in 1966, we received an enquiry from a building firm called Lawdons to paint several dozen large executive houses they were constructing on the old Bickley Hall Preparatory School site near Bromley. Normally we would not work as sub-contractors to a building firm, as 'new work' is notoriously difficult to execute profitably. As the contract was practically on our doorstep we decided to make an exception, and submitted a tender at rates somewhat higher than our general price level owing to the anticipated problems one always seemed to have when working for builders. For a start, the specification for most new work was totally inadequate to produce a decent finish, and because the painters were the last trade in they were expected to make good any faults (and usually there were many) left by the other trades, notably the carpenters. As it happened, with the realistic rates we had achieved, the internal work on over 50 large detached houses on the estate was completed without any serious problems.

The external work, on the other hand, was a different proposition. Many of the externals had extensive areas of shiplap wooden cladding, and during the estimating stage nobody had thought to question the specification for this section of the work. The specification wording for this boarding was *Prepare for and apply two coats of Bourne Seal.* So, without thinking about it, that is what we did.

Within a few weeks Lawdon's Staff Architect, who had prepared the specification, Geoffrey Huyton, called me to the site, where the Bourne Seal was beginning to flake off in several areas. He asked what we were going to do about it. I checked with our foreman, who assured me that all the work had been carried out correctly and in strict accordance with the specification, so there must have been something wrong with the paint. I therefore called a representative of the manufacturer, who informed me that the specified paint, Bourne Seal, was not an appropriate material for external cladding. It was formulated especially for obtaining a hardwearing floor paint for school gymnasiums and similar locations.

He added that he found it hard to understand why a qualified architect would specify such a material for treating external cladding. I duly reported what he had said to the architect, who immediately blamed us for not checking the suitability of using Bourne Seal. His argument was 'as old established and experienced contractors you should have known not to use it, despite it being specified by me'.

My view, which I expressed very strongly, was that as a qualified and experienced architect he should have known, or if not known he should have at least checked, as to its efficacy for the work in question.

Ultimately, and after a costly exchange of letters by the two firms of solicitors involved, Lawdons had to agree to pay us to strip the faulty work and redecorate with a more appropriate material. This contract seemed to be ill-fated regarding the materials used, for this was the first contract we had carried out using Dulux paints where a major problem had arisen over the 'chalking' of externally-applied white gloss. We suffered from the same problem on several further external painting contracts before the chemists at Dulux solved the problem. I bring to mind that it was a technical problem and something to do with the inclusion of insufficient, or the wrong type of, oil in the manufacturing process. The effect was that the white gloss looked perfect after it had dried, but then, after several weeks, a thin chalk-like coating gradually grew on the surface which took away the sheen, and if you drew your hand over the area a small amount of chalk would be left on your fingers. We were glad when this contract came to an end. Although I had no idea what the future held for Lawdon's Bickley Hall Estate, I could never have imagined that less than two years later, my wife Ann and I would be in a position to purchase one of the houses to accommodate our growing family.

During the summer of 1966 were we entrusted by the works engineer of the BP oil refinery on the Isle of Grain in Kent to paint huge areas of large oil pipes that ran from one section of the refinery to another across fields where cattle continued to graze. After normal preparation, the specification called for a priming coat of red oxide followed by two coats of aluminium paint.

There were no problems up to the stage of applying the aluminium, but on the first morning after we had commenced the first coat of this attractive silver-coloured material, our men noticed that some of the cows in the vicinity had brightly coloured silver tongues! It seemed they had a predilection for the taste of aluminium. The next day it was even worse, some of the cows seemingly having told their mates about this new delicacy, as all the cows now had silver tongues. Quite apart from any harm this paint might do to the cows, it was costing us a small fortune because of the number of times we had to redo the work. Eventually we persuaded the farmer that, in the interests of his animals, he should remove them to another location until the paint had a chance to dry.

A further very strange and most unusual situation arose towards the end of 1966. One of our supervisors, Peter Trew, came into my office one day looking quite crestfallen. 'I'm really sorry, guvnor' he began. 'You know I've got a very good driving record, but I'm afraid that I've got to report a car accident I had this morning which wasn't my fault. This woman came in the back of me while I was waiting at a roundabout in Streatham'.

I duly completed an accident claim form and thought nothing more about it until, that is, he knocked on my office door two days later. 'You're never going to believe this, guvnor, but I've had another accident, this time a woman drove in the back of me while waiting at traffic lights in Chatham – and, you're really never going to believe this, it was the self-same woman who hit me two days ago!!'

There was another amusing situation in the office at about this time. I had always been interested in the Stock Market, and even while at school as a 15-year-old I kept records and graphs of the share movements of a few well-known companies such as Dunlop Rubber, EMI, and ICI. In 1963, at about the time Pip joined the firm, I started dabbling with shares for real and did very well with Dunlop Rubber on three occasions. Typically, I would make a small purchase, say £100, of Dunlop shares at, say 22s 10d and sell a few months later for about 26 shillings; I would then wait for the shares to fall back to, say, 23 shillings and sell again when perhaps they reached 28 shillings. I began discussing share dealing with Pip, who was also interested, and on the basis of a tip he was given we both bought some shares in a fairly obscure firm called Golden Hope Rubber, based in Malaysia.

We both held these share for a considerable period, during which time some sizeable dividends were received, and finally sold for a fair old profit when the company was taken over.

One day Pip came to me and told me that one of his sons-in-law, James, had recently emigrated to Australia and was working for a major silver and zinc mining company called Mount Isa. He said that James had told him that if the mine had a major silver strike he would send a telex to let Pip know so that he could buy some shares before anyone else in Europe as they were twelve hours ahead of London time.

Pip promised to let me in on this, and a couple of months later he came running excitedly in to my office, shouting 'I've had a telex from James – there's been a major strike at Mount Isa'. So immediately we were on the phone to our brokers, placing orders for as many Mount Isa shares as we could afford.

A few days after that, a disconsolate Pip came to see me to give me the bad news. 'You know the telex I received telling me about the strike?' he began, and I sensed there was some bad news coming up. 'Well, I've now had further details. The telex should have stated that all the men had gone on strike for more pay and nothing at all about a silver strike!'

I was flabbergasted at the time, but we both had a jolly good laugh about it later and for many years afterwards we would occasionally remind each other 'do you remember the strike at Mount Isa?'

Another prestige contract came our way in the autumn of 1966, which was for the painting of the huge Palm House at Kew Gardens. A specially-designed birdcage scaffold had to be erected, and as with all such high-profile contracts, it was a worrying period for me until the work was completed and the scaffolding removed from site.

Also in 1966, following a successful contract to redecorate the Head Office of the Hawker Siddeley aircraft factory at Kingston-on-Thames, we were awarded the prestigious contract of painting their factory at Dunsfold Aerodrome in Surrey, their main production facility and proving ground. This was the same location where, in 1953, Squadron Leader Neville Duke famously had broken the sound barrier for the first time. Duke became involved in the testing of Hawker's new family of experimental jet fighters that culminated in the production of the Seahawk for the Fleet Air Arm and the P.1067 (later named the Hunter) for the RAF. He was appointed the company's chief test pilot in 1951. On 7 September 1953, flying the all-red Hunter WB188, he set a new world absolute air speed record of 727.63 mph.

The Dunsfold Aerodrome site was therefore very famous, certainly in aviation circles, and our work had to be meticulously planned from the scaffolding perspective, for we were to work in the hangar roof steelwork above the area where a very important order was being fulfilled producing jet aircraft for a Middle East customer. We had to take out special insurance cover. If even a putlog were dropped on to the production line and had gone through a tailplane, for example, the cost could have exceeded a quarter of a million pounds.

It was while this particular contract was in progress that I came across the strangest sight I have ever witnessed. I had driven down to the aerodrome one morning, and after negotiating the narrow lane leading to a rear entrance that happened to be my nearest point of access to the location where we were working, I was approaching the guarded entrance gate when I glanced over to my left. I was astonished to see in a clearing a large jet aircraft just hanging in the air. It was neither moving forwards nor backwards, and after a few seconds it started very slowly to descend vertically to the ground.

I just could not believe my eyes. As I was gathering my thoughts, my car was suddenly approached by two men dashing out of the guardroom by the gate and two more rushing over to me from each side of the road. The scene was quite chaotic for a few minutes with each of them shouting instructions to me such as 'what are you doing here?', 'sign this form', 'you never saw what you think you saw' and 'you are forbidden to mention this to anyone , including your close family'. Evidently I had approached at just the wrong moment.

Several months later I read in the daily paper about this fantastic new invention of a vertical take-off jet plane. The press release stated: *'The Hawker Siddeley Harrier GR.1 was the first production model derived from the Kestrel. It first flew on December 28, 1967, and entered service with the RAF on April 1, 1969. Construction took place at factories in Kingston upon Thames in southwest London and at Dunsfold, Surrey. The latter adjoined an airfield used for flight testing.*

Some years later BAE systems took over Hawker Siddeley and both factories have since closed.

Hawker Harrier AV-8A vertical take-off jet aircraft with the thrust nozzle seen directed along the normal axis

One side issue of working for Hawker Siddeley at Kingston-on-Thames was that I got to know the Plant Engineer, Harry Paterson, very well. One day Ann and I, together with our new baby daughter, Penny, were invited to tea with Harry and his wife Sybil at their home in Purley near Croydon.

I often think about the time I spent with Harry at Littlehampton. One day when I was out to lunch with him the conversation got around to fishing, and it transpired that Harry was a keen sea angler. He said that he knew the captain of a small fishing boat based in Littlehampton and had been out with him on numerous occasions. Obviously I was supposed to say 'Why don't we arrange to have a day sea fishing, then?' So I fell for the bait, if you'll pardon the pun, and a couple of weeks later Harry rang to say the forecast was good for the following day, so was I free? I drove to his house, picked him up with all his fishing gear, and we presented ourselves at the appointed place and time on Littlehampton beach.

As we left the shore I remember thinking how nice and calm the sea was and what a wonderful day for fishing. Little did I know how things would pan out. After going about three miles out to sea the captain decided this would be a good place to drop anchor, after which he proceeded to light up a huge half-smoked cigar. The smell was pretty powerful, but as I also smoked the occasional cigar I told myself not to worry as I should be used to it. After about an hour of catching nothing, not even a nibble, I suddenly felt a huge tug on my line and as I hauled it in I could see that it was an ugly looking eel about 18' long. 'Oh, hell' I called out 'can I cut the line? – I don't want to pull that into the boat'. The captain said 'that's no problem, we catch eels all the time in these waters – carry it on the line and into the middle of the boat and I'll look after it'.

I did as he commanded and while he held the head of the eel in one hand he deftly removed the hook with the other. Once it was freed, the eel started to wriggle and jump around. As cool as a cucumber and evidently very used to handling such situations, the captain took a sharp long bladed knife and thrust it directly down straight through the middle of its skull, firmly pinning it to the deck.

This action certainly stopped the wriggling, but as I looked at the poor creature with its pleading eyes, and then caught a large whiff of the half smoked cigar coupled with the pungent smell of diesel from the engine and the boat's movement, I suddenly felt violently ill. I was seasick on an off until we reached the shore a few hours later.

Over 50 years of dealing with vehicle accident claims, there have been a number of strange events, although very few were more unusual than the incident involving a supervisor called Phil Weeden. In August 1969 he had been driving through Broadstairs in Kent when his van was hit by a car coming straight at him out of a side road. A little old man got out and they started to exchange details.

Phil told me that, at precisely the moment when he was asking for his name, the old man's eyes seemed to be looking up at the sign above a fish and chip shop opposite to where they were standing. 'Salmon', the man had said. 'What do you mean - salmon?' Phil had asked. 'You asked me for my name, and it's Salmon' he had insisted. 'Stop being silly or I'll call the police' said Phil. Phil had then asked 'What's your first name, then?'. 'I don't use it as I don't have to' he had said. Only after much banter and disbelief on Phil Weeden's part did it become clear that the little old man's name was indeed Salmon.

He was in fact Lord Salmon, Lord Justice of Appeal at the time, one of the most senior and respected members of the House of Lords. Less than three years later, in January 1972, he was created a Life Peer with the title Baron Salmon of Sandwich in Kent (just down the road from Broadstairs).

On leaving school, Alan Ward's first employer (where he learned the rudiments of the building industry) was a small general contractor based near Shooter's Hill, South London, called R L Ruggles & Son Ltd. Ron Ruggles, the founder, was approaching retirement, so he asked Alan and myself if we were interested in buying him out. After a brief investigation of the work in progress and business assets etc, we concluded that there was very little to buy other than the yard, so we advised Ron to sell the yard privately and wind up the company. Within a few days, however, we were approached by Len Alexander, a director of a reputable firm of old-established industrial painting contractors, Messrs W J Brooker, based for very many years in the Medway Towns. He said he was not getting a fair deal where he was, and did we have any suitable openings?

I asked him if he had ever considered running his own firm, and before I knew it I was suggesting that we could buy just the trading name of R L Ruggles & Son Ltd and set him up with a generous remuneration package in offices in South London, where he could introduce clients who were well known to him. At the time I had a collapsible bicycle which I kept in the boot of the car, and I found myself the next Sunday parking the car in Streatham and cycling up and down likely roads looking for a suitable yard and offices. Len also did his own research for premises and came up with the ideal location not far from Streatham High Street. He started to trade in the autumn of 1966 with just himself and a lady book-keeper.

Initially I used to visit him regularly, monitoring performance each week and generally proffering advice, but when it seemed he was well on his way and didn't need any more guidance, the visits waned somewhat to about once per month.

The financial arrangement I had with Len Alexander was that the company would be trading as a subsidiary of John Fairhurst & Sons Ltd with our firm holding 75% of the shares, leaving him with 25% (at no initial cost to himself), but of course we would be loaning money interest free for the working capital and would pass suitable enquiries his way from time to time. Additionally, to match his shareholding, he was entitled to 25% of any trading profits earned. When the draft accounts had been completed for the first year ending in August 1967 and were showing about £3000 pre-tax profits he approached me to say that now that he felt confident and was able to proceed without my periodic visits, could he please make a realistic offer for the remaining 75% shareholding and buy us out. This wasn't my idea at all, as I could foresee that he was going to preside over a growth company and it was likely to be very successful in the future. As he now dealt directly with all the contacts, including the ones we had passed to him, and as I knew that what he was saying was right and that I didn't have the time to run the firm myself, I felt that I really had no alternative but to accept the price he was offering, which was £10,000, based upon a multiple of three times current profitability.

So that was the parting of the ways with Len Alexander, but I can never think of him without bringing to my mind what happened at the office Christmas party of 1966 when he had only been running Ruggles for a few months. I was well acquainted with the tremendous amount of work that he had put into getting the firm off the ground, but not being aware at that time what he had in mind for the future of Ruggles, I took the opportunity at the party of seeking out his wife to say how much I appreciated all his efforts and to apologise for any detrimental effects this might have had on his home life. It just so happened that his wife, whom I had never met previously, was very similar in appearance to Pete Trew's wife in height and age, with the same length dark hair and both wearing a similar style and colour of dress. So I went up to the woman I thought was Len's wife and spent a good five minutes heaping praise on her husband and how much I appreciated all his hard work.

It did occur to me that she looked at me quite strangely once or twice, wondering why I had been so full of admiration for someone who she knew for certain would never put himself out unnecessarily in the line of duty! I shall never forget that particular Christmas party when I mistook Len Alexander's wife for the wife of Pete Trew, and the ensuing peculiar conversation.

After the experience with R L Ruggles & Son Ltd, I kept thinking that it might be prudent to start a completely new company in a different line of business. One night, in the very early hours, I sat up in bed and thought 'I know, what about a contract cleaning company?'

The more I thought about this, the more I was attracted to the idea. Initially I thought of it as being a hobby business, but if it proved to be successful, and if I could persuade my younger brother, John, to come in with me, this could prove to be a great platform with which the family could legally avoid some of the punitive death duties (the forerunner of Inheritance Tax) that would have become due on our father's death. John and I decided to go ahead with the formation of a separate cleaning company, and I was the one who came up with the alliterative name North Kent Cleaning Company Ltd. Although the intention was to share the ownership of the firm, I expressed my concern to John that if we were to own 50% each then problems could arise if, for whatever reason, we were to fall out in the future, so we formed NKCC, with each of us having a 49% shareholding and the balancing 2% being held by the Senior Partner of our Accountants, David Shetly. If we so chose, we could take on some of the contracts previously carried out by John Fairhurst & Sons Ltd and as luck would have it, within a week of formation, we managed to divert a small cleaning contract for the United Glass factory at Charlton which would normally have been sent to Fairhurst. The work entailed vacuum cleaning all the steelwork in the roof of the main bottle production area.

The only way this could be done effectively was to use a special vacuum cleaner manufactured by Nilfisk for such a purpose, which was strapped to the shoulders of the operator to allow the freedom of one arm to hold on to the steel trusses and the other to hold the nozzle.

This job could only be done at weekends, and as we had no employees at that time it was left to me to deal with it. Anyway I wanted the experience of seeing what such a machine was capable of, so with very little start up capital, we hired one of these machines and for the next three Sundays I went down to Charlton and climbed up into the steelwork and completed the job on my own. Very shortly afterwards Alan Ward was talking to the manager of a plant hire firm based at Hawley near Dartford called Hawley Plant Co. He gathered that he was seeking quotations for regular daily office cleaning for the office block, and reported this back to me. Of course I said we would be happy to give them a quotation, but knowing nothing of pricing such work, I placed an advert for a cleaning manager and a young man called Peter Medway was the only person to answer it.

Although only 20 years old, Peter had been working as a manager for a major window cleaning company which also undertook office cleaning, so I said we would engage him with the proviso that he would only join us if we landed the Hawley Plant contract. It seemed that we were in fact the only firm offering a quotation, although of course we were not aware of this at the time.

With Peter's ability to price the work and with a few contacts that he already had, the company began to expand. In order to maintain his interest, I agreed with John that we should transfer 10% of the shares to Peter Medway. On looking back, it was quite extraordinary how we managed to operate in those early days, as the only office accommodation we could afford was a small rented office within the single-storey office block from which John Fairhurst & Sons Ltd traded in Palace Road, Bromley. When I say 'small', I do mean very small, for the total area of the office was five feet by three feet, with a fitted desk 15 inches deep stretching along the longer wall.

This tiny space had to accommodate two people, my brother John and Peter Medway, and the only way they could get into this 'cubbyhole' was by the use of a sliding door. If the three of us had a meeting, one of us had to stand outside, and the one and only filing cabinet had to be stationed in the area just outside the door.

After trading successfully like this for a while, Peter became a little disillusioned at the prices he was able to achieve for cleaning contracts compared to what he perceived would be much more lucrative work when he saw at close quarters the level of profitability that Fairhurst were able to achieve by specializing in painting and decorating work. To some extent this was encouraged by some of the Fairhurst staff, who were quite happy to pass some of the smaller painting contracts to NKCC.

The name North Kent Cleaning then became inappropriate for approaching clients for decorating work, so it was decided to change the company name. As Peter was the type of person to beaver away to achieve his goals, the new name I came up with was Beaver Decorating & Cleaning Company Ltd. At the same time, and in order to preserve the office cleaning contracts, I arranged for the formation of a subsidiary company called Beaver Office Cleaning Services Ltd.

The office cleaning element was still quite important to the firm's revenues, especially the largest of them, which was the main office block at the Walls Sausage Factory in Park Royal, North London. I often think about the time I spent at this factory. The occasion was in the summer of 1969 when Peter Medway took his annual holiday and I found myself volunteering to supervise the contract while he was away. The ladies who worked on this contract for us had a working slot to complete all their tasks between 4 am and 8 am.

I shall never forget the awful stench that greeted me that first Monday morning when I arrived on site just after they arrived. I found it difficult to understand how anyone could possibly work in the factory with such a terrible smell of offal. Once inside the office block the smell was more bearable, and I stuck it for a week working alongside the women. My motive for this was to see exactly what was involved and how long each task took to complete. The specification was quite complex, requiring some items such as cleaning venetian blinds once per week, the complete stripping and re-sealing of floor areas once per month, and of course many items such as waste paper baskets, ashtrays and general dusting every day.

Although the work required a gang of eight cleaners working for four hours, every so often one or two of them failed to turn up, so the others had to 'cover' for them. I could see that the rates we were getting for this work were unrealistic if all the work was to be carried out correctly as per the specification. When I consulted Peter Medway about this on his return he said 'Almost all cleaning contracts are like this. To come out of an office cleaning contract with a profit depends on how much you miss or leave out. While everyone will notice if the wastepaper baskets have not been emptied, very few will query if the tops of the doors and tops of some filing cabinets have not been attended to or if the blinds are only cleaned once every two months'. He went on 'With window cleaning contracts, it is standard practice to price the work at cost and make 5% profit by missing out one window in every 20'.

I remember thinking what a terrible business this was to be in and feeling glad to stick with what I knew – painting and decorating. Having said that, even decorators would try to get away without applying the correct number of coats of paint or emulsion. One often heard the phrase 'Oh yes, guvnor, I gave it two coats – one up and one down'!

Talking of missing coats of paint, one of the strangest incidents I ever encountered was when we had been decorating a GLC primary school with Ron Murrell, one of our long standing foremen, in charge. Apparently he had been having several difficult encounters with the clerk of works throughout the contract. The clerk had on numerous occasions accused him of 'bouncing' a coat – a euphemism for missing a coat of paint. It seems that our Ron was determined to get one over on the clerk of works, and when I visited the site on the final day he came up to me with a wide grin and rubbed his hands together.

'I've caught him at last' he cried in triumph. 'You've just missed the clerk of works and he has passed all our work without even giving us a snagging list. I got away with only one coat of emulsion on all the ceilings, and now that I've caught him out and he has passed all the work I'm going to go back now and give all the ceilings a second coat'!

By the spring of 1971 the two Beaver companies were trading so successfully that they were able, from their retained profits, to pay cash for their own small freehold offices in Streatham. It was at that juncture that I had a meeting with my brother John to discuss how we were to proceed. Until then, Peter Medway had been the only one of three directors working full time in the business, with John working some of the time for Beaver while also carrying out his estimating tasks with John Fairhurst & Sons Ltd. I was only involved with finance and general administration, and realised that the firm had got to the point where it required the full-time services either of John or myself, so the outcome of our meeting was to agree which of us it was to be. We decided by the age-old and highly successful method of tossing a coin, and John won!

This was very welcome to me as it left me free to concentrate on expanding John Fairhurst & Sons Ltd. I set about this with relish, and the next five years saw some enormous changes.

CHAPTER EIGHT

Trading at home and overseas

Between 1971 and 1978 Beaver Decorating & Cleaning Company did not expand as I thought it might, but it was always very profitable, so much so that I was able to draw a fairly substantial dividend every year. One of the reasons for the high ratio of profits was that at the time of the major move from Bromley to Streatham in 1971, Peter Medway had approached John and me with a request to be given a further 15% shareholding to take his stake to 25%, leaving John and me each with 37.5%. Peter had been very motivated by this arrangement.

When I moved home from Chislehurst to Bromley in 1977, I thought how nice it would be at this stage in my life to no longer require a mortgage on my house. I also saw that I was spending less and less time with Beaver owing to my commitments by then at West Drayton and Southampton, so I approached both John and Peter to see if either of them was prepared to buy me out. John said he was not interested, but thought that Peter might. Peter agreed to acquire my 37.5% holding for £10,000, which went towards carrying out certain improvements to the new house but, more especially, to enable me to be mortgage free.

I also thought that John and Peter would be pleased to no longer have my involvement and that they would now be free to develop the firm as they thought fit without any interference from me. However, a few weeks after the share transfer had taken place, I was amazed to discover that when John realised how much I had been paid for my shares he had also approached Peter to see if he could do a similar deal and sell out completely. It later transpired that, following the deaths of his wife's parents in Beckenham, John and his wife were intent upon forging a new life for themselves in the West Country.

It was at about this time that an incident occurred that the contracts supervisors would never let me forget. Unusually for me, I was travelling by bus one day to collect my car from a service. As I sat on the top deck admiring the scenery I suddenly realised that a building coming up on my right was the Labour Exchange in Holbeach Road, Catford, which we had painted once before in 1962. I noted that the condition of the exterior paintwork didn't look too bad and then recollected that we had received an enquiry for redecorating this very building a few days earlier, so if I could unearth the 'dim book' (dimension book) going back seven years it would save a trip for an estimator to measure it up again. Upon returning to the office, I found the information I needed, worked out a price, and duly submitted the tender when the time came.

Eventually we learned that we had been awarded the job and the task of carrying out the work was passed to Pete Trew with, as was customary, a target for the cost of labour to complete it. After visiting the site and ordering the materials, he came to tell me that he thought the price was ridiculously low.

We then went through the specification and it was at that point I realised that, in the intervening seven years since we carried out the work previously, an extension with four further rooms had been added to the rear of the main building. Worse still for me, Pete said that when he had met the Accommodation Officer on site to discuss when and where we were to start, he had been told that, although our firm's tender had been accepted despite the price being much lower than the other contractors, there was no record of any representative from our firm ever attending the site to measure up.

Pete confronted me with this information and I had to admit that, as I knew (or thought I knew) the building, I had worked up an estimate based upon what I had observed on the bus. This story got around the firm very quickly and for many years afterwards whenever a query arose over a perceived low labour target the cry would go up 'did you measure it from the top of a bus?!'

One day in the spring of 1971, when we were in the throes of organising the men for a busy Easter programme painting several schools for the GLC (Greater London Council), I received a telephone call from an inspector from the Inland Revenue to say that he, together with a colleague, wished to make an appointment to inspect our records to ensure we were dealing correctly with our tax and National Insurance obligations. I agreed and made a date to see them about ten days later.

They duly arrived, went into the office with the wages clerk, and started poring over our records, so I left them well alone. An hour or so later they called me in to ask questions about one particular aspect of our weekly site wages summary. On those summaries were listed the total wages incurred for each current contract, a total of about 20 contracts in progress for any one week. Underneath the total of these costings was a section entitled Expenses, which gave the weekly amount of site expenses for each office-based employee including myself.

At the bottom of each sheet was a further section entitled Special Expenses, and against each of an average of about eight contracts were listed small round sums ranging from £5 to £20.

'What are these?' the senior man asked. I replied 'they are small cash expenses paid for help we have received on site, such as a 'thank you' payment to an accommodation officer on a London nightwork contract for taking in and storing a load of paint that can only be delivered during the day when our men are not on site.

He then started looking down the list and picked one item out at random. 'What would that be for?' he enquired. I said 'I believe that was to the employee of another contractor for the use of a long ladder to save us having to get our own'. He then pointed to a larger amount of £20. 'And that?' he asked. I said 'I don't know, I'll have to ask one of the supervisors'.

He looked at several wages summaries and enquired 'Who authorises and who pays these cash sums?' I said 'on occasion, I pay them myself but they are usually paid by, and at the request of, a supervisor. In any event I am the person who authorises every payment'.

He continued perusing the sheets and came to a payment of £15 charged against a primary school. 'Who would have received that payment ?' he asked me. I replied that I didn't recall, but could find out. Then he suddenly pointed to a contract entitled IRO Bexleyheath, against which a payment of £10 had been listed. 'IRO, IRO' he repeated, and started to jump up and down and went red in the face 'IRO, that's an Inland Revenue Office, isn't it?' Who had that, who had it, tell me who would have had that in an Inland Revenue Office?'

He seemed to be going quite mad at his discovery. I repeated as I had done before 'I can't recall off-hand, but I'll find out for you'.

'I'll have to take this further' he said, and the two of them departed.

The very next day, without any warning or appointment, two more men arrived on the doorstep and announced that they were from the Inland Revenue. Although they did not divulge their precise roles within that organisation, I later learned that they were from the Fraud Office in London. The senior of the two said his name was Mr Fudge, a name I shall never forget for the rest of my life.

He had a long conversation with me about the cash payments we had been making. His investigation had shown not only that these payments had been going on for many years and had been escalating over that period, but also that our associated company, North Kent Cleaning Company, had been doing the same thing, albeit on a smaller scale.

Eventually, he seemed fairly satisfied that there was no fraud intended, and I told him in my defence that we had been completely open about these payments and had made no attempt to hide them in any way.

He then said 'How do I know that you have not benefited personally from all or any of these cash withdrawals?' I told him there was no question that I had benefited in any way, as it could never be in my interest to do so.

'How so?' he asked. I replied 'For the simple reason that I have a substantial personal financial interest in this company and one of these days it will be sold. The going rate is eight times pre-tax profits, so even with the tax saved from withdrawing cash for myself I would still be well out of pocket if the company were not to declare its full profits each year'.

He closed the meeting by stating 'Nevertheless, I need to know the name of each recipient, together with the reason for the payment, for each of your companies going back for a period of five years. If I am not satisfied I will have no alternative but to issue you with a demand for personal taxation on the total amount'.

Within two days a letter arrived from Mr Fudge confirming his demand and giving me a month for a satisfactory reply. I wondered how on earth I was going to be able to accede to his request, and it worried me sick as there was no way I would be able to raise the funds if the tax burden were to fall on me personally. We were talking about an average of eight weekly payments for the main company and four for North Kent Cleaning. This totalled up to about 3000 names I had to provide, and in many cases there was no actual name known.

I commenced my immense task with meetings with the

supervisors, who were able to provide me with a lot of the information. However, even after delegating the details of North Kent Cleaning's payments to the manager of that firm, I was still left with over 2000 names, together with 2000 reasons for the payments, so somehow I just had to get on with it.

I felt that the only way I could deal with such an enormous task was to take myself completely away from both the office and home environments for a short period to give my total concentration to this chore. Two complete days should suffice provided there were no interruptions.

An ideal opportunity arose when, that weekend, Ann began to discuss a short holiday for the four of us and Torquay was mentioned. I immediately thought that if I were to go down and check out the hotel we had in mind, I could spend a couple of days to concentrate fully on the Inland Revenue information.

In one way, though, the timing could not have been worse for Ann, as she was pregnant with Lucy and did not fancy being left alone even for only a couple of nights. I stayed for three nights at the Victoria Hotel in Torquay and spent two complete days sitting in my car in a car park overlooking the sea surrounded by paper and notes and not even stopping for lunch. After dinner in the hotel restaurant I went to my room and carried on plumbing the depths of my mind to come up with the necessary facts requested by Mr Fudge.

On returning home I was convinced I would now be able to provide the Inland Revenue with sufficient information to satisfy them, but after posting several sheets of paper to Mr Fudge with almost all of the details he sought, I never had a reply or acknowledgement and never heard from him again. I thought how very rude he was, and left it at that.

We had a very strange experience on a contract carried out in the summer of 1971 at an old Army camp called Hobbs Barracks, near

Lingfield in Surrey. It had a long and interesting history dating back to the First World War, and in May 1968, HM Frederick IX, the King of Denmark, as Allied Colonel-in-Chief of the Queen's Own Buffs, visited the barracks for an inspection of the troops. However, by 1970, Hobbs Barracks was surplus to military requirements and stood empty, being taken into care by the Department of the Environment.

While the site was unoccupied, the DOE took the opportunity to have the outside of all the barrack huts painted, and we duly commenced work on what should have been a straightforward job. The most important part of any painting job is, of course, the preparation, and as the windows and sills were in pretty poor condition our estimator had allowed for a considerable amount of re-puttying of the glass.

He had not bargained for what happened subsequently. On arriving on site one morning soon after commencement, our foreman painter was both surprised and annoyed to find little holes in large areas of newly applied putty, mainly on the bottom edges. The men could not understand how this could have happened, but thought that maybe some youngsters had somehow managed to bypass the perimeter fence and had been playing some sort of game involving the windows.

But the next day there were more holes in the putty and it was getting beyond a joke. The following day was the same, and the men were having to send for more putty. As this was now becoming a costly operation, the foreman decided that the men should draw lots for one of them to remain behind to see who was causing this damage to their handiwork.

The painter nominated for this task afterwards said he was bored stiff with nothing to report until about 4.30 in the morning, when dozens of birds started to swoop down from the surrounding tall trees and commenced furiously pecking away at the putty. The penny dropped, and we realised that the birds were after the linseed oil in the putty!

After that we covered our re-puttying each night with wire mesh to prevent any further damage, and once the priming and undercoating stages were under way we had no further problem with the birds. But at the end of the contract we calculated that we had used four hundredweight of putty against an estimate of one hundredweight, to say nothing of the wasted hours in labour costs.

In 1972, the barracks briefly came to life when over 700 Ugandan Asians occupied it as a temporary refuge, having been thrown out of their country by Idi Amin, who forced over 80,000 non-Ugandan citizens to flee the country, the vast majority leaving behind most of their wealth and possessions.

The summer of 1973 heralded the start of the most frightening contract we had ever taken on. The work for which we had submitted the most competitive tender was for the cleaning and painting of the 625-foot high Thames Crossing Tower at Northfleet in Kent for the CEGB (Central Electricity Generating Board). The specification called for wire brushing and applying a suitable metal primer, followed by two coats of Micaceous Iron Oxide, which is a high-build urethane-modified alkyd-based coating for the protection of steel against corrosion. This was one of two extremely tall steel towers which carried the electricity cables across the River Thames from Essex to Kent.

We employed the services of a specialist team of climbers from Northampton, but things did not get off to a particularly good start, with the site engineer insisting that the men wore safety harnesses and the men explaining that the use of such equipment was totally impracticable when working on steelwork several hundred feet from the ground. They insisted, probably correctly, that it was far more dangerous for them to be continually clipping and unclipping a safety harness, as the most likely time for a slip and consequent fall was the period between unclipping, moving to a new location, and clipping on again to the steelwork. They said they had painted hundreds of transmission towers (pylons, to everyone else) simply by monkeying the steelwork, and they certainly would not risk their lives by wearing safety harnesses!

As can be imagined, I was quite ill with worry for the whole period of the contract, but especially during the period when they were working on the arms near the top of the tower, which protruded about 50 feet out on each side. While this part of the contract was being carried out, which took about a fortnight, I had virtually no sleep and kept thinking about my being responsible for these brave painters working away 50 feet out and about 600 feet into the sky. As there were vehicles parked in the area of the tower base, any spraying of the final finish was not permitted. I knew, of course, that if we were able to use a spray this would speed things up considerably, but the site engineer reiterated that this would not be possible owing to any overspray landing on the vehicles below.

I put my thinking cap on and carefully calculated the mathematics involved. I took into account all the factors concerned, starting with the maximum number of droplets of overspray that would arise from such an operation, then calculating the minimum wind speed that would be encountered, the height involved and the vast area in which any errant fine droplets of paint might fall.

I considered that by the time the spots arrived in the parking area they would be at least eight feet apart. Given the size of the average vehicle, there would be no more than two tiny spots of paint per vehicle, which I believed no one could possibly notice. Anyway, in practice, at that height and given the fact that any droplets would have to pass through a vast amount of latticed steelwork, I thought that most of the remaining overspray would be sucked up into the atmosphere.

It was a great pity that spraying was disallowed, as once having successfully completed this particular contract we could have approached the CEGB to spray future transmission towers and saved them many hundreds of thousands of pounds. But it was not to be.

In any event the contract was so successful that further contracts were awarded to us by the CEGB for long lines of much smaller transmission towers throughout Kent and Sussex.

View of steelwork from the ground   *The 625' high Thames Crossing Tower*

Other interesting painting contracts undertaken for the CEGB during the 1970s included the main turbine hall at Bankside Power Station (later to be converted to the Tate Modern Gallery), work at Dungeness B Power station on the Kent coast and a rather more complicated contract at Sizewell A Power Station near Leiston in Suffolk.

Sizewell A was complicated. It was the first nuclear power station we had worked on, so our operatives had to undergo an intensive screening process which made the whole operation much more expensive than our estimator had envisaged. We were fortunate to complete the work at cost, without even enough gross profit to cover our overheads.

* * * * * * * * *

In 1976 there was an extreme shortage of work in the UK, so we decided to start looking overseas. At the behest of John Akerstrom, the Sales Manager of our major paint manufacturer at the time, Macphersons Paints, I had the necessary inoculations and flew to Jeddah in Saudi Arabia. I had been told there was a great deal of work to be had there, especially for experienced painting contractors.

The outgoing flight on a Lockheed Five Star (with over 300 passengers) left on time from Heathrow and arrived almost on schedule at Charles de Gaulle Airport, Paris, to take on additional passengers. However the flight was delayed in Paris for 90 minutes, so I did not eventually arrive until 1.30 am, to discover that John Akerstrom and his Saudi agent, Mohamad Althukair and son Khalid, had been waiting for nearly two hours to collect me and usher me through the complicated customs procedure.

It transpired that Mohamad was well acquainted with the immigration officer, and it was in fact the officer who personally carried my suitcase out of the main airport building to the car park, which was teeming with people even at that time of night. Both Mohamad and Khalid Alkuthair were extremely pleasant and courteous, and they arranged to collect me at 8.30 the next morning.

Mohamad had apparently mistaken John's instructions to reserve a room for me at John's hotel that night and had in fact booked me in for the following night instead; he therefore had to make urgent arrangements for any hotel that would accept me at such short notice, so I ended up in a very downmarket hotel at the other side of the city for this first night (or what was left of it by the time I got there).

The hotel was of a very poor standard, and although it had its own bathroom I felt I could not use it. The very small old-fashioned bath was utterly filthy, as were the floors of both bedroom and bathroom. From an inspection it was clear that several people had already slept in the bed sheets before my arrival, so I sat in a chair and dozed off.

I managed only about three hours of sleep that first night, owing to excessive noise from the air-conditioning unit. I ventured into the bathroom to discover that the peculiarly-shaped bath (about three feet square by three feet deep) had cobwebs at the bottom with spiders running around in it!

On the ground floor, in a large restaurant area, there was fly-covered food laid out as a self-service buffet, and two or three other guests were having breakfast. I didn't fancy any of the offerings, indeed I didn't even recognise what any of them were, so I returned to my room and ordered room service. From the list supplied, the only item I fancied was a toasted cheese sandwich, so I ordered this together with a bottle of apple juice to drink, which cost eight times the price of one in England.

Apart from being taken out one evening to an open-air restaurant where we were treated to lamb on skewers, toasted cheese sandwiches with apple juice remained my sole diet for the entire week. Unsurprisingly, on returning home, I found that I had shed over a stone in weight during the week.

On the Monday, having had very little sleep, I was up at 6.30 watching the mad dash to work. This was an extraordinary sight, with cars brightly decorated with carpets fore and aft on top of the dashboard and rear parcel shelf. I saw two workmen on a small moped which looked as though it would hardly carry them and many others looking like building workers going to work carrying their bedrolls, many walking barefoot. Above the sound of men shouting to each other and the continual roar of motor bikes with ineffective silencers all I could hear was the incessant noise of car horns.

I went down the uneven stone stairs to the reception area and was duly collected right on time and taken to Mohamad's small air-conditioned office behind the shop, where he sold hundreds of gallons of Portaflek each week. He had a very pleasant disposition and looked very smart in his crisp clean white robe.

I was in his office for over an hour discussing business and my experience of applying various decorative materials. During that relatively short period however, he and many others in nearby shops and offices left what they were doing on two occasions to go to the local mosque to pray. I gave him an outline of our business and some sales leaflets together with photographs of some intricate work we had done painting and gilding the main gates and railings of Buckingham Palace. At 1 pm John and Walter called for me and I was taken to their hotel where we had toasted cheese sandwiches in their room.

In the afternoon, I was taken on a long car journey to the edge of the city where there was clear evidence of a major construction boom in progress, including dozens of half-built factories with masses of steelwork awaiting protective painting. John reckoned that the work prospects were excellent and said that his Portaflek sales alone would produce a minimum annual turnover of £600,000. Portaflek is a specialist coatings product made by a firm called Sissons and was used extensively throughout the UK, especially in toilet areas and staircases.

Portaflek gives a hard-wearing coating with an attractive multi-coloured fleck appearance. It is manufactured by suspending tiny coloured fragments of cellulose in a water-based material similar to emulsion, and applied by low-pressure spray. Because of the composition of the material it is not possible to apply it by brush. It is supplied in the usual five-litre cans, and sold for about £9 per can out there.

I was told that local labourers earned about £90 per week, although really good tradesmen earned considerably more. It appeared that money was no object if the standard of workmanship and advice on decoration schemes was right. The accommodation situation there was diabolical, and a good room virtually impossible to obtain. The bill for that first night in my grubby hotel was £40. Rented accommodation, where it could be obtained, was very expensive, with a typical cost of about £6000 a year for a room shared by two people. I didn't feel very hungry all the time I was in Jeddah as it was so hot.

In the new hotel to which I was taken they provided an efficient room service, so that evening I ordered the usual toasted cheese sandwich and a bottle of apple juice. In the afternoon I enjoyed a really nice cup of coffee with Mohamad in a local coffee shop and then visited his retail shop (DIY type) and it was extremely busy. Mohamad told me that he also had a warehouse for larger orders.

At his shop I helped to solve a problem of rollers drying out too quickly with a small local contractor. The contractor was deaf and dumb, but he was a talented actor and made himself easily understood using sign language.

That evening I was able to see a great deal of the market and bazaar area as darkness fell and there were masses of people about, seemingly very wealthy locals. I observed that less than one in a hundred was European and was quite surprised by the number of physically disabled people. I even saw one man walking on all fours using two pairs of sandals. Several people were walking round the market smoking shisha pipes, and I witnessed fantastic displays of various spices together with their evocative aromas and the wonderful smell of local bread being baked.

I met Ahmed, the shop manager, and had a long discussion with him about costs and margins of decoration work. He was staggered to learn of the low profit margins earned in the UK. I discovered that Mohamad bought Portaspray units for £200 from Macphersons and sold them for £500. This appeared to be a typical markup on most business deals. It really was a completely different world from the one I was used to, with the deaf and dumb contractor apparently buying about 100 gallons of Portaflek per day. At £9 per gallon I calculated that he must be spending about £200,000 per year on this material, giving him a turnover of about £1 million with a net profit of some £200,000!

During the evening, Mohamad told me that in his old house in 1974 he was quoted a sum exceeding £3000 for decorating a room of 40 square yards and 10 feet high. The specification was for ceilings to be coated in combed plastic and walls hung with good-quality wallpaper. This equated to about £16.50 per square metre, more than double the rate typically achieved in the UK. The usual working day there was from 7.30 am to 1 pm and then from 4.30 pm until 9 pm. There was no night life whatsoever, and TV and radio in the hotel were both of a very poor calibre.

Petrol cost the astonishingly low price of 7p per gallon and car tax was only £8 per year. Most streets were one way, which was just as well with the standard of driving being so appalling. As happened in many other countries, the indigenous race, the Saudis, did not perform any manual tasks and almost all menial tasks were carried out by Yemenis. I saw only three European women all day, and for that matter very few local women. All economic functions were undertaken by men.

In every office one visited one was offered, at approximately 20-minute intervals, a small glass tumbler of hot sweet tea (chi); no milk was available, but this made a very pleasant drink in such a hot climate. I noted that it was not quite as humid that night as the previous one, but understood that the temperature in the shade early that afternoon was just over 90 degrees.

You certainly took your life in your hands when you attempted to cross a road, and I recalled having to run very fast earlier that day to avoid being struck by a motorcycle. Both cars and motorbikes were driven, and treated, rather like toys, with some cars emitting the sound of a barking dog when reversing while many made bird noises (swallow whistles) when the brakes were applied.

On the Tuesday I remembered that, on retiring to bed the previous night, I was bitten by a mosquito and didn't get to sleep until 1 am. I was fast asleep when knocked up by John at 8.15 the next morning. Once again I visited Mohamad's shop and was collected by him in his big black Mercedes. He told me that one petrol station had run out of petrol on his way to meet me. He explained that his new car bought the previous week had cost him about £10,000, including 3% import duty.

Earlier in the morning I witnessed the last few strokes of a man in the main street being flogged for drunken behaviour in a public place; it was more to shame him than to impart physical pain, they said, though in addition to this he received a sentence of one month in jail. I was told that the previous month in Riyadh three men had been beheaded for attacking a girl.

In mid morning I kept my appointment with the Manager of the National Commercial Bank. This was a most imposing building, constructed mainly of marble, and although it was extremely busy there was not a European in sight.

The Manager was very courteous and tried to be helpful, although I did feel that he wasn't giving me all the attention that I was used to with a bank manager. All the time we were talking, he was busying himself signing dozens of documents.

I was given the inevitable glass of chi while he told me he was convinced that there was a good demand for quality work, especially if advice on suitable materials was given as part of the service. He said that the price for two coats (without specifying which materials) had increased recently from 2-3 riyals to 5-6 royals per square metre.

Back in Mohamad's office, I had a long discussion with Sada, a Yemeni with eight children, who was Mohamad's under manager and also acted as an interpreter for another under manager called Hood. As they were both employed by Mohamad I felt that between them they would have a pretty good idea about the overall situation with the painting trade in the Kingdom.

They both confirmed that the current going rate for preparation and applying two coats of oil paint was 6-7 riyals per square metre and Portaflek was 12 riyals. A first-class decorator would expect to earn 1600 riyals per week (but they stressed that this would not be all the time).

They said it should be possible to rent unfurnished accommodation for eight bachelors for 35,000 riyals per year, and Sada suggested that I should bring ten tradesmen out from England. I said they would require regular earnings of 1,200 riyals per week and he thought this not unreasonable. By now I was getting several conflicting stories: the bank suggested 6/7 riyals for two coats, Sada the Yemeni saying 6/7 riyals and Mohamad at least 10/12 riyals. Portaflek cost 9 riyals a metre for the material alone and Sada said you would get 12 riyals for supplying and applying this material, while Mohamad says you would get 18 riyals.

Sada said that publicity brochures were a must, as nobody else produced these and Mohamad confirmed that, in his opinion, it would be necessary to rent a shop on Main Street and that the annual rent would amount to about 35,000 riyals.

I worked on all the figures I had been given and concluded that, because of the high labour/material ratios, the prime cost of applying two coats of oil paint would likely be about the same as applying a coat of Portabond and Portaflek, ie 9.5 riyals per metre.

In the afternoon, I met up again with Mohamad and visited his new house that was being constructed on the City's outskirts. Back at his office we discussed the various prices for two coats of water-based paint (emulsion), two coats of oils and Portaflek.

He then introduced another dimension which we had never considered in the UK. From his conversation it seemed that any prices he had been discussing to date were deemed to include a skim coat of a plaster-type substance to cover all the 'brickwork', which was in fact a cheap type of block work, or breeze block as we knew it, so it made sense to me that some sort of material would have to be applied before any paintwork. In this situation I had been used to this treatment being undertaken by specialist plasterers and I was unsure that our decorators would be skilled enough to carry out this work.

Mohamad then arranged for a meeting with various interested parties, one of whom I understood to be a sheikh with some influence in the construction industry. There were nine of us sitting in a circle, and apart from John and myself, all the others were Saudis, including an interpreter. I began by showing them photos of the main gates and railings at Buckingham Palace and explained that our firm had used a specially-formulated paint with all the gold spear heads and coats of arms on the main gates being treated with 22-carat gold leaf.

The photos and some copies of our recent company brochure were handed round, and there was great approval with some hand clapping. One of the Saudis said he often visited London and was most impressed with the high standard of work we had carried out to various important London landmarks.

I later gathered that many wealthy Saudis made regular visits to Europe, especially London, where they can gamble huge sums of money in the casinos, something they are forbidden to do in Saudi Arabia. Eventually the conversation got around to discussing the benefits that our firm could bring to Jeddah with a much higher standard of redecoration.

'Redecoration' said one of them, 'what is this redecoration?'. I then explained that, although I had seen for myself the vast amount of new painting work going on everywhere, our firm did not in fact carry out new work, which would involve working as sub-contractors to a main building contractor.

This came as a complete bolt from the blue to me. All along, they had all been talking about new work, and this had included John, Walter and Mohamad. Once again, one of them asked 'what is this redecoration?' in a very confused voice. I tried to explain, but to no avail. One of them then said 'we all understand the word décor with wallpaper to match lights and curtains, etc, but what is redecoration?' Once more I found myself trying to explain. Another said, 'When you construct a building you put glass in the window frames, for example, but after five years or so you wouldn't consider re-glazing would you? So once you have painted a building why would you ever want to repaint it?'

Eventually the penny dropped. Through the interpreter it transpired that there was no equivalent word in Arabic for the word redecoration.

On hearing this it dawned on me that when you see pictures of old buildings in the Middle East there is indication that they were once covered in some sort of limewash, applied dozens, sometimes hundreds, of years earlier but never touched again. It seems that places like Jeddah, where it only rains (albeit very heavily) about once a year, protection against the elements is not the priority it is in Europe.

* * * * * * * * *

In the summer of 1972 we found ourselves carrying out a most unusual office redecoration contract for the MPBW (Ministry of

Public Building & Works). This was in an office block in London which we were warned was top secret; we were told we must never divulge its location. The security system was quite incredible, and it took a considerable time for our operatives to be security-vetted and issued with the necessary passes to enter the building. The work had to be carried out at night.

The most extraordinary element of the contract, however, was the procedure for operatives wanting to visit the loo. Each painter had two armed guards, one on each side, to accompany him there and back! We thought it had been bad enough a year or so earlier when we had encountered the strict security involved in repainting some underground shelters in the Clapham Common area which were destined to be used in the event of a nuclear attack, but the security there was nothing compared to the secret London office building.

I received a 'wake up call' in the summer of 1977 when Tommy Mulholland, the Managing Director of one of our competitors, Hygienic Cleaning & Decorating Company, was attacked while carrying a large sum of money from the bank to pay the weekly wages. Acid was thrown into his eyes and he was completely blinded. The incredibly brave Tommy not only continued to work but after much practice and expert guidance ended up playing 'blind golf' for England.

Our insurers had always been aware of the dangers facing our staff when drawing money from the bank, and until that moment they had required us to warrant that at least one person would be present for every £1000 being carried. As the sums involved were quite large, often £4000 or more (in today's terms this would have amounted to about £20,000), it meant that up to five people would be necessary to collect the weekly cash withdrawal from the bank. I thought this was a preposterous idea as there would be nothing more obvious to would-be wage thieves.

For a period of several years, I decided to deal with this predicament alone by spreading the money all over my body, in each shoe and a little in each pocket. In addition I always carried a water pistol filled with black ink which I would have used to identify any assailant.

It should be remembered that the reason for this cash requirement for weekly-paid operatives stemmed from the original Truck Act of 1831 which in its time replaced no fewer than 19 statutes by a wide prohibition against contracts for artificers' wages being specified in other than 'current coin of the realm'. Its 27 clauses applied to a dozen specified trades but excluded agriculture. Fortunately this problem was solved so far as I was concerned by the passing of The Truck Acts (Repeal) Bill (2nd reading in the House of Lords on 30th March 1983) which decently buried the carcases of five outdated laws listed in the schedule. We would now be permitted to pay our weekly wage earners by cheque or transfer the money by Autopay direct into individual bank accounts.

One major difficulty we faced with the change was that many of the men did not want their wives to know how much they earned – incredible, but true.

In 1978 a friend of Alan Ward called Don Barnes, who had successfully launched a Group Twelve subsidiary called Group Twelve Membrane Coatings, was promoted to assist in the day-to-day control of our other Group Twelve companies. In 1980 he was taken on a business 'jolly' trip to the USA by one of our paint suppliers, and on the plane he met up with Gordon Kay, the representative of a major thermal insulation contractor. To cut a long story short, on arriving back home he introduced Gordon to Alan and me with the idea of setting up Gordon with his own trading company using his many contacts from his present and past employers.

I carried out some research into the market we were talking about and it seemed that this specialist field did not have too many competitors. I discovered that the main market for Gordon Kay's expertise was for spray applied intumescent coatings to steelwork on new construction projects, designed to prevent the steelwork from twisting in the event of fire. I was thrilled at the prospect of rejoining the spraying fraternity within which I had been reared, though I was less enchanted when I realised that the clients for this service would almost always be large building contractors. From past history I had developed a natural aversion to working for such organisations.

Once I had conjured up a suitable name for the new firm, Kaytherm Services Ltd, it was up to Gordon to locate suitable office and storage facilities. He wanted to be geographically central to the southern half of England, and he managed to find suitable premises in Milton Keynes. Trading started off well enough with two very nice contracts, but within two years the recession of the early 1980s began to wreak havoc with the construction industry, which nosedived into substantial losses, and quite suddenly the market for Kaytherm's work dried up almost completely. After suffering almost £50,000 of trading losses in three years, we decided to call it a day and sold the firm for a nominal £1 to a competitor.

For quite some time, the Fairhurst Organization had evolved by trading as two completely separate groups, first the main Fairhurst Group trading as John Fairhurst & Sons Ltd with branches in Bromley, West Drayton and Hove and John Fairhurst & Sons (Southern) Ltd covering Hampshire, second the Group Twelve Group with subsidiaries Group Twelve Decorations Ltd, Group Twelve Advertising Ltd, Group Twelve Membrane Coatings Ltd and Bulfords (Builders) Ltd.

Our advertising and promotional material gave the impression that the group was just one entity rather than two, so by early 1981 we started to plan the best way of merging the two. One way or another 1981 turned out to be a very eventful year. In April, the Sussex area office based at Cowfold had outgrown their rather small premises and we purchased the freehold of a corner shop with suitable storage in Hove, where we could give an even better service to the Brighton Area Long Term Maintenance Contract that we had held for many years.

By 1981 health and safety was beginning to be taken more and more seriously, and many of our competitors had followed our lead by setting up their own safety committees. I suppose I had no alternative but to accept as a compliment the discovery that some of the safety policies being issued by certain competitors were almost exact copies of our own. Evidently someone in our organization had passed our details to friends employed by these competitors. It was a little galling to think of all the hours I had spent in setting up our safety systems, only to find that they had simply been copied.

To keep ahead of the game I discovered a company called Hinton & Higgs who had recently been established as specialist safety advisers to the construction industry, and in June 1981 we appointed them to visit all our sites on an ad hoc basis and report their findings direct to me, leaving a copy of their recommendations at the site.

This system worked extremely well for a number of years and really concentrated all of our operatives' minds on the importance of health and safety in the workplace.

In September 1981 we finally and officially merged all companies and branches into one. John Fairhurst & Sons Ltd acquired for cash the entire shareholding of Group Twelve Ltd. In the same month the newly-established Fairhurst Group Retirement Benefit Scheme acquired as an investment the freehold property in Chandler's Ford which had been rented by John Fairhurst & Sons (Southern) Ltd for the previous eight years.

To condense the name of the Retirement Benefit Scheme to a more manageable size, we shortened the name to the Fairhurst Group RBS. This was many years before our Bankers, National Westminster

Bank, were taken over by the Royal Bank of Scotland and thereafter started referring to themselves as the RBS Group.

Bearing in mind the way the firm was growing and the length of time it was taking to form new companies, I hit on the idea of going through all the motions of forming a company with the intention of keeping it on the shelf without trading, merely to be there in case of need. This company was called John Fairhurst (London) Ltd.

CHAPTER NINE

Tragedy and triumph

In November 1981 my mother was no longer able to cope with my father's increasing memory loss due to the onset of Alzheimer's disease, and her doctor recommended that he should be looked after full time in a ward at a hospital in Croydon which specialized in Alzheimer's patients. Little did we know how soon we were to lose him.

In the early weeks of 1982 I was knocked sideways by three events which happened in quick succession. On January 31 came the sudden death of my father. This was followed by a major burglary and break-in at our Head Office in Bromley, and worst of all by the appalling murder of my friend and colleague Ron Allen, the MD of Bulfords (Builders) Ltd.

Although the death of my father, on 31st January 1982, was not totally unexpected at the age of 83, I was hit much harder than anyone else in the family. Not only had I worked so closely with him for so many years, but more importantly, because of my decision 20 years earlier to rename the company after him, I could not look anywhere without seeing his name on letterheads, invoices, even calendars and desk diaries.

The burglary took place a few days after my father's funeral. A gang cut a large hole in the office wall and removed the safe, as they were unable to open it on site. It was eventually found opened up in Keston Ponds with all its important contents such as holiday stamps, contracts ledger, etc. totally ruined. It took us many weeks to get our books back into some sort of order.

The third event, the murder of Ron Allen in mid February, was of course by far the worst tragedy of the three. Ron was a young qualified quantity surveyor in his thirties who was married with a small daughter. Nobody knew precisely what happened, as he was alone in his small office at the time, but it seems that two men came in off the street, grabbed pickaxe handles they found in the corner of the yard, and burst into Ron's unlocked office demanding the safe. There was very little need for a safe as money was never kept on the premises, but they probably did not believe Ron when he told them we had no safe. With no-one else about they evidently laid into him and he died later of his injuries in hospital.

The strange thing about this case was that although the police set up a portable incident room at the end of the road and took various statements and interviewed a lot or people in connection with this terrible crime, the one person in our firm who dealt with him most often and on a regular basis, and who therefore probably knew Ron Allen better than anyone else other than his wife, namely me, has to this day, 30 years after the event, never been approached by the police and never interviewed. It was as though I never existed.

Although we put up a substantial reward for information leading to an arrest, nobody was ever charged with Ron Allen's murder. As I was never interviewed, I can only assume that either the police were totally inept or, more likely, were well aware of who the culprits were but were unable, for whatever reason, to get sufficient evidence for an arrest.

In the immediate aftermath of these events I really felt I was beginning to crack up. Ann saw how I was feeling and suggested that I have a complete week's break away to pull myself together. Tenerife was suggested as being suitably sunny in late February, so I booked a flight and spent a week at one of the best hotels in North Tenerife, the Hotel Botanico. This was a great help in my coming to terms with my immediate problems, and I returned refreshed to face the business world again.

On looking back, it was as if 'someone up there' was saying 'you've had enough', and within a few days of returning from my week's break, I was interviewing Kathy Lynch, one of the contenders to replace Joan Short, my secretary for the past 17 years, who was retiring. She was already down to a four-day week.

The main requirement was to find someone who was an experienced book-keeper, generally financially aware, but most importantly a person who would be totally loyal to me and the firm, as she would be dealing with all manner of confidential matters.

Kathy was appointed. Within a few weeks of joining us on 22nd March 1982, she confided that at one point she had been on the verge of resigning because Joan had given her the impression that she might not retire after all!

I did realise that there was a clash of personalities when Joan kept querying almost everything that Kathy did, but when I challenged her on this she told me that she was only looking after my interests. Once Joan had left, everything ran much more smoothly in the office and Kathy and I really worked well together although, like Joan, she was only prepared to work four days a week. At her interview she explained that her husband had his own tailoring business in Orpington and as he worked Saturdays, Monday was his day off and she would also like to join him for a day together on Mondays.

In retrospect, I was aware that I was in a very poor mental state at the time Kathy started with us in March 1982 and I am certain that having someone who was totally loyal to me and with whom I could discuss business matters with confidentially stopped me from going over the edge.

In about 1980 the tax authorities introduced a new tax charge on the private use of fuel in company cars. Until then, employees were required to pay tax on the benefit-in-kind value of the use of a car, which was also deemed to include the private use of fuel. We therefore issued an Internal Memorandum to all drivers of company cars explaining about the new tax and saying that from now on they would be expected to pay for their own petrol when the car was used privately, and spot checks would be made to ensure that this new ruling was being complied with.

Then in 1983 I received a call to say that an inspector would shortly be making a visit to see that we were adhering to all the current tax rules. His first mistake was to confront Alan Ward with his monthly expenses and state that Alan should be paying more tax on his entertaining expenses. He asserted that he, the tax man, had no such benefits and was limited at lunchtime in his office to such sandwiches as he had brought for the day, whereas Alan was often entertaining clients with steak lunches and fine wines, all on expenses.

'How would you like to live like this?' retorted Alan. 'The entertaining part of my job is a real health hazard – how can it possibly be classed as a benefit if it's taking several years off my life?'

The tax man had no reply to that, and never mentioned the subject again. He did make it clear, however, that he was not happy with the system we were using for administering the car fuel benefit, which largely relied upon the honesty of each driver. Although we told him about the spot checks we took to ensure compliance, in practice we had never done any.

The upshot of the inspector's visit was that he asked me to write in and confirm our procedures, which I did, but I never heard from him again – at least, not until I had a further visit to deal with this same issue in 2003, 20 years later. In the intervening years we had become a lot more lax on the subject of private fuel, and it was obvious that both we, as the company, and the individual drivers of our company cars were going to be hit hard.

The inspector went through the usual motions of going back five years ('and I'll go back six if I feel like it' he said), and the total fine, at an average of about £8,000 per year, came out at almost £40,000.

It was then that I suddenly remembered the confirmatory letter that I had sent to one of the inspector's predecessors 20 years earlier. I asked him about it.

'I've got nothing on record' he said. I thought, well I have, and spent several hours up in my office loft going through various files until I found what I was looking for. My reasoning was that, as they had not replied to my letter of 1983, then it was realistic to suppose that our system of checking was acceptable. One of my arguments in that letter was that, with all our drivers at that time being regular employees with many years of service, they would not jeopardize their positions by not putting in private fuel at their personal expense.

Once I had found the letter and passed a copy to the inspector, he said he would have to look at it again. Having then perused the letter and the length of service of current employees, he had to agree that those drivers (quite a number of them) who had been employed by us since the letter had been written would be exempt from any fines.

The revised total to pay was now down to just over £17,000, a saving of some £23,000! Who says it doesn't pay to keep correspondence for many years, and not just the statutory six years?

In June 1986 we completed the painting of the prestigious Hammersmith Bridge over the River Thames. The contract involved a massive scaffold. To gain access, the scaffolders had to rig a 40-foot-long cradle and suspend it beneath the inshore section of the bridge, using it to paint the areas on either side. In order to deal with the underside of the central section, the cradle was mounted on a barge and floated into position. Access to the remainder of the work, above parapet level, was from platforms, using a special technique of descending steps following the curvature of the main suspension cables. This was adopted so that traffic and pedestrians were scarcely aware that the work was in progress.

The scaffolding and painting of Hammersmith Bridge, 1986

One day in June 1990, I was driving through Chislehurst and past the yard gates of a small competitor whom I had known for many years, a local builder owned by John Smith called J Smith (Chislehurst) Ltd. We had only come across this firm over the years when we had both been tendering for the annual GLC school painting programme.

This time the gates looked different. They had been newly painted and the yard behind seemed to be buzzing with activity. I knew John Smith was due to retire some time soon, and guessed something was up.

When I got back to my office, I did a company search on the firm. I was amazed when I saw what had been happening. For a start, the registered office was now based in Hampshire, at the same address as our own company accountants, James Todd & Company. Not only that but the Company Secretary was none other than Carol Buck, my colleague Alan Ward's secretary!

My search also revealed that two more companies had come on the scene based at the same address, all registered at the James Todd address. They were called Southern Paint Services Ltd and Moderngood Flooring Ltd.

I was absolutely flabbergasted, and wondered what the devil was going on. A few weeks later, the problem still paramount in my mind, I was invited to the annual NatWest Bank Golf Tournament. While going round the course with my bank manager, he noticed that I was very quiet and withdrawn and asked me what the problem was. I told him. He was very surprised at my story, but his advice was to do nothing for now unless I was certain that the company was suffering.

His attitude seemed to be that I should not be too surprised about Alan Ward, as he was a born entrepreneur, and if it didn't affect me I should accept what he was doing for the time being. As for Carol Buck, she was only doing Alan's bidding. His strongest comment was reserved for David Shetly, our accountant for the past 30 years. He felt that, as a professionally-qualified person acting as a personal adviser to me and the company, his part in going behind my back like this was quite reprehensible.

Almost exactly a year later, on Monday 3rd June 1991, I had a meeting with Alan Ward in our Bromley office. I made a note in my diary:

During a long conversation today regarding future strategy etc, Alan said he could well have a proposition (regarding a property deal) shortly. He would have preferred to carry out all work in association with JF & Sons but got the distinct impression that I would not have been interested. 'It started off in a small way but events have escalated further than anticipated'. He saw no harm if it did not affect the main company performance in the same way that I had operated Beaver some years before.

He went on to reveal the details and outline his proposal for JF & Sons to purchase the three J Smith companies, of which the main asset was the freehold bungalow and yard at Whitehorse Hill in Chislehurst. The agreement was reached and signed on 15th July 1991 to acquire these companies for a total consideration of £320,000 in cash. As Alan had rightly surmised, the freehold premises would be ideal for a new head office, as we had grown out of the original offices in Palace Road, Bromley. Planning permission had already been sought for a single-storey office block in the yard behind the bungalow and Alan was confident of approval being granted. In due course, a wonderful new office facility was constructed and the move took place in 1993.

It will be remembered that our company was originally registered with limited liability status on 30th August 1941, so with August 1991 approaching I wanted to use the opportunity of publicizing the fact that we had survived in business for 50 years. This was achieved in three main ways:

First, I had hundreds of special black-and-gold stickers made to place on all letterheads and invoices, proclaiming '50 years of Service from 1941 to 1991'.

Second, we ordered 200 leather-bound road atlases, specially overprinted with the same '50 years of Service from 1941 to 1991'. These were distributed to important clients and senior members of staff.

Finally, on 4th September 1991 at some considerable expense and effort, I personally organized a major golf society meeting at my local club, Sundridge Park, to which over 70 golfers were invited, including clients and staff representatives from each company, subsidiary and branch. The following is the speech I made to the assembled gathering that evening on 4th September 1991:

Colleagues and friends. Today is the highlight of our Golden Jubilee Year. It is the highlight, not only because it is the main celebration, but because, so far as I can ascertain from the archives, 4th September 1941 was the actual day that the first contract was commenced – so when we were all teeing off this morning it was exactly 50 years ago to the minute that the very first brushful of paint was being applied. That very first contract was for the Ministry of Works to paint two Nissen huts at Wrotham Army Camp.

For those of you who are familiar with the Wrotham/Mereworth area, these same two huts are still visible halfway down Seven Mile Lane and only until six years ago the original coating was still in evidence.

John Fairhurst, my father and our founder, was born near Preston in Lancashire at the end of the last century, and came down south to volunteer for military service in the 1914-18 War.

In common with many of his friends at the time, he had been influenced by the famous poster campaign of the day 'Your Country Needs You', and although only 15 years old, he said he was 16 to gain acceptance. He saw action in the trenches at the Battle of the Somme and was very lucky indeed to come home alive. When the Second World War broke out he was too old to be enlisted compulsorily, and with four young children at the time, you can imagine the two words he used when asked if he would consider volunteering again – no thanks – or something similar! Instead, he undertook fire watching duties at night all through the London Blitz, from the roof of the National Provincial, now NatWest Bank in Bromley. This was the same bank and the same building where the Group has held all its major accounts for the past 50 years and, coincidentally, where John Fairhurst had his own small office in Bank Chambers at that particular branch. When he came downstairs to tell the Manager that he proposed, as part of the war effort, to set up a company to carry out camouflage work to aircraft hangars, etc, the Manager's exact words were 'you're going to do what? – you must be stark raving mad, John!' This proves, of course, that while your bank manager's advice might well be right most of the time, it certainly isn't right all of the time.

We could not possibly have survived for 50 years without the loyalty and dedication of the best staff that any service company could wish for, *together with the co-operation of some really super customers, and my fellow directors and I thank you all for your loyalty and support over many, many years. Thank you in particular for supporting us here today.*

One interesting fact that illustrates the point concerning staff loyalty is that we had playing with us today 15 directors, managers, surveyors and supervisors representing the company and its 7 trading subsidiaries, and these 15 gentlemen have no less than 250 years of service between them – I think that says a great deal. I am so grateful to so many people that it would be invidious to mention individual names. I am grateful to the staff, the operatives, the many customers who have become personal friends over the years and the supporting services of our bankers, accountants, insurers and others – but above all I am grateful to the Lancashire lad who settled in Bromley and had the foresight, the energy and the courage to start our company 50 years ago, so, wherever you are – thank you, Dad.

The period between 1991 and 1994 was a very busy time, especially with the assimilation of the J Smith Group of Companies, and this period was not helped by the UK having yet another recession. It was during this particular downturn in trading activity that my thoughts turned to all the other recessions we had managed to overcome which seemed to arrive with such regular monotony every ten years or so. Just out of interest, I started doing some research to investigate the timing of recessions and difficult trading conditions over a 100-year period, and came up with the details given in Appendix B.

At our peak in the mid 1980s, we were trading with 16 separate units, some merely branch offices while others were fully-fledged subsidiary companies. With the closure of the Gibraltar operation and certain other loss-making activities, the number of units had decreased by 1995.

While Alan Ward and I were in the car travelling to a meeting at Chandler's Ford in the spring of that year, he told me he had been giving a great deal of thought to the way the group was organized and the various names we traded under. He suggested it would be better, for many reasons, if we all traded under the umbrella of the same corporate identity.

'It's important that we don't lose the name Fairhurst' he said. 'As Ward Abbotts Painting is the largest and most successful subsidiary, I wondered what you would think about merging the two names to become Fairhurst Ward Abbotts? More important, this would be abbreviated to the three initials FWA.'

As I drove, I started thinking about the simplicity of this idea and how much better it would be for all of us to be working for the same name. I began to think of all the great names in the business world, almost all of whom marketed and identified themselves with initials. Some had three initials and some had two or four, but the vast majority seemed to get by very well with three. Such iconic organisations as ICI, GEC, AEI, the BBC and ITN sprang to mind.

The more I thought about it the better it all sounded, so from the first day's trading of our new financial year on 1st September 1995 the parent company began to trade as Fairhurst Ward Abbotts Ltd (FWA) with the West Drayton office (previously trading as Fairhurst Pippard Ltd) changing to FWA West Ltd and the Hampshire office (previously trading as John Fairhurst & Sons (Southern) Ltd) to FWA Southern Ltd.

We began to be recognised as the FWA Group, and with the advent of computers I knew it was important immediately to register the domain name fwagroup.co.uk. In order to give a professional appearance to our stationery, I employed the services of a specialist design firm to advise on a totally new FWA logo. Historically, blue had always been used by John Fairhurst & Sons Ltd as the official company colour, while the Abbotts group had always favoured orange, so it was important to utilize these two colours in the design.

Finally, to emphasize the new corporate identity, we purchased a group of 20 consecutive cherished numbers for our vehicles, ranging from M1 FWA to M20 FWA.

Between 1995 and 1996, the FWA Dartford Office under Barry Brown carried out the complete shotblasting and repainting of Grosvenor Railway Bridge in London. Also known as the Victoria Bridge, this was the first railway bridge to span the Thames into central London and had been constructed almost 150 years earlier when the engineers were under instruction to build a bridge with piers conforming to those of neighbouring Chelsea Bridge, just 150 yards upstream.

This contract was an utter disaster from beginning to end. It lost us over a quarter of a million pounds (without any addition for overheads), and almost broke us.

The problems began before any painting could take place, as the surface had to be shot-blasted to a bright finish. The main problem we were faced with was a change in environmental law which meant shot-blasting contractors could no longer allow tons of spent lead shot to fall into the Thames. Instead, the shot had to be bagged up and taken by boat way downstream to be dealt with as hazardous waste.

This was an enormously expensive operation, and although justifiable claims were submitted which reduced some of the loss, this contract went down as the biggest loss-maker by far that we had ever endured. It made us all quite ill, and Barry decided to retire early as a result of the sheer strain of it all.

Before he went, however, he assisted in finding a suitable replacement to run the Dartford office. I employed a London recruitment agency for this task and several possible candidates were interviewed during 1996. Eventually, from a final short list, they came up with their recommendation to employ a very bright young manager called Paul May from Ian Williams & Co, who had made a name for himself in the West Country. He was only 28 years old, but to compensate for his relative lack of practical site experience he was a trained 'systems' man and within only a few months of joining FWA he had successfully gained for us the coveted Investor in People accreditation. Not only that but the systems he implemented ensured that FWA passed with the highest number of points from the other 26 firms attempting to gain Investor in People recognition in Kent that year.

However, although Paul had a certain amount of entrepreneurial flair and possessed an engaging personality, he seemed unable to keep costs within bounds and I'm not sure if he ever knew how to produce a cash flow forecast, or, if he did, how to keep to it. From all the initial high expectations, Alan and I began to run out of patience with Paul and had to let him go before he did too much financial damage.

At the time, the new head office we had constructed in Whitehorse Hill, Chislehurst, was employing some 16 members of staff and Dartford almost the same number, making about 30 office staff in all. There was only one thing for it – the Chislehurst operation would close down and the staff would all transfer to Dartford under Alan Ward's watchful eye. In the event, some of the staff did not wish to make the change. Where there was duplication of duties, we had to let some of the Dartford employees go as well. We ended up with a nucleus of 22 staff, and never looked back from that point.

In order to ensure that there was sufficient office space for the merged operation at Dartford, Kathy and I vacated the independent bungalow building which had been the location for the Group Administration Office - I had constructed this within the grounds of the Dartford office some years earlier - so we now had to find alternative accommodation. As Kathy and I lived within three miles of each other in the Maidstone area, we both thought it made sense to rent somewhere small not too far from our homes.

Having been used to operating independently in my own office for over 30 years, I found it difficult to adapt to working from rented rooms, where, for instance, allocated parking meant nothing to some people. I found myself falling out with other tenants over this and similar issues.

After renting like this for three years, I suddenly thought of the concept of constructing my own office within the grounds of my home in Yalding. When I came up with this idea originally, I did not think there would be any realistic hope of the local council giving approval to such a proposal, especially as the ideal spot for such a project in the corner of my garden actually fell within the conservation area; however the first-class local architect I employed was able to persuade the council to grant permission, with the proviso that a very large silver birch tree could not be disturbed. Its roots would have to be bridged with a huge steel joist and the construction of one elevation actually took place on top of this massive RSJ.

Once the new office had been constructed and fitted out, Kathy and I worked happily from it for several years, until the sale of my majority shareholding in 2006.

In 1999, FWA was involved in major and very costly litigation in connection with a large term contract let by the London Borough of Southwark. Once the contract had been awarded, both the council and one of our competitors were of the opinion that it was subject to TUPE, the Transfer of Undertakings (Protection of Employment) regulations. TUPE was designed to protect employees' terms and conditions of employment when a business is transferred from one owner to another. Employees of the previous owner automatically become employees of the new firm on the same terms and conditions. It's as if their employment contracts had originally been made with the new employer. Their continuity of service and any other rights are all preserved. Both old and new employers are required to inform and consult employees who are affected directly or indirectly by the transfer.

TUPE regulations apply in all business transfers when a business or undertaking, or part of one, is transferred from one employer to another. This can include mergers where two companies close and combine to form a new company. In very many cases the TUPE regulations are applied to protect employees when a contract is assigned to a new contractor during a re-tendering process.

In this particular case the London Borough of Southwark had entered into a contract with one of our competitors for the maintenance and alteration of void domestic dwellings in 1996. The contract was then put out to re-tender as two separate contracts in December 1998. The two new contracts were to be divided into two geographical areas, referred to as Areas 1 and 2. Southwark regarded this as a TUPE transfer.

The original contractor tendered for both areas but was unsuccessful. Southwark awarded the contract for Area 2 to FWA in April 1999. As these were newly-created geographical areas, we could not see how TUPE could be applied and therefore refused to engage some of the employees. We were especially influenced by the discovery that the original contractors, having lost the contract, had taken away their best tradesmen to work for them elsewhere and put poorer-quality men in their place, assuming we would be forced to take them on.

We were of the view that there had been no TUPE transfer and refused to take on some of the employees. We argued that under the old contract, the employees were not assigned to the new Area 2 before the transfer and therefore their contracts had not transferred via TUPE. Our competitor took the opposite view, and on that basis, did not continue the employees' contracts.

The employees began proceedings against FWA for unfair dismissal. During the proceedings, the Employment Tribunal adopted a multi-factorial approach by assessing all the material before it and, attaching such weight as appropriate, concluded that, 'having regard to the overall picture', there was in fact a transfer.

The case considered whether there could be a transfer of part of an undertaking when a local authority puts out a major contract to re-tender, but splits that major contract into two separate contracts defined on the basis of geographical coverage of the local authority area. It also dealt with the question of assignment of workers to a part of an undertaking when they are absent due to sickness (as was the case with one of the employees) at the point of transfer. In short the Tribunal concluded that the division of the contract into two new distinct regions did not disapply to TUPE and that a sick worker is to be treated no differently to any other.

Our solicitors were amazed by the Tribunal's decision and advised us to appeal, as they believed that we had a clear cut case and the Tribunal's decision was wrong in law. Large sums of money were then spent in employing a top London barrister to deal with our appeal, and everyone was even more amazed when we eventually lost the appeal. Our legal adviser suggested that we would have an excellent case of winning if we felt that we could fund an appeal to the House of Lords, which we duly did. It seems that the legal advice we took was wrong, as the three Lords who heard this case came out in favour of our competitor 2:1.

It was evident that we had been breaking new legal ground with this case and, as such, a great deal of interest had been generated in the outcome. At that juncture it occurred to me that it was quite possible that someone in authority had realised that the UK could not afford for us to win our case, for it would mean that any other council or public authority in future could sidestep the TUPE Regulations simply by changing its geographical boundaries.

Again, with advice from our solicitors, we were told that the only course of action we could now take was to appeal to the European Court of Justice. By that stage we had lost faith in their advice!

The New Millennium started with the most fantastic and rewarding experience, for during the very first week we received a formal letter from Buckingham Palace confirming that, as of 1st January 2000, Fairhurst Ward Abbotts Ltd had been granted Her Majesty the Queen's Royal Warrant of Appointment. After working personally on so many contracts, both directly and indirectly over a 40-year period for the Royal Family, here was the official recognition that I had dreamed of.

I was so very proud of this achievement, which I saw as the pinnacle of my working life. If only my father had been alive at a time like this. He would have been over the moon. Although there were a few other specialist decorators and a handful of builders who had the distinction of holding the Royal Warrant, so far as I could ascertain FWA was the only firm to hold the warrant as both builders and decorators.

Once all the work of erecting the Coat of Arms at our Head Office and arranging for these to be added to our commercial vehicles and letterheads had been completed, the citation for FWA on the Royal Warrant website read:

'*Maintaining and improving a diverse range of property, including some of the UK's most famous landmark buildings, has been at the core of Fairhurst Ward Abbotts' (FWA) operations since the 1930s. Delivering maintenance services, decorating, minor works and specialist projects across building and mechanical & electrical disciplines, along with specialist finishing services and window installation, FWA offers the complete solutions for the maintenance and management of property within London and the South East. Quality sits at the very heart of the business and the direct employment of our highly skilled trades and craftsmen illustrates this commitment. We invest in our people, ensuring they remain highly motivated and equipped with the skills to meet today's ever-changing challenges. As such we have one of the lowest levels of staff turnover in the industry. As a professional business, we have a track record of precision execution and works of the very highest standards, and we hold all the expected industry accreditations, including ISO 9001, ISO 14001, CHAS, Constructionline and Exor. Health & Safety standards are uncompromising, and our exemplary accident record illustrates our continual investment. In respect of our ongoing work with the Royal Household, we are extremely proud to hold the Royal Warrant. With offices in Kent, Central, West and South London, we serve London, the Home Counties and the South East. Services are provided to a broad range of clients, spanning both the public and private sectors. Our customers often come back, ensuring a high proportion of repeat business year-on-year. Good business is about traditional values coupled with dynamic, modern management. This is our model at FWA. We respect our peers, clients and staff and we are, in turn, respected.'*

After talking to an acquaintance later in 2000, and after he had congratulated me on the award that year of the Royal Warrant of Appointment, the conversation got around to why some firms were successful and others less so. This subject began to intrigue me, and I spent some time considering what precisely was 'success' and how could it be defined? First I consulted the dictionary and discovered its definition to be: The accomplishment of an aim; a favourable outcome; the attainment of wealth, fame or position; a thing or person that turns out well (from the Latin 'successus' meaning 'advance, happy outcome')

Then, I thought, there must be several criteria at play when it comes to defining success for a trading company other than being based merely on turnover or profit levels.

For a start, just to stay in business for many decades must clearly be one important aspect and to have a happy and motivated workforce must surely be another.

After much deep thinking over a long period, I finally came up with five major criteria that would define success for most types of business:

Finance
- Strength of balance sheet
- Average percentage return on capital
- Average gross and net margins on sales
- Bad debt record

Administration
- Length of association with the company's bankers
- Length of association with the company's accountants
- Length of association with the company's auditors
- Length of association with the company's Insurers

Personnel
- Average length of service
- Qualifications and experience
- Pay and conditions
- Health & safety record

General
- Number of years since formation
- Number of years under the same ownership
- How the company is perceived by the trade in general
- Industry awards
- Membership of appropriate trade associations
- Number of clients who are 'blue chip' customers
- Percentage of repeat business

I then got to thinking. If each of the above items were to be awarded points out of ten and then all the points added up, I honestly could not come up with the name of any competitor who would score more points than FWA.

Many were much larger in terms of turnover and many more boasted higher levels of profitability, but when everything was taken into account, in particular the number of years in business and the quality of the client list, there was no painting and maintenance contractor I was aware of in the UK who would be able to score more points on my 'success criteria chart'. With famous London landmarks such as The Bank of England, Buckingham Palace, Windsor Castle, the Albert Hall, the Victoria & Albert Museum, the House of Lords, the Houses of Parliament and the National Gallery, for instance, being world-renowned locations, it was conceivable, if not likely, that our firm was the most successful in the world in its particular specialist field.

For a full list of important buildings and locations where FWA have carried out painting and maintenance work over the years, please see Appendix C.

On a less serious note, I do remember a stand-up comic many years ago giving his definition of success, which I always thought highly amusing:

Definition of Success
At 4, success is: not needing nappies
At 12, success is: having friends
At 17, success is: having a driving licence
At 20, success is: having sex
At 35, success is: having money
At 50, success is: having money
At 60, success is: having sex
At 70, success is: having a driving licence
At 75, success is: having friends
At 85, success is: not needing nappies

Carol Buck, Alan Ward's secretary for 30 years, and I had a secret mission in March 2004. The occasion was to mark Alan's 40 years of service. With a great deal of luck, we managed to keep the whole affair private, with Alan knowing nothing whatever about it. He was a member of the London Golf Club near Brands Hatch, and we had arranged for as many as we could of Alan's friends and working colleagues to meet up at the club, timing it so that we could all welcome him as he came off the golf course.

There was a crowd of about 60 to greet him and it was a huge success, especially as it came as a complete surprise. I had prepared a speech in advance and it went as follows:

'Thank you all for coming here today. I know that many of you have very busy schedules and your presence here is very much appreciated – especially for those who work very closely with Alan, it must have been extremely difficult to keep this event secret and Carol and I are thankful to you all for joining in the subterfuge.

We are here to celebrate Alan Ward's 40 years of service to FWA. The number 40 has always been a number of some significance, from the 40 days and nights of Biblical fame, the fact that this is the number of years the Government has set as being required for full pension entitlement, a short sleep is referred to as 40 winks, the winds of the South Seas being the Roaring Forties, and the area of sea between Scotland and Norway is known as the Forties. Also the depth of the sea is reckoned to be 40 fathoms, and the penultimate score in a game of tennis is 40-love, not 50 or 60 love. Even Ali Baba had 40 thieves.

40 years with the same firm is a very long time in anybody's book, especially having to work with an old scoundrel like me! In fact I shall be celebrating 50 years with this firm in three years' time, but I don't want to make too many plans as I'm very aware of the old Cornish saying 'if you want to make God laugh, tell him your plans for the future'.

Talking of long service reminds me of the story of the two men, both well into their 80s, still working full time and chatting in the boardroom before the AGM. One says to the other, 'tell me honestly, Jack, how do you feel now you're in your eighties?' and Jack replied 'You know I feel like a new born baby. I've no hair, no teeth and now I've just wet myself!'

Many of you here today will have known Alan for most of this period, but I believe that I have known him the longest.

I am aware of at least three of you here today who have known him for almost 39 years and there are many of you who have known him for over 30 years. Just out of interest I did a quick calculation yesterday to confirm that between those of us present here today, the total number of years that we have known Alan exceeds 1000 years.

As this is a special occasion, I trust that I may be forgiven if I reminisce a little.

It was apparent from the beginning that Alan was destined for commercial success in his life. One morning towards the end of 1963, my secretary at the time came in to tell me that a young paint rep from Murray & Jones would like to see me. She was quite a large middle-aged lady who was very adept at warding off reps (if you'll pardon the pun) and the like and I was intrigued to see who had breached her defences.

On that first morning I was so impressed with Alan's manner that I asked him if he had ever considered working on the other side of the fence marketing the services of a contractor. He said he would be very interested, and in fact he started with us very shortly afterwards. However, after only a few weeks I was disappointed when he was persuaded by Murray & Jones to re-join them. After only a couple of months or so, he telephoned to tell me that he thought he had made a big mistake and could he please rejoin.

So, although Alan did in fact commence with us a little over 40 years ago, it was not until 31st March 1964 that his continuous employment began.

From the outset he was highly successful in attracting contracts from various industrial concerns, notably the Ford Motor Company, the Ministry of Public Building & Works and the Greater London Council.

He was so successful, in fact, that had he continued in that role, we would not have been able to cope with all the work he generated, so it was decided that, in addition to sales, he would act as a contracts manager, running his own jobs.

I shall never forget the occasion when, after about five years, he arranged for the two of us to take out to lunch the Works Engineer from Vauxhall Motors at their Dunstable Plant where the Bedford Trucks were made – an extremely nice man called Bert Colver, Alan will remember him well. After a pleasant lunch, Alan went outside, I believe to bring the car round, and Bert Colver and I went to the gents. While we were standing there side by side (admiring each other as men do on such occasions!) he said to me, 'Look, Colin, I hope you won't take this amiss, but I would like to give you some advice. I'm due to retire in a year or so and I've been in management most of my working life, and once in a blue moon you come across someone a bit special –someone who is going to go places. In my opinion, Alan is one of those people, so my advice to you is to make sure you look after him'.

I've never forgotten that advice – I've never acted upon it either, but I've never forgotten it! In actual fact, it's Alan who has looked after me rather than the other way round.

Alan is the type of person who Gets Things Done – and if he can't do it, then he knows someone who can.

He typifies the old adage, 'if you want something done, ask a busy man'. One of his main attributes, one which I greatly admire, is his ability to get immediately to the nub of the matter rather than floundering around the periphery, and he is forever searching for ways to improve any situation. It was Alan who, almost 20 years ago to the day, was instrumental in the acquisition of the Abbotts painting business, although it was my idea to rename it Ward Abbotts Painting.

I well remember the occasion when, 10 years ago, we were on a car journey to our office near Southampton and he said 'I've been thinking, don't you consider it would be a good idea to merge our main company, John Fairhurst & Sons with our largest subsidiary, Ward Abbotts Painting and call it Fairhurst Ward Abbotts? It's such a long-winded name we could trade using the initials FWA.'

However, I was a little reticent later when, in the early years of the Internet I did a search for FWA and came up with various results including America's version of Interflora, Flowers With Amour and in the UK, Family Welfare Association. But today we are celebrating another meaning of the initials FWA – Forty With Alan, so would you please come up here and accept this special gift, Alan. You spend so much time doing things for other people, it gives me great pleasure to do something for you.

While I am here, I have in fact another presentation to make. This will come as a complete surprise to the recipient, but the young lady who did most of the organisation for today, Carol Buck, herself will be celebrating 30 years with FWA in a few months' time – so I thought it would be opportune to use the occasion to commemorate this milestone with a small token of our appreciation.

CHAPTER TEN

Subsidiaries and skulduggery

In 1972 David Hills, a director of one our old competitors, Abbotts Painting Contractors, contacted Alan Ward to say he was very disillusioned by some of the decisions being taken by his board, notably by Peter Abbott, the son of Benge Abbott, the founder. He was seriously thinking of tendering his resignation. Did we have a suitable position for someone of his experience?

Alan and I arranged to meet David for lunch in Bromley to discuss his situation. He appeared to be pretty knowledgeable about the trade and was evidently very ambitious; he was also a similar age to ourselves, being in his mid thirties. My ears pricked up when he said he had once worked as a contracts manager for Abbotts of Southampton and was fully experienced in pricing and running MTCs (maintenance term contracts).

I told him that we had been carrying out an increasing volume of work recently in the Southampton area and perhaps we should consider opening a branch office down there. Alan and I talked this idea over after lunch at our office and I suggested that, as David was new to us and to avoid the risks involved in controlling contracts so far away, we should form a separate subsidiary company. We both thought David would be the ideal person to develop our work in Hampshire, as he was evidently very ambitious. I further suggested that since he was a director of his present employer he should be taken on as Managing Director, and we should register a new company to be called John Fairhurst & Sons (Southern) Ltd.

David Hills joined us a month later and set about locating suitable premises from which to trade. Eventually he was sent details from a local estate agent of a modern end-of-terrace retail unit with offices above the shop and with side access to a large car park and yard area to the rear. Storage for small plant, paint and stores might have presented a problem, but this was overcome by erecting a block of three concrete slab garages at the bottom of the yard area. The rent was reasonable as the location, in Chandler's Ford, was not in a prime position, but it suited our purposes as the town was midway between Southampton and Winchester and only a short distance from the motorway network.

Within three months David had seven office-based staff, including Lou Delrue, the Sales Manager. It hadn't taken him long to land three long-term painting maintenance contracts at Southampton West, Bulford Army Camp near Salisbury and the UKAEA (United Kingdom Atomic Energy Authority) establishment at Culham, to the east of Abingdon. Several other large individual projects were also landed at the Ford Motor Company truck plant in Southampton and IBM headquarters building near our office at Hursley.

The contracts being awarded during this early period were many and varied and ranged from redecorating a string of public houses across Hampshire and Dorset to painting the steel superstructure of a lightship while it was bobbing around out at sea.

Within a very short space of time, the total number of office-based staff were really too many for the first-floor offices of the Chandler's Ford shop, so David submitted planning permission for a change of use for the ground floor retail area to offices. When this was refused, being ever ambitious, he persuaded me that he should install suitable shelving etc and open it as a retail shop selling paint and sundries.

As major contractors we had always enjoyed preferential

discounts on leading brands of paint, so the idea made sense to me and the trading name of Southern Decorating Supplies was established. An experienced local paint representative personally known to David, Malcolm Harper, was engaged to run it.

David thought he could see benefits in supporting Southampton Football Club, and to be fair, most of his staff were also avid supporters. He had arranged for a large company advertisement to be erected in a prominent position in the main stadium and reserved a box for entertaining purposes. After home matches it was not unusual for members of our staff to mingle with the players, and they got to know several of them to talk to. It was on one such occasion that David met one of the star Southampton players, Mike Channon, and talked him into coming to our offices to officially open the Southern Decorating Supplies shop.

I was told which day this was to be and drove down to Chandler's Ford to witness the opening ceremony. The next day a photograph appeared in the local Southampton paper showing Mike Channon halfway up a ladder, pulling on a cord which released a large banner across the shop front. It was quite a coup for David to persuade a man of Mike Channon's local celebrity status to open the shop. He was the main goal scorer for Southampton that year, which followed the call from Alf Ramsey to make his debut for England in October 1972.

Although Channon's England career was short-lived, he played well enough in a 1–1 draw against Yugoslavia at Wembley to be selected for two subsequent qualifying matches for the 1974 FIFA World Cup, though he wasn't eventually in the team for either. However, he won his second cap in a famous 5–0 hammering of Scotland at Hampden Park in February 1973, scoring his first international goal in the process.

But despite all the excitement and anticipation, the shop was a dismal failure. One of the selling points was having Malcolm Harper permanently on call to give decorating advice to customers, but nobody seemed interested and it was apparent that the limited parking space in front of the shop prevented some potential customers from buying paint owing to the difficulty of carrying it back to wherever they had parked their vehicles. The final straw came when I learned on one of my regular visits that the shop had suffered its worst trading week since opening. I was told that on one day they had only had one customer whose only purchase had been a sheet of sandpaper. The sales for that particular day totalled five pence!

We really had no option but to close down Southern Decorating Supplies after only about three months, and poor Malcolm Harper found himself without a job.

By the end of the second financial period, ending 31st August 1974, the bulk of the work was on long-term contracts on schedules of rates. Because of the nature of such contracts, which covered a three-year period, the turnover, or value of work executed, had to be classified as work in progress. As was customary in those days it was generally accepted that, in order to present a fair set of accounts relating to such work, all contracts that were still in progress at the financial year end would be treated by the addition of 10% to the basic cost of site wages and materials to cover the cost of overheads and a token sum on account of presumed profit.

I was becoming quite concerned by the volume of work in progress, so when they landed a large long-term contract for the MPBW (Ministry of Public Building & Works) for every type of public building throughout East and West Sussex I decided that both the size and type of work involved warranted this contract to be treated separately from the Chandler's Ford operation. Apart from anything else, I was most concerned that they were quite clearly growing too big too quickly and, above all, they were now requiring large sums of working capital which I managed to obtain by a meeting with the local National Westminster Bank Manager and by a guarantee from the parent company.

David Hills had, in anticipation of running this contract himself, already arranged to appoint an experienced manager, 'Mac' McKeown, to control this contract. Therefore when I told him that this work was being taken away from him, I confirmed that I would still employ Mr McKeown to run it. In the light of what was shortly to occur, this was one of my better decisions at that time.

Eventually, some months into the third year, it became clear that things were not going well with either the Southampton West or the Bulford Camp contracts. In order to prevent a further drain on our capital it was decided to terminate both of these contracts.

In keeping with all Government long-term contracts at that time, although it was the original intention that they should run for the full three-year period, either party was able to terminate on 13 weeks' written notice. Shortly afterwards, when our privately-appointed quantity surveyors (PQS) had measured most of the orders, it was clear that considerable losses had been sustained. The problem of having to face these losses was, however, greatly exacerbated by the prior decision, which had been the company's policy since the inception of maintenance term contracts, to add 10% on the cost of site wages and materials ostensibly to cover the inherent cost of overheads and a small contribution towards profit.

There had never been any problem with this arrangement in the past as contracts always ended up making enough profit to cover overheads and this method of accounting was generally used throughout the trade. Of course, in the event that no gross profit was earned at all the system became unstuck so, for instance, on the Southampton West term contract the maths ended up as follows:

SOUTHAMPTON WEST MTC

Year 1	
Cost of Wages & Materials	£175,000
Add 10% to work-in-progress	£17,500

Year 2	
Cost of Wages & Materials	£240,000
Add 10% to work-in-progress	£24,000

Year 3 until termination	
Cost of Wages & Materials	£86,000
Add 10% to work-in-progress	£8,600

Total Costs for the Contract	£501,000
Final value of measured work	£448,000
Gross Loss	-£53,000
To this loss, add the 10% included in previous years, which in the event never materialised	£50,100
Total loss for the contract	**£103,000**

The trading situation at Bulford Camp was much the same. and I confronted David Hills with these appalling figures and asked him if he really knew the rudiments of contract costing and the relationship between turnover, gross profits, overheads and net profit. I spent a long time explaining the basics of contract management from an accounting point of view and I believe that, finally, he realised that he had been found severely wanting in that direction. I really thought he had flipped, though, for when I was departing he started talking about establishing a subsidiary company to carry out work in the West Country.

I was concerned enough about one particular contract, UKAEA

(United Kingdom Atomic Energy Authority) at Culham, to take the file home with me. The next day I telephoned the Senior Surveyor at Culham to enquire as to when a recent invoice to him would be settled. He became quite agitated and asked me if I had any control over the finances of John Fairhurst & Sons (Southern) Ltd. Was I not aware that, following a call from David Hills two weeks earlier, this account had already been settled?

This sum was quite clearly listed as outstanding from the information received from David, so I immediately wondered how many other amounts, listed by him as being money due, had in fact already been paid. Little wonder then that the cash flow had dried up; there was obviously very little cash due on any of the current contracts and I had been given false information.

I arranged with Alan Ward for the two of us to travel down to Chandler's Ford the next afternoon and we stayed the night at the Potter's Heron Hotel near Romsey. First thing next morning we went to the office, arriving before any of the staff. Fortunately I had had the foresight to arrange for another set of keys to be cut some months before for emergency purposes, so we were sitting in David Hills' office when he arrived for the day and confronted him with what I had discovered.

He had no excuse and meekly accepted our demand for him to be dismissed immediately and without compensation. We took his car keys and arranged for a driver to take him home, promising to forward any private possessions that afternoon.

With my ability to type, I had already prepared a letter of resignation for him to sign, and this he did without demurring.

Once he had left the office we went through his desk drawers and in one of them we found several original invoices, all completely false, that he had raised internally for various clients and passed to the book-keeper to register as payments due. In another drawer I found several scribbled notes. I was astonished to find one particular note the details of which I remember quite clearly. He had jotted down several figures, seemingly arising from an earlier conversation the previous week when I had been discussing contract costings with him and attempting to explain the difference between gross and net margins. He had scribbled '£15,000 @ 20% = £3,000 less overheads giving gross margins of ? ... what does all this mean? – I don't know!'

But the most extraordinary insight into how his mind was working and how he was evidently suffering from delusions of grandeur, on an adjoining sheet he had written down a whole list of hypothetical names, starting with his own subsidiary, John Fairhurst & Sons (Southern) Ltd.

John Fairhurst & Sons (Southern) Ltd

John Fairhurst & Sons (Wessex) Ltd

John Fairhurst & Sons (Portsmouth) Ltd

John Fairhurst & Sons (Plymouth) Ltd

John Fairhurst & Sons (Midlands) Ltd

John Fairhurst & Sons (East Anglia) Ltd

John Fairhurst & Sons (Northern) Ltd

John Fairhurst & Sons (Scotland) Ltd

John Fairhurst & Sons (Europe) Ltd

As a parting stab into my already tender gut, I was told later that David Hills, despite all the losses mounting up, had even had the temerity to have an extension built on to his house with all the costs being charged to the contracts! However, as all the costs had been 'lost' this allegation could not be proved.

Straight away I called the Sales Manager, Lou Delrue, into the office and asked him if he would consider looking after the affairs of the company on a day-by-day basis until we decided what to do about the disastrous situation in which we found ourselves. Lou was a very affable character and had been working in the painting contracting industry, albeit as a sales representative, for many years and had built up a good client following. Moreover there were at least three members of staff who seemed to be very knowledgeable and were happy to work for Lou and try to rectify matters.

I went down to see Lou a week later and was encouraged to see that he seemed to be getting to grips with things despite being thrown in at the deep end. Above all, he had the right attitude and I came away feeling a lot more cheerful than I had done the previous week. Two weeks later he was formally appointed General Manager and awarded an appropriate salary increase. In due course his persistence paid off, and slowly but surely he turned things round until, after four years, the huge trading losses incurred under David Hills had been eliminated and the balance sheet went into the black for the very first time.

One of the main reasons for his success, I believe, was the exceptionally generous profit-sharing scheme he was offered. Although this was based upon being rewarded with 25% of the net trading profits for him to have and also share with his staff, it was also complicated by being based upon the company achieving a pre-tax profit ratio of 5% of turnover (which was the average margin being achieved by other contractors at the time); for every 1% above that 5% target he would receive a further 2^1/2% in profit sharing. Thus, if the net profit were to be 7% of work executed, for example, he and his staff would receive 30%. Conversely, if the profit ratio were to be 4%, they would receive 22^1/2%.

Fortunately, at the time of adopting this scheme, a limit of 50% profit sharing was agreed, neither party ever dreaming that this figure was a realistic possibility. By limiting the growth in turnover and concentrating on maximising profits on each contract, the team was able to earn huge bonuses. This suited me absolutely, because apart from having a very happy workforce, it was self-financing and generated cash for the parent company.

Over the ensuing ten-year period from 1975 to 1985, the turnover grew only from just over £400,000 to about £700,000, an annualised rate of little more that 5% (and these were during highly inflationary times), but with pre-tax profitability increasing from £21,500 to £155,000, which resulted in a collective bonus of the maximum under the scheme of £77,500 (50%). Every year, however, I had to rein in Lou's ambitions for what he thought he personally should be entitled to and what he considered would be a fair bonus that each staff member should be awarded. With a typical collective bonus of £60,000, for instance, his idea would be to take £50,000 for himself, £3,000 each for the Estimator and Contracts Manager, and £1,000 for each of the remaining four members of staff. However, by the time I had sat down with him to persuade him to release more to the people who had been instrumental in making such high levels of profit, the final outcome would typically be for Lou to receive £30,000 with £6,000 each for the Estimator and Contracts Manager and £2,000 for each of the other staff members.

I then persuaded him not to take the whole sum in cash, with the inevitable high level of taxation, but to take two thirds in cash, with the firm paying the balance into his pension plan. This would be very tax effective for him, and the company would save the National Insurance contribution.

So, after an appalling start thanks to David Hills, John Fairhurst & Sons (Southern) Ltd under Lou Delrue was trading very profitably. Until, that is, 1977, when there was a terrible setback, and the company was on the brink of going into liquidation.

This came about through a fire caused by our decorators while painting the exterior of King Alfred's College at Winchester. One of the team had been burning off old paintwork from a window sill of a double-hung sash which had been left slightly open, and the flame from the blowlamp had caught the bottom edge of a curtain.

Within a few minutes the building was ablaze. The foreman ran to get a fire extinguisher from about 50 feet away, but by the time he had climbed the ladder the fire was well established and too dangerous for him to proceed. The fire brigade was called immediately and got the fire under control very quickly, but not before £20,000 of damage had been suffered. I then had the problem of dealing with our insurance company in settling the claim from the College's insurers, Clerical & Medical Insurance Company.

Some years before this occurrence our brokers had discussed with me the adequacy of our insurance cover for such an eventuality. It seems that our insurance company, General Accident, had been dealing with a number of cases of fire damage by the use of blowlamps when burning off old paintwork and our brokers wished to discuss with me the wording on a new warranty they had introduced to the insurance policy. Basically, there was now a requirement when using blowlamps for there to be a two-gallon water-based fire extinguisher within easy reach of the operatives.

I remember saying that this would be extremely difficult in our case with the number of contracts we were carrying out, but in any event all our work was to Government and other public buildings where they all had suitable fire extinguishers on every floor. If it was a large building there would be several on each floor. The broker told me that this would be in order, provided they were within reasonable reach, which I took to be a distance of no more than, say, 25 yards.

When it came to dealing with the assessor on behalf of General Accident for the King Alfred's College fire, a report came back that they were not prepared to cover us for this particular incident as our blowlamp warranty had not been adhered to. They insisted that to be 'within easy reach' meant by the foot of the ladder being worked on and certainly no more than ten feet away. I contended that this was ridiculous and totally impracticable, but they insisted that their interpretation was correct and absolutely refused to pay out on the claim.

I was then left to deal with the situation on my own, so I contacted Clerical & Medical Insurance and explained that John Fairhurst & Sons (Southern) Ltd was a relatively small subsidiary and there was no way that we could afford the £20,000 involved. I went on to tell them that if they sued for the full amount this would financially cripple the firm and would inevitably lead to its liquidation and they would receive nothing. However, as a goodwill gesture, I managed to obtain an agreement to a sum which we could just about manage. This was for a total payment of £10,000 in full and final settlement, payable in instalments of £2,500 per quarter for 12 months. They agreed, very reluctantly, to my proposal and we were able to put the whole episode behind us.

Over the years the Chandler's Ford operation became very profitable in its niche market and traded successfully under the management of Lou Delrue until, on one visit in 1992, he approached me to say that he had decided to retire early at the age of 63. It seemed that his main reason was that he was still in shock from the recent death of his younger brother, and this had concentrated his mind on having some enjoyment from life before he went the same way.

When Lou retired his assistant took over, but while trading profitably, it never again reached the dizzy heights Lou had managed to achieve. Both Alan Ward and I felt that the new manager did not have the same level of control shown by his predecessor. There was also a rumour that his contracts manager had taken his eye off the ball and was having an affair with the book-keeper. The manager denied that this was happening, but when, on one of my monthly visits, I needed to go to an archive office on the first floor I found a mattress leaning up against a wall!

In 1995, along with all other trading units of the Group, John Fairhurst & Sons (Southern) Ltd ceased to trade under that name, but carried on as a branch office of the parent company, newly named Fairhurst Ward Abbotts Ltd (FWA).

The premises at Chandler's Ford had been acquired by the Fairhurst Group Retirement Benefits Scheme back in 1983 and the value had increased considerably. On the run-up to my own impending retirement, the trading operation (once again reverting to the name of John Fairhurst & Sons (Southern) Ltd) was sold in 1999 to the Mears Group, which was a competitor and a public company. As part of the deal, we continued to rent the premises to Mears for a further three years until the property was eventually sold in 2003.

The Sussex Area Office 1974

When I took Mac Mckeown away from David Hills back in 1974, I confirmed that 'Mac' would be kept on and that I was going to oversee the large maintenance contract covering East & West Sussex myself.

I felt that with such a large geographical area to cover, and with what appeared to be realistic rates for this work, the MPBW deserved to have a dedicated team to administer it. My first task was to arrange for a base from which to operate and, after drawing a blank from each estate agent I contacted, I saw an advertisement in the Brighton Argus for a very small office with garage space available to let in the heart of a small village in the middle of Sussex called Cowfold.

Although neither I, nor anyone else I ever talked to, had ever heard of this small village, it was in fact in an ideal location for this particular contract, being right in the centre of the contract area. The tiny premises were just about big enough to house Mac, his newly appointed supervisor Max Buxbaum and a part-time girl to look after the 'phones and perform other light clerical duties.

From a fairly shaky start, Mac and Max began working well as a team and soon the little branch was running profitably, albeit with only one contract. Mac was able to give each order his personal attention and his attitude towards costs was quite remarkable. He was trained by a very old and respectable decorating contractor called Perrott Grenville Ltd and had worked for them for many years, managing their Brighton office before joining us. Just how he found the time I never knew, but it was quite clear from discussions with him that he knew every item of stock and equipment for which he was responsible. Every single paintbrush, and its degree of wear, was known to him and his reputation with the operatives was that he was a man who never missed a trick.

The original Sussex term contract ran for the usual period of three years, but through competitive pricing (for which I was largely responsible) this contract was retained in 1977 and again in 1980. When even more buildings were included in the immediate Brighton area, and we retained the contract once again in 1983, we felt that the client would receive an even better service if we relocated to Brighton. We managed to find suitable premises in Hove, which were much larger and more appropriate for our needs than the Cowfold location, and our Sussex office thrived there until, finally, we lost the term contract in 1986 and moved the three office-based employees to a new building in Crawley.

A friend of Alan Ward, Bryan Hills, had approached us as he had recently lost his managerial job with his current employers, who had allowed the decorating firm which he had managed for many years to go to the wall. He said that he had many contacts and would be able to arrange for the transfer of his Crawley Office lease to our firm.

The timing seemed just right for us, having just lost the Sussex term contract, so we would be able to start with existing employees from Hove. Shortly after we opened this office for business, however, Stancia, the book-keeper from the old Hove office, said that the Crawley office was too far for her to travel each day and handed in her notice. At about the same time Max Buxbaum decided to emigrate with his wife to New Zealand to live with his daughter.

At the time the only contract of any consequence which was running was a long-term contract at Wakehurst Place in Sussex, part of the Royal Botanic Gardens at Kew. This contract had been secured by Bryan Hills at unrealistic rates and was losing money. With all the other problems we had at the time, particularly in Gibraltar, we decided to close this office to concentrate on other matters.

The West Drayton Office

In 1973, very soon after the Chandler's Ford office had been opened, a rare opportunity arose for us to establish a presence in West London. We had spent considerable time and effort submitting tenders for various painting term contracts all around London and the South East area. One day, quite out of the blue, we received a letter asking us to confirm that our prices still held firm for a three-year painting contract at the RAF Station West Drayton establishment which we had submitted some two months earlier; after this amount of time had elapsed we had assumed by then that it was to be yet another abortive attempt at gaining a further MTC .

RAF West Drayton in West London was a Royal Air Force station and the main centre for military air traffic control in Britain. It was co-located with the civilian London Terminal Control Centre to provide a vital link between civil and military flying and airspace requirements.

On looking again at the rates for this work I now recalled my submitting very high prices as it was quite a long way for our operatives to travel. In the unlikely event that we were awarded this contract, we would certainly be able to manage to run it without too much trouble.

Rather like the large Sussex area contract we landed at about the same time, I thought if we were to gain a contract at these rates the client deserved a first-class service, and to that end I started to look at all the options. It so happened that, during the three-year period prior to David Hills setting up his office in Chandler's Ford, we had carried out a number of jobs in the Southampton area which had been estimated for, and run, by Richard Pippard, the son of Pip. I was aware that, at the time, he was disappointed when he was passed over for the Chandler's Ford operation but as he was very young and had got married only recently I doubted if he would want to move house at that point in his life. The possibility of opening an office at West Drayton, however, was a different kettle of fish, as it would be possible to drive to work each day from his new house in Farnborough.

When I put the idea to Richard he was delighted at being given such an opportunity, although of course this was tempered by the thought of such a long drive each day. Anyway, he travelled up to attend the inaugural site meeting at RAF West Drayton and was most fortunate to be approached by the foreman painter of the previous contractor, who made it clear that he would like to join us. The pair of them managed to locate suitable office and storage premises at the end of the same road as the main entrance gates to the RAF Station, and a 12-year lease was duly arranged, with me being required to act as a personal guarantor.

Richard was offered, and gladly accepted, the same generous profit-sharing scheme I was later to set up with Lou Delrue. Within a relatively short space of time, he had organised the office with a supervisor and a lady book-keeper. Then, once the term contract was generating profits and he could afford the time, he engaged the services of a friend of his to drum up sales and was soon dealing on a regular basis with the London Fire Brigade and carrying out work at various fire stations all over London.

Another client, who had been passed to the West Drayton office by Alan Ward, was the large head office block occupied by the North East Thames Regional Health Authority in Eastbourne Terrace, West London, where Richard's team carried out work on a regular basis for ten years. The generous profit-sharing scheme had the same effect on Richard Pippard as it had on Lou Delrue, in that the growth in turnover was a lot less than the prevailing rate of inflation yet the resultant net profits grew to the point where Richard and his team were in receipt of extremely hefty annual bonuses. As with Lou, large sums were invested in their individual pension schemes.

When the initial contract period of three years was up, the West Drayton office successfully re-tendered for two further three-year periods, so the work at RAF West Drayton spanned nine years. In 1983 we decided to hive this branch off as a separate subsidiary company, so in recognition of Richard Pippard's record, it was called Fairhurst Pippard Ltd. It traded very successfully under this title until 1995.

When the parent company in that year changed its trading style to Fairhurst Ward Abbotts Ltd (FWA), it was agreed that the West Drayton operation should remain independent, so Fairhurst Pippard Ltd changed its name to FWA West Ltd. However, shortly after this, in 1997, everything at this unit went awry. The reason was that, on holiday with his wife Jean in America that year, Richard met a younger English girl with whom he was besotted, and he seemed to completely lose the plot. His new lady friend lived in Somerset, and for some reason none of the rest of our senior management team could understand, he could see no practicable reason why he should not be able to continue to run FWA West despite moving to Somerset. It seemed evident that work was now of secondary importance to Richard. The turnover of this unit declined and the profitability nosedived.

Alan Ward and I had a heart-to-heart meeting with Richard one evening and made it clear that we were not prepared to allow him to carry on running the company from so far away. We ended up agreeing an acceptable financial package for Richard to leave and his contracts manager was put in charge. From that moment on, however, the business went downhill, as Richard had kept everything tightly to himself, so no one knew what to do without him. FWA West was beginning to lose money rapidly, and we were on the verge of closing it down when I realised there was someone who might be interested in taking on the challenge of turning it round.

It so happened that when I contacted the executive recruitment agency I employed to find a replacement for Barry Brown, the MD of Ward Abbotts Painting, upon his retirement in 1997, they advised me, among a dozen or so other applicants, that the two most likely contenders for the position were Alan Boswell and Paul May. They had recommended the latter because he was younger and they were a little concerned that Alan had been used to controlling a firm with a much higher turnover and might be too big for the job we were offering. So, after much thought, and as recommended by Barry, we chose Paul as his successor.

Soon after Paul joined us I was discussing matters in general with him and it came out in conversation that, coincidentally, Alan Boswell had been Paul's boss when they both worked in the Bristol area for one of the UK's largest maintenance contractors, Ian Williams & Co. I thought nothing ventured, nothing gained, so I immediately made contact with Alan, who was still searching for a suitable position. When I outlined the dire current situation at FWA

West Ltd, yet with our pedigree and connections the opportunity it offered to anyone who had the knowledge and management skills to turn it round, he jumped at the chance, and joined us early in 1998.

Alan did not take too long to get to grips with the West Drayton operation and he managed to land a very large long-term maintenance contract (all trades) for Network Housing Association. This enabled him to recruit staff of a high calibre which, in turn, enabled him to obtain further profitable work.

I often reminisce about the history of the West Drayton office and what a pity it was that Richard Pippard decided to get divorced and go and live in Somerset when things were going so well (at the time I called it 'trading his wife in for another one'). They were good times for me and I enjoyed the 15 year period when, typically, once per fortnight I would drive from the Bromley area to West Drayton, where I would go somewhere pleasant for lunch with Richard, spend an hour or so back in his office discussing work, and then motor down to the Chandler's Ford office for another hour or two of discussion before heading back home – a total journey of some 250 miles – arriving back home in time for dinner at about 8 pm.

I will always remember the story Alan Boswell once told me regarding a meeting he was due to have with a senior official of the Network Housing Association at their offices in Wembley. It seems that he was sitting in a waiting room and the door to the corridor was slightly ajar. He heard voices coming down the corridor and one man was saying, in what Alan described as a very cultured public school accent, 'It makes my job really difficult with all these immigrants we are employing – there are so many of them now'.

The remark made Alan cringe and he thought 'you can't say that sort of thing, especially here in an area where there are so many immigrants!' Then, as the two men walked past, he caught a glimpse of them through the gap in the door, and they were two of the darkest-skinned Africans he had ever seen!

By September 2000, the inevitable situation arose where a competent manager wished to realise his dream of running his own company. This was when Alan Boswell had a series of meetings with Alan Ward and myself with a view to purchasing the entire shareholding of FWA West Ltd. The timing of such a deal suited me admirably, since I was now well into my sixties and planning for some sort of retirement or semi-retirement.

When I reflected on the dire situation we had had with the West Drayton operation only three years previously, I was pleased to sell the company in a management buyout to Alan Boswell and his two fellow directors for £290,000 spread over a three year period.

Group Twelve Ltd

While carrying out a painting contract for the Ford Motor Company in 1974, one of the Plant Engineers whom Alan Ward had been meeting on a regular basis suggested that there would be other work available, apart from industrial painting, but it would be difficult for him to place any such work with a specialist painting contractor rather than a general building contractor.

Alan came to discuss this problem with me, and it was clear that not only with Fords but also with certain other major clients, we could obtain contracts for other trades if we established a general contractor trading under another name. Some of the 'other trades' mentioned were suspended ceilings, partitioning, flooring, roofing, carpentry and joinery, electrical and plumbing and general construction work. We worked it out that, in addition to painting & decorating, there could be up to a dozen specialist trades which we could accept by using experienced sub-contractors.

With this number of trades involved I suggested that we form a separate company, not associated directly with the main company of

John Fairhurst & Sons Ltd other than common directors, to be called Group Twelve Ltd. Operating with little or no overheads, this company traded highly successfully for three years. Because there was no pressure to extract excessive remuneration, the balance sheet improved rapidly, so much so that we decided to hive off some of Fairhurst's work into separate specialist subsidiaries coming under the Group Twelve banner.

One of these, under the day to day management of Peter Trew, was Group Twelve Decorations Ltd, which set out to specialise in high-class redecorations to public houses etc. Another, under the management of Don Barnes, was Group Twelve Membrane Coatings Ltd, which specialised in the application of spray-applied coatings to encapsulate asbestos.

One day in 1975 a friend of Alan Ward called David English came to see us. He told us he had been working for one of the UK's leading suppliers of book matches for advertising purposes and was intent upon starting his own business in this field. He told us he had found suitable premises to house four special printing presses at an address near Sidcup, so Alan and I had a discussion and decided to finance him by forming a separate company to come under the Group Twelve banner.

This company was to be called Group Twelve Advertising Ltd, but would trade under the name of Admatch. One of the benefits of this was that the offices and workshop in Sidcup was far too large for Admatch on its own. It was on two levels and rented from a firm called Aerosigns which was surplus to their requirements. It occurred to me that the first-floor offices would be ideal for me, as the time had come for Alan and me to split up. There had been several instances at about that time of an employee coming to me for a decision on a particular matter and then approaching Alan to see what he said. This 'playing one off against the other' had obviously caused problems.

Another reason for me leaving Alan at Bromley was to allow myself to concentrate on getting to grips with the 1974 Health & Safety at Work Act, which I could see had to be addressed and taken seriously. Finally, with several branches and companies now trading, I felt that a separate administration office could deal with all the mundane aspects of the business – all the matters which, although important, nobody else was really interested in, such as Health & Safety, banking, auditors and accountants, insurance, advertising, pension scheme, staff salaries and printing & stationery.

So, shortly after Admatch had started trading, I moved to the new Group Administration Office, as I liked to call it, with my long standing book-keeper/secretary Joan Short. We were joined by Group Twelve Membrane Coatings, as there was sufficient room for all of us on the first floor of this building.

My very first task after settling in to the new office was to establish the first Fairhurst Group Safety Committee, with myself as Chairman and producer of all the paperwork, including meeting agendas, typing the minutes and setting up systems and procedures.

My second project was to organise our first national trade exhibition. I had been approached by a promotion firm to see if we would be interested in taking a stand at the 1975 PEMEC show (Plant Engineers & Maintenance Exhibition) at Earls Court. This was quite an undertaking, as it involved liaising with stand designers and ordering special leaflets to distribute on the stand.

Alan introduced me to a friend of his who was a tailor in Woolwich, who had agreed to make a matching light grey two-piece suit for each of the four members of staff who would take turns manning the stand. The centrepiece of our stand was one moveable wall which depicted an artist's drawings of all the various types and structures our firm painted. 'From pylons to palaces' was the slogan, and against each drawing was a coloured, lit-up circular area of about eight inches in diameter on which the subject of the drawing was printed. Each circular area was of a different colour and was lit from behind.

When a flashing timing device was added it certainly drew attention from anyone passing the stand. The exhibition lasted for a week. It was very hard work but we gained many useful leads which resulted in a considerable volume of factory painting work and, more importantly, we received an excellent review in that month's *Plant Engineer* magazine, which really put our name on the map.

At about the same time, when the timing was right for Peter Trew to begin trading with Group Twelve Decorations Ltd, we found suitable premises from which to operate at an address at the far end of Orpington High Street. The only problem was that the property had a relatively long lease and, as was quite usual at that time, I was required to personally guarantee the payment of rent.

This subsidiary got off to a flying start with Fairhurst passing them two key clients, namely Trumans public houses and the Woolwich Building Society. Over the next few years the firm traded successfully, making small but useful contributions to the annual Group Twelve accounts, but it came to an abrupt end with the sudden and totally unexpected serious illness of Peter Trew. Neither he nor his doctors knew precisely what the problem was, but he was unable to return to work again and his deputy was put in charge.

One weekend early in 1975, while browsing through the 'businesses for sale' advertisements in the local Bromley & Kentish Times, I chanced upon one for a small, old-established building business with its own yard and office in Penge. Out of curiosity, I went along to meet two of the four Bulford family members who were the joint owners and directors of this very small jobbing builders, which had been established by their father in 1912. The firm owned a nice little yard which was, in fact, its principal asset, but I immediately saw it as an ideal adjunct to our existing business as we seemed to be forever sub-letting small building jobs and I saw the advantages of having such a firm 'in house'.

After negotiation, which included the agreed continued employment of an elderly office clerk called Flo, we purchased the share capital for £12,000. Through a connection with a competitor, Cristpin & Borst, Alan knew of a bright young qualified quantity surveyor called Ron Allen whom he thought might consider the opportunity of joining us to develop Bulfords (Builders) Ltd and take a stake in the company, with a generous profit-sharing package that had proved to be so successful elsewhere. Ron was pleased to have been given the opportunity, and was duly appointed as Bulford's Managing Director.

At the time local councils were spending huge sums refurbishing their housing stock, and Ron and his team excelled in pricing and carrying out this type of work. As with many quantity surveyors, Ron was quite pedantic regarding the wording used in specifications and generally saw things only in black and white. A lack of flexibility on his part saw the firm often making claims which none of the clients liked. He never realised that if he had only softened his approach to contractual matters many clients would have had a much more amenable attitude.

Ron could be quite belligerent at times, and often was when I called to see him in his Penge office. After knocking politely on his door, as was my custom (even when the door was open), he wouldn't look up but would carry on writing or whatever else he was doing for maybe 20 seconds before acknowledging me.

Bulfords continued to trade quite successfully until Ron's dreadful murder in 1982, as detailed in Chapter 4.

CHAPTER ELEVEN

Gibraltar adventure

Before we ever actually carried out any work in Gibraltar, we received an enquiry to paint a bridge and associated steelwork at the North Mole over ten years before landing a contract out there. This was in November 1972. Rather than turn down this opportunity, I decided to go out on my own and submit a tender for the work.

My plane duly set off from Gatwick and after the two-hour flight was preparing to land. However, after circling the Rock twice, a message was relayed from the Captain to the effect that he was very sorry but the seas were too high at the end of the runway and he would not be able to land. Instead we were to go on to Tangiers for the night, where we would be put up in a hotel and attempt the journey back in the morning.

The stewardess seemed completely unfazed by this and told me she wasn't at all surprised, as quite a high percentage of flights at this time of year never made it at the first attempt. A few years later they extended the runway at Gibraltar and there were no similar problems after that.

I spent a pleasant evening in Tangiers and shared a room at the Hotel Rif with the BBC overseas correspondent for the Iberian peninsular. He knew the hotel and the general area very well and took me for a walking tour of the local souk. We had a long conversation in the hotel bar that evening and I found him to be a most interesting person. We agreed to keep in touch, but for some reason never did.

The next morning I was becoming very stressed, as the plane for Gibraltar was not due to take off until 9 am and although it was only a very short flight the tender had to be received in Gibraltar by 11 am; this would give me only about an hour to get to the North Mole, measure or size up the work, and complete the tender form for handing in by the deadline. Being in a fairly isolated position, the job seemed to be an ideal one for spray painting, but I saw that the specification strictly forbade any spraying. Anyway the contract was submitted by hand and in due course we learned that we had been unsuccessful.

The following July I took the family on a two-week Mediterranean cruise from Southampton on Shaw *Savill's Northern Star*, which was in fact the sister ship of the *Southern Cross* in which I had returned from New Zealand some 15 years earlier. Coincidentally, on this cruise with the family, one of the ports of call happened to be Gibraltar, so while the family were looking at the shops in Main Street I walked out to the North Mole to have a look at the bridge I had tendered for. There, as large as life, were six Moroccans working away with, guess what? Two large petrol compressors were humming happily away, complete with all the associated spraying equipment!

Several years later, in 1983, there was yet another recession in the building trade. Such recessions arrived steadily approximately every 10 years or so and, once again, painting contracts were very hard to win and there were few opportunities. At about this time it seems that the British Government was becoming concerned by both the cost and general standard of maintenance painting being carried out on its behalf in Gibraltar. For some years the Ministry of Public Building & Works (MPBW) was responsible for all this type of work, and a very senior surveyor let it be known to us that should our firm ever be interested in receiving tenders for work in Gibraltar, we would be looked upon very favourably by the powers that be. We were told that the same firm of contractors, with a head office in Shropshire, had been the sole suppliers of this service in Gibraltar for many years, and evidently had become very complacent about their situation.

Back at our Bromley office we all thought that the prospect of working in Gibraltar was an exciting one, so we readily agreed for our name to be put forward for any future major projects. In April 1983 a large and complicated set of contract documents was received which required a price for the complete external painting of walls and all other previously-decorated surfaces to six huge blocks of flats. Despite all the measurements being detailed, as usual, on a prepared 'bill of quantities', it was of course necessary for our senior estimator to fly out to inspect the work and assess general site conditions, not least to determine the amount and extent of any scaffolding or other access equipment that might be necessary to carry out the work.

He reported back that the work to the six blocks was a painting contractor's dream, and we duly 'sharpened our pencils' in an effort to secure the job. In due course we learned that we had won the contract by quite a narrow margin, which of course was very pleasing to hear, but naturally the incumbent Gibraltar painting contractor was horrified that it had failed to secure this large contract.

Along with the letter of acceptance from the MPBW was a note requiring us to obtain from the Gibraltar Government a licence to operate there. This required me to fly out and attend what I was given to understand would be a brief meeting with a Gibraltar Government official. Instead, when I arrived at the appointed room in the Mackintosh Hall, I found a large oval table with a dozen men sitting round it. They immediately asked me to sit down at the head of the table while they fired all manner of questions at me. How many Gibraltarians did we intend to employ on this project; as the work was all external, what arrangements would we be making for any inclement weather; what percentage of the materials would be sourced locally; how many tradesmen from England would we be providing, were we aware of the acute shortage of accommodation, etc.

As one would have expected, the two trades union officials were the most vociferous, and it became clear to me that the older of the two was very disgruntled about a firm from England having secured the contract. He was really quite nasty, expressing some extreme left-wing views about contractors coming out from England to 'take away work from the locals' and make a profit from the situation.

I produced my old faithful photographs of some of our work in England, particularly those of the gilding and painting of gates and railings around Buckingham Palace (the same ones I had used to great effect a few years earlier in Saudi Arabia). They had impressed them in Jeddah and they duly impressed once again in Gibraltar, so eventually, after almost two hours of (sometimes heated) discussion, it was agreed unanimously to provide us with the necessary licence to operate.

After the meeting I walked out of the building alongside the belligerent union representative, who, to my amazement, suggested that we go across the road to one of the many pubs just off Main Street for a beer. He apologized for his attitude at the meeting but explained that he was well known not only for speaking his mind but treating all and sundry in a generally rude manner, and had his reputation to think of! After a couple of beers we parted good friends. Shortly afterwards we received the hard-won licence to operate as painting contractors in Gibraltar.

We had ordered the materials but had not actually started work on this contract before we received an enquiry for the three-year painting term contract on a schedule of rates. If we were to take working in Gibraltar seriously, we felt we really must try to secure this particular contract, as the stability of having three years of guaranteed work in front of us would be fantastic. Not only that, but it would provide much-needed internal work while we undertook the external flat painting project.

We were duly awarded the contract, much to the chagrin of the incumbent contractor from Shropshire, and it was important to take steps straight away to set up an office on the Rock with a suitably experienced manager to run it.

It so happened that Alan Ward had been having a discussion with a representative of the paint suppliers who we were intending to use in Gibraltar when he offered to introduce him to a man called Brian Callaghan, who was English, but had lived in Gibraltar for many years. He had married a Gibraltarian girl who was a member of the Bassadone family who had several business interests in Gibraltar, including the Caleta Palace Hotel (since renamed the Caleta Hotel). Brian was the manager of the hotel and, because of the amount of building and refurbishment work continually being carried out, he had recently purchased a small building company, Guncrete Ltd, so that he could have priority for any work he needed to have done at the hotel.

Originally, Guncrete had been a specialist in concrete repairs, but it also carried out small building repair contracts. They had a yard up near the Rock Hotel but operated from a rented office within the Caleta Palace Hotel. This small building firm had four employees under a Gibraltarian manager/estimator/supervisor called Mesod Belilo.

It was agreed that, on his next visit to England, Brian would come and meet Alan Ward and myself to see if there was any benefit in our two companies getting together to our mutual advantage, as he had been told of our success in landing the Gibraltar painting term contract. After a long discussion, taking into account all the advantages and disadvantages, we agreed to take a controlling interest of 60% in Guncrete Ltd and to change its name to Fairhurst Guncrete

(Gibraltar) Ltd. We would be able to operate from the same office in the hotel and use the yard facilities. The yard was all-important for us as our contract was going to need a good deal of secure storage space for the containers of paint that we would shortly be ordering.

When I flew out to Gibraltar and explained to Mesod the rudiments of what we had in mind he was absolutely delighted. When I told him of our plans to introduce a generous profit-sharing scheme, he was overjoyed and said he had always hoped for such an opportunity.

We transferred funds to the new company prior to any work commencing and sent out one of our supervisors, Brian Evenden, who had been with us for many years, to manage the orders. They were raised on the term contract, with the first job being to redecorate the exterior of the Royal Naval Hospital. The orders came thick and fast, mostly to married quarters, but we were finding it exceedingly difficult to generate any profit on these initial orders and it seemed that the rates we had submitted with our tender were too low, bearing in mind the general calibre of the workforce.

In addition to the three-year painting term contract based on a prescribed schedule of rates, we successfully tendered for some large individual projects, but they all seemed unable to generate very much gross profit, insufficient to cover overheads. It did occur to me that in the UK we took what we used to call the Protestant work ethic for granted. In Gibraltar they loved the idea of profit-sharing but were not motivated to work any differently to the way they had always worked. Whether this was due to the much warmer climate or what I suspected to be an underlying drug culture, I never knew.

The reason I mention a drug culture is that it was well known at the time for dealers in mild drugs such as marijuana to use South Western Spain to bring in their products from Morocco. It was common for them to approach the coast of Spain by night, bury or hide the drugs ashore, and then return to collect them by car the following day. Also I heard about it first hand from Brian Evenden. I took him out to dinner on one of my many visits to the Rock and on one occasion he related to me the story of how he had been involved in a very brief experiment with drugs. He had been out one evening with some of the lads and had been offered some cannabis in the pub.

The accommodation he was renting was a third-floor flat with a long balcony shared with other flats. He told me that when he went home at the end of the evening, then came out of the lift and attempted to walk along the corridor to the door of his flat, he kept walking but seemed to remain in the same spot, never getting any nearer to the door. Having failed in his attempt, and being desperately worried about what was happening, he had stayed where he was on the balcony and lay down and promptly fell asleep until morning. He said it really had taught him a lesson and he would never touch the stuff again.

The book-keeping system was not of the standard I was used to, and made it very difficult to get an accurate picture of the financial state of the contracts, so on one particular visit from England I took with me my PA, Kathy Lynch, who was a first class book-keeper, to try and sort things out and get a better system in place. This worked for a while, but as soon as she was out of sight and had returned home, they reverted to the method of costing that they were used to.

Later on, and after my complaints to our 40% partners, the contract costing system was transferred to a new but untried computer system introduced by Rodney Stansfield, the recently appointed Chartered Accountant who had been brought in from Yorkshire to oversee and manage the Bassadone Group finances.

I wasn't certain, but I believe it was Rodney who was instrumental in persuading Brian Callaghan not to honour what I assumed would be usual in a partnership situation where the cost of financing would be pro rata to the shareholding, that is, if our jointly owned company required additional finance, it would be provided 60% from us and 40% from them.

But this aspect of the 'partnership' idea with the Bassadone family was a farce, as they were very happy when we provided additional funds but they refused any help in that regard, their argument being that we had the controlling interest so we should be responsible for providing any additional working capital.

On looking back, Fairhurst Guncrete (Gibraltar) Ltd was losing money from the outset. After struggling to halt the losses for four years, and with total trading losses approaching £300,000, we had little alternative but to call it a day. With some contracts still in progress and certain employment contracts to honour, I decided in consultation with my fellow directors to dispose of our 60% interest by selling it to the Bassadone Group. They agreed to take it on but would not budge from their initial offer of a nominal £1 for our entire shareholding, and to give some idea of the type of people we were having to deal with, we still haven't been paid that £1!

The following is an extract from the final decision-making meeting held on 17th June 1986 detailing the reasons why we should offer our controlling interest of 60% to our 40% partners for a nominal sum:

As a result of recent meetings with both our Partners and others in Gibraltar likely to affect our trading in the future, it has been decided that one Partner or the other should now take 100% control and the following are the main reasons why it has been decided that the Gibraltar Partners should be left to run the Company with 100% shareholding.

As little as one month ago it was thought that the Company was trading at or about break-even and that with two profitable contracts recently commenced the Company should be trading profitably within the next few months. However, for various reasons, it now seems unlikely that the Company will trade at anything other than a substantial loss for the period ending August 1986 and further that even if profits were to be generated in subsequent years these would not be substantial enough to warrant the time necessary to produce such profit.

The following are the main reasons for this decision:

1. Problems now seem likely with one of the two major contracts with regard to building work which at best will now be executed at cost having been under-priced by a former Director who left our employ in March.

2. From a meeting last week it is evident that the newly-appointed Director, Mike Lawrence, has his heart in surveying, in particular measuring term painting contracts, and does not see his future role as running a jobbing/painting contracting business and his employment in this role is likely to be terminated by him in the not too distant future thus leaving us without a competent UK orientated Manager.

3. If we were to retain 100% control then our Gibraltar Bankers would require our UK Bankers to supply a guarantee for the £50,000 overdraft. Our UK Bankers would not be at all keen to do this and in any event would certainly require a reduction of the same amount in our UK facilities.

4. Approaches were made by the Property Services Agency on last week's visit for re-imbursement of an alleged over-payment of £4,600 on the very first order of the recent term contract and it seems likely that most of this will have to be repaid.

5. Further losses are now coming through on current work as a result of no gross profit being generated but at the same time overheads are continuing albeit at a smaller amount. Losses shown on the computerised balance sheet we receive monthly have increased from £5,000 to £10,000 to £11,000 to £17,000 over the past four months and it seems likely that, although carrying a certain amount of profit in work-in-progress, the accounts will actually show a trading loss approaching £30,000 for the period ending August 1986.

6. *Disappointment with the final building contract which was being managed on a fee basis by the Director who left our direct employ in March. This was a new £45,000 contract anticipated to produce some £8,000 gross profit but it is now likely that the most we can hope for is a gross profit of some £1,500/£2,000.*

7. *From discussion in Gibraltar last week it now seems that a major problem is looming on the horizon regarding union/labour problems and this will affect not only our work but all work being carried out in Gibraltar.*

8. *When we went to Gibraltar over three years ago our opinion was that the total market for our services was of the order of £3,000,000 p.a. and that we could realistically anticipate approximately 25% of this being one of four contractors. Recently it has become clear that half this market is not available to us as this is work now carried out directly by the Gibraltar Government (responsible for housing, schools and other public buildings). This work is now all being done by direct labour and although invitations were being sent out to quote for this work none of it is being done by private enterprise. Also cut backs in the PSA programme are barely sufficient to off-set an increased private sector market.*

9. *This increase in the private sector market is, however, subject to a history of bad debts and we would not wish to enter this market to any great degree. The market therefore available to us is unlikely to exceed £350,000 (less than half what we expected at the outset) and we have estimated that in a good year the maximum profit that could be derived from our Gibraltar activities is £20,000 p.a. (against the £50,000 thought possible at the outset). Even if this £20,000 were to be achieved then it would still be subject to profit-sharing and the costs of a senior Director from the UK with his time and flight costs added on, the conclusion was that we should pull out of this operation and concentrate on the UK market.*

Although, *prima facie*, substantial trading losses were incurred with our three year foray into the Gibraltar market, the experience was used to great effect in our UK sales and marketing efforts during subsequent years. I am certain that with the advent of changing clients' attitudes where the lowest prices did not necessarily secure work but the overall experience of the contractor counted as an important factor, much work was gained that would otherwise not have been the case.

Our only other sortie into working overseas was in the early 1980s, when one of our specialist subsidiaries, Kaytherm Services Ltd, won a contract in Saudi Arabia to carry out the spraying of an epoxy intumescent paint to act as a fire protection coating to steelwork in a factory roof which was sub-contracted to us by the international construction firm of Taylor Woodrow & Co.

CHAPTER TWELVE

The sale of FWA

For at least six years from about 1997 to 2003, the question of succession planning had been discussed regularly at our board meetings. As happens with most family-controlled businesses, no firm conclusions were ever agreed. I had been studying for quite some time the types of problems encountered by similar-sized enterprises when the question of retirement arose and was familiar with the fact that most business owners fail to plan seriously for their own succession.

I was well aware that smooth succession planning is something that takes a lot of time, and the eventual handover needs to be carefully planned and executed if it is to be successful. I learned that even where a business owner has no plans to retire, succession planning is needed in the event of something dire happening such as disability, serious illness or even sudden death. I knew that it was received wisdom to develop a plan for succession several years before the actual event. I read somewhere that some experts in this field advise that the planning should begin as long as 12 or even 15 years before retirement of the owner, but I was of the opinion that three to five years would suffice in our particular case.

One difficulty which I had to accept was that my close colleague of over 40 years, Alan Ward, was almost three years younger than me yet, although we talked about it, I felt his heart was not really in it so far as planning his own retirement was concerned. He actually said on more than one occasion that he would like to carry on working for as long as possible. I also felt that I was not ready to be put out to grass at the normal retirement age, but when I thought about the question seriously, I did not really fancy the ultimate responsibility beyond, say the age of 70.

If I had decided to retire some years earlier, then of course there was the possibility that Alan would have been prepared to buy me out, but the older we both got the less inclined he was to consider this option.

Many owners of family-controlled firms make the mistake of assuming that their children will take control when the time comes, but I knew that in my case, as also with Alan Ward, this would be most unlikely. For a start none of our children worked for the company and my son Robert had made it clear to me many years earlier that, following a highly successful start to his chosen career in the academic world, there would never be any possibility of his taking over.

The difficulty of dealing with recessions every ten years or so made the timing very challenging as I realised how important it was to have at least three or four good trading years in succession behind us before attempting to market the firm. In the absence of a serious recession, I was able to foresee the very real possibility of being able to post increasing turnover and trading profits for 2005 to follow the two good years of 2003 and 2004.

Here at long last was the opportunity of showing the required three-year rising trend in trading fortunes. Therefore in the summer of 2005, at yet another board meeting to discuss the future, it was agreed that I should investigate the market for firms who specialised in the sale of private companies. For many years it had been the usual practice of retaining one's own accountants to deal with such a disposal, but latterly I had noticed a distinct trend to employ the services of only the larger firms of accountants who invariably had specialist divisions for this type of work.

A case in point was when Mike Turl was looking at the next stage of development for his successful Mears contracting firm. He employed the services of his own accountants, who just happened to be one of the largest and most successful accountancy practices in the UK, Grant Thornton. We ourselves had previously had dealings with Grant Thornton when they were appointed as receivers to deal with our acquisition of the Abbotts Painting business in 1992.

As stated in the foreword to this book, every businessman gets one lifetime opportunity to really go for the big time, and my father's opportunity came in 1948 on the death of Ian Williams. My own opportunity arose in 1995 when I saw an advertisement in the *Financial Times*, placed by Grant Thornton, seeking a suitable company to either merge with, or take over, one of their clients, a fast-growing building maintenance firm. I was intrigued, and made an appointment to meet the partner concerned, together with the MD of their client, a company trading under the name of Mears Ltd.

A meeting was arranged at a hotel near Heathrow, and from discussion, it seemed that Mike Turl, the MD, felt that he had taken Mears as far as he could on his own and was now in search of a similar firm with which to merge.

Coincidentally, at the time, our firm's annual turnover was very similar to that of Mears at about £12 million. The two companies would have fitted well together, as the turnover of Mears was almost entirely derived from long-term 24-hour responsive maintenance work (all trades) for housing associations and councils, whereas our own company's work consisted mainly of individual projects for prestige clients such as the Royal Household and nationally-known museums.

I got the distinct impression from Mike Turl, however, that although he sought an alliance with another similar firm, his real ambition was for another firm to take over Mears, still retaining his services, so that he could give more time to his young family. Mike was a very bright and intelligent quantity surveyor by profession, with a special aptitude for computerising the whole of his organisation to the point where his head office knew every nail and screw that was stocked on the various sites and an automatic re-ordering service had been established to ensure stock levels were maintained.

I gave it a lot of very hard thinking before letting Mike and his accountant know that I thought Mears would be a little too much for us to swallow. Mike eventually received the offer he wanted and, shortly afterwards, Mears had their shares quoted on AIM (the junior Stock Exchange).

The growth since then has been nothing short of phenomenal. At the time of writing these memoirs they were employing some 12,000 people and enjoyed annual sales of approximately £500 million, with an operating profit of £25 million – a fantastic achievement in so short a period.

I did not think that we could follow the Mike Turl example and employ our own accountants to assist in the sale of shares in FWA, as I did not believe they had the expertise required. I knew that to sell an organisation of our size and complexity would necessitate assistance either from a national firm of accountants or from a professional firm whose sole business was that of arranging mergers and acquisitions. From a study of such organisations on the Internet, I came up with a firm based near Newbury in Berkshire trading under the name of BCMS Corporate. I never did discover what the initials BCMS stood for, but I know I chose well, for in 2007, the year after our sale was completed, their refreshingly different approach to mergers and acquisitions was recognised by Coutts Bank, which honoured them with the highly-coveted 'Best Family Business of the Year' award.

Certainly, from the very first exploratory meeting with their senior negotiator, I found each member of their team highly professional to deal with. One of the main reasons for employing the services of

BCMS was that their statistics showed that 65% of their successful sales involved companies in the service sector.

Right at the start I was issued with a comprehensive document detailing the various stages of what they called 'The BCMS Process' which, initially, involved three preparatory meetings.

1. Initial client meeting (personal introductions, running through the research process, running through the marketing documentation/process and checking the development of the M&A (Mergers & Acquisition) information checklist).

2. Dry run meeting (prepare for face to face meetings, 'coaching' and details of risks/benefits).

3. Business plan meeting (meeting with BCMS Financial Controller) to discuss and formulate business plans and presentation of the research list

After that came the sale proposal, which included:

1. Information memorandum which needed to be approved.

2. Approval of proposal letter to prospective purchasers.

3. Approval of the Powerpoint presentation.

The next stage was for the BCMS Prospect Generation Team to make telephone calls to prospective purchasers; this process was anticipated to be completed within eight weeks. After that it was the turn of the BCMS Project Manager to talk individually with those prospects who had received the comprehensive information memorandum. This was to establish the reason for their interest, discuss strategic synergies and their ability to purchase, etc. Next came arranging to book initial prospect meetings to allow face-to-face talks.

All the foregoing took many weeks of preparation so that, from the initial client meeting on 19th October 2005, it took until mid

March 2006 for face-to-face meetings with prospective purchasers to commence.

To summarise, the whole process took the following form:

1. Company and product initial brief
2. Preparation for the market
3. Desk research
4. Preparation of the sales proposal
5. Going live to market
6. Ongoing review of process and results to date
7. Fine tuning - working with initial offers
8. Conclusion - running with an accepted offer

The final outcome of all these efforts was that the number of potential purchasers approached totalled 196, of which serious expressions of interest numbered 27. After all the negotiating, the eventual number of competing bids was down to just seven. Five of these were either from competitors or other similar organisations involved in the construction industry. The other two offers were from management buy-in teams.

From the outset, it had never been my intention to dispose of my controlling interest in FWA for money alone, as other factors were also important to me. I was not too keen, for instance, on selling to another larger organisation where our trading name, built up so meticulously over 50 years, would be swallowed up and lost soon after the take-over.

Another consideration, probably the most important to me, was that any larger firm would have its own administration department and I could foresee that in any take-over several of our loyal office staff could lose their jobs overnight. When discussing and agreeing the way forward with Alan Ward, it also had to be taken into account that it was his wish to carry on working for the foreseeable future and proceeding with a management buy-in would allow his continuation, indeed it would be imperative for the new management to continue to employ Alan's services in some form or another.

It was at this stage that BCMS warned me about potential purchasers requiring 'Due Diligence' to be carried out. Although I had heard of this procedure I was unprepared for the depth of work that had to be undertaken by the purchaser's financial advisers. I was told that, typically, the following details would be asked:

Annual and quarterly financial information for the past three years
1. Income statements, balance sheets, cash flows
2. Forecast versus actual results
3. Management financial reports
4. Breakdown of sales and gross profits
5. Current backlog by customer
6. Accounts receivable ageing schedule

Financial Projections
1. Quarterly financial projections for the next three years
2. Major growth drivers and prospects
3. Predictability of business
4. Pricing policies
5. Explanation of projected capital expenditures, depreciation and working capital arrangements

Capital Structure
1. Current shares outstanding
2. List of all shareholders with shareholdings and options,
3. Summary of all debt instruments/bank lines with key terms and conditions
4. Off balance sheet liabilities

Other financial information

1. Summary of current tax positions, including net operating losses carried forwards
2. Stipulate general accounting policies
3. Schedule of financing history for equity, warrants, and debt

Description of type of service provided

1. Major customers and applications
2. Historical and projected growth rates
3. Market share
4. Speed and nature of technological change
5. Timing of new products, product enhancements
6. Cost structure and profitability

List of top 12 customers for the past three fiscal years and current year-to-date by application

(name, contact name, address, phone number)

List of strategic relationships

(name, contact name, phone number, revenue contribution, marketing agreements)

Revenue by customer

(name, contact name, phone number for any accounting for 5 percent or more of revenue)

Brief description of any significant relationships severed within the last three years.

(name, contact name, phone number)

List of top 12 suppliers for the past three fiscal years and current year-to-date with contact information
(name, contact name, phone number, purchase amounts, supplier agreements)

Description of the competitive landscape within each market segment including:
1. Market position and related strengths and weaknesses as perceived in the market place
2. Basis of competition (e.g., price, service, technology, distribution)

Marketing and sales strategy and implementation
1. Discussion of distribution channels
2. Positioning of the Company and its products
3. Marketing opportunities/marketing risks
4. Description of marketing programmes and examples of recent marketing/product/public relations/media information on the Company

Major customers
1. Status and trends of relationships
2. Prospects for future growth and development
3. Pipeline analysis

Principal avenues for generating new business

Sales force productivity model
1. Compensation
2. Quota average
3. Sales cycle
4. Plan for new hires

Indicate ability to implement marketing plan with current and projected budgets

Management and personnel organization chart

Historical and projected headcount by function and location

Summary biographies of senior management, including employment history, age, service with the Company, years in current position

Compensation arrangements
1. Copies of key employment agreements
2. Benefit plans

Significant employee relations problems, past or present

Personnel turnover
1. Data for the last three years
2. Benefit plans

Pending lawsuits against the company
(details of claimant, claimed damages, brief history, status, anticipated outcome, and name of the Company's legal advisers)

Pending lawsuits initiated by company
(detail on defendant, claimed damages, brief history, status, anticipated outcome, and name of company's legal advisers)

Description of environmental and employee safety issues and
liabilities
1. Safety precautions
2. New regulations and their consequences
3. Copy of safety policy
4. Copy of Environmental Policy

Summary of insurance coverage
Summary of material contracts

In the event, the process of due diligence was far more exhausting than I could have envisaged and I felt quite drained by the whole process. On more than one occasion I wondered if we were doing the right thing.

By the end of April 2006, however, we were well on the way to deciding to accept an offer from a highly experienced two-man team who had been successfully running a much larger building firm for a number of years. Their names were Kevin Brush and Dave Brown. When I returned from a week's holiday in the middle of May, however, I discovered that a potential disaster had been unleashed on all proceedings, as I heard that on the very day I left for my holiday on Friday 5th May it was discovered that our accountant had made a major error in the first draft of the annual accounts which could now jeopardise the whole transaction. We did eventually manage to retrieve the situation, but for a while it was touch and go.

Although we had decided to proceed with 'Newco' (the name Kevin and Dave's financial advisers had thought up for the proposed new venture) we realised that there was a large element of risk involved. However we calculated that this risk was outweighed by the possible financial outcome if all went according to plan. The essence of the arrangement was that a new holding company (FWA

Holdings Ltd) would be established, which would own the entire shareholding of the trading company of Fairhurst Ward Abbotts Ltd. The purchasers would pay in cash a sum which was slightly more than the offers from other interested parties, and the balance would follow after a minimum period of three years.

This meant that they would immediately acquire a 60% controlling interest (with Kevin and Dave each holding 30% in FWA Holdings Ltd and with Alan and myself each left with a 20% stake). The snag was that, between them, the purchasers had only about 21% from their own resources to put on the table.

With Alan and I and other members of my family having received cash for our 60% holdings, we then had to lend them back 30% of the purchase price at an

agreed interest rate over a three-year period. On completion, they immediately raised the balance of almost 50% by utilising a significant amount of cash that the firm was holding on deposit and, thanks mainly to our long and highly-successful relationship with NatWest Bank (originally National Provincial and now RBS) over a 65-year period, our bankers were prepared to finance the not inconsiderable balance. In short, it was a classic case of a highly-leveraged deal, but Alan and I were convinced that the new controlling directors were the right people to carry FWA forward to its next phase of development.

The one aspect that surprised me somewhat when the deal was completed in October 2006 was that between them, the two purchasers had decided, for the time being at any rate, that profit and turnover levels at FWA were insufficient to sustain two highly-paid executives. It was arranged that Kevin would not work full time in their new venture for the present and that Dave Brown would assume the role of managing director. Kevin would attend board meetings and keep in close touch, but without active participation on a daily basis.

Kevin, who had many contacts at a senior level in the trade, was appointed as a director within the Rok organisation. Rok was a relative newcomer to the building maintenance industry, but the firm had been built up rapidly over the previous ten years from its base in the West Country and by 2007 was trading with group sales of about £1 billion. Rok was not a competitor of FWA, so there was no conflict of interest. I was a little concerned by their arrangement, because throughout our negotiations it had been Kevin rather than Dave in whom I had had most confidence, possibly because of the two he came across to me as having a personality more suited to the type of work we had always carried out. Anyway, that was how they decided to manage, with Dave full time and Kevin, although available for consultation, only attending the occasional meeting.

When the initial three years from the date of the sale were due to expire in October 2009, Alan and I wrote a formal letter to Dave Brown stating that we now wished to exercise our right to be paid the final amount for our joint 40% shareholding all as per the Sale Agreement. Shortly afterwards I had lunch with Dave. He explained that there were insufficient funds to pay us the full amount at that time, and the only realistic way for the terms of the agreement to be fulfilled was for us to be paid over, say, a seven-year period.

Having discussed this new development with our solicitors, there seemed to be no alternative but to accept the situation. A new and comprehensive agreement was drawn up for payment over seven years, commencing with the first quarterly payment in February 2010.

I am sure that this new arrangement was not too displeasing to Alan as it would mean his continuing involvement with assisting the purchasers over a much longer period than originally envisaged.

Although new and exciting contracts were being accepted, a problem became apparent in December 2009 concerning the adequacy of the person in charge of the accounting function and it was agreed that a change should be made in that important department. Also, from the value and type of contracts now within FWA's reach, Kevin had seen the potential for the firm to really go places in the very near future. Accordingly, Dave agreed at this time to step aside from his responsibilities as managing director and allow Kevin to head up the team in a full-time capacity.

Kevin's first priority was to employ the services of Steve Evans, an experienced qualified accountant, to get to grips with all monetary aspects of the firm. This proved to be quite a daunting job for Steve, as many of the financial practices required a complete overhaul and indeed a new computer system had to be installed to cope with the complexities and types of contracts now being carried out.

During the early months of his leadership, after ensuring that the financial reporting systems were in order, Kevin set about using his considerable managerial expertise to establish FWA as a force to be reckoned with in the decidedly specialized field of conservation, restoration, refurbishment, conversion and extension of historic and ecclesiastical buildings and monuments. This was achieved by the creation of a new division to undertake such work and the introduction of Chris Maryon, a highly qualified Operations and Conservation Director, to run it. Within a relatively short period, Chris was enjoying relationships with English Heritage, The National Trust, Historic Royal Palaces, The Landmark Trust, the Crown Estate and many other similarly high-profile clients.

The types of work coming under the day-to-day control of Chris Maryon were becoming wide and varying and included contracts at Castle Acre Priory, King's Lynn, together with Kensington Palace and Hampton Court Palace.

In addition to Steve Evans as Group Finance Director and Chris Maryon as Director of the Conservation Division, the following senior appointments were either confirmed or introduced at this time:

Dave Brown	Director of London Residencies Division
James Vevers	Director of Arts and Culture Division
Dave Westwood	Director of New Build Division
Matt Dauncey	Director of Social Partnerships Division
Geoff Taylor	Director of Pre Construction Division

Thus the stage was set for a transformation of FWA's fortunes. Despite being in the middle of what was, and continues to be, the worst recession with which the UK has ever been faced, the value of work executed increased substantially in the period from 2011 to 2012 - a fantastic achievement, doubtless helped by the establishment of an office in Huntingdon, Cambridgeshire.

On 20th October 2011, FWA celebrated 70 years of success at its newly-completed Look Out project in Hyde Park. Commissioned by the Royal Parks Foundation, the Look Out Centre is a green educational facility in the heart of London for use by children and young people. Built around a landscape designed with ecology in mind, the new 406-square metre facility underpinned FWA's environmental expertise through the use of sustainable timber, natural ventilation and lighting, and a range of energy and water-saving measures. The end result was a comfortable, modern and environmentally-sympathetic space set in one of London's most historic parklands – a fitting venue for FWA's 70th anniversary celebrations.

As this book goes to press, it has been announced that one of the largest, most prestigious and exciting projects ever to be undertaken by FWA has been awarded. This is for a multi-million-pound refurbishment contract to certain areas of Chatsworth as part of the Duke of Devonshire's £14m masterplan for restoration.

I am so very proud of all that the new management team has achieved in so short a period.

POSTSCRIPT

Working wives, and other matters

In my retirement years, and in fact during the run-up to retirement, Ann was forever telling me how unfair I had been regarding what she referred to as my 'not allowing her to go back to work in the 1970s'. It was not a matter of 'not allowing' but trying to explain why it made no economic sense for her to go to work. Most people these days would not understand the financial implications of a working wife in the mid 1970s, as very few couples would have been in our position. I just happened to be fortunate enough to be earning enough to bring me into the top tax bracket at that time.

There are still some people around who remember the tax system in the 1970s and certainly those working in the financial sector, especially accountants, will know how iniquitous the tax treatment was for married couples until Margaret Thatcher's government got to grips with it soon after being elected in 1979. It does seem quite extraordinary now, but in 1975, for instance, the top rate of income tax for anyone earning over £20,000 per year was 83%, and to add to this misery any so-called 'unearned income', i.e. interest earned from savings, attracted a surcharge of 15%. In effect, therefore, if one earned over £20,000 a year and had income from savings or other invested capital, the top marginal rate was an incredible 98%!

As if this wasn't enough, until Margaret Thatcher's Government changed the law to tax husbands and wives separately, a wife's earnings were added to her husband's, so in 1975 when Ann expressed a wish to go back to work, albeit in a part-time capacity, I had to explain to her that I would be out of pocket. She did not believe me then, and to this day she still does not believe that the rates of tax at that time were so grossly unjust.

If she were to have returned to work as a part-time nurse, for example, she would have earned about £25 a week. Although she herself would have only been taxed a modest amount, at the end of the tax year her earnings would have been added to mine and as, at that time, the top slice of my earned income came into the 83% tax bracket, the net income from Ann's employment would have been only a little over £4 per week. If one then added the cost of actually getting to work (by car was the only feasible way) then we would have made an overall loss. This is how it would have worked out:

Ann's gross weekly income	£25.00
Net amount post tax at top marginal rate of 83%	£4.25
Less cost of running car 6 miles each way 12 miles x 5 days = 60 miles @ 12p	£7.20
Overall weekly loss	**£2.95**

At the time of writing this book, 55 years of my life have been spent with FWA, of which 25 years have been as Chairman and CEO. I could not possibly have managed with this responsibility over such a prolonged period without the tolerance and general forbearing nature of my wife. During all those years she has had to put up with my complex working hours, particularly during the first few years of our marriage in 1961 when I was involved in supervising nightwork contracts in London and would often not get home before two or three in the morning. 2011 was the year we celebrated our golden wedding anniversary, and I want to pay tribute to Ann for her fantastic support over those 50 years.

Another person to whom I am indebted is Kathy Lynch, my PA for 25 years until her retirement in 2006. I know I could not have managed without having someone on hand to discuss the periodic occasions when financial crises loomed and generally having someone available to listen to my problems and constant complaints.

I am very proud of my three children, who had to put up with my bad temper on the many occasions when things weren't going to plan. I am especially thankful to my son Robert, who acted very professionally as the Company Secretary for a ten-year period which ended only when my controlling interest was sold in 2006.

I am also proud of his academic success since leaving Eltham College in 1995 - not just for the starred double first in English he attained at Pembroke College, Cambridge, but for being awarded Procter Visiting Fellow at Princeton University, USA in 1991, followed by a Doctorate in 1994, Junior Research Fellow, Fitzwilliam College, Cambridge, 1995-96, Fellow and Tutor, Emmanuel College, Cambridge, 1996-2002 and Fellow and Tutor, Magdalen College, Oxford, from 2002 until the present time.

In addition, his media work has included writing regular arts features and reviews for the *Daily Telegraph*, contributing to UK and US radio and television programmes and acting as the historical adviser on recent BBC adaptations of *Jane Eyre* (2006), *Emma* (2009) and *Great Expectations* in 2011.

Every Saturday I turn hopefully to the *Daily Telegraph* review section to see what, if any, book he has been asked to review. His reviews are always a joy to read.

Robert's first book, Victorian Afterlives, was published in 2002 and his second, Becoming Dickens (Harvard University Press), was published in 2011 in readiness for, and in celebration of, the bicentenary of Dickens' birth in 1812. *The Book of Shadows: Victorian Magic and the Making of the Modern World* (Princeton University

Press), is due for publication in 2012. Apart from his own books, he has also edited the following published books:

- *Charles Dickens, A Christmas Carol and Other Christmas Books* (Oxford World's Classics, 2006)
- *Charles Dickens, Great Expectations* (Oxford World's Classics, 2008)
- *Tennyson Among the Poets: Bicentenary Essays* (Oxford University Press, 2009)
- *Henry Mayhew, London Labour and the London Poor: A Selected Edition* (Oxford University Press, 2010

But for all Robert's academic achievements, my proudest moment came in 2009 when I received a photograph of him meeting the Queen and Duke of Edinburgh during their visit to Magdalen College. This for me was especially poignant as I had been working for the Queen and the Royal Family for over 50 years decorating and generally maintaining the Historic Royal Palaces of Buckingham Palace, Windsor Castle, Hampton Court Palace and others, yet I had never met Her Majesty in the whole of that time. Anyone reading this will, I am sure, fully understand why I am so proud of my son.

Robbie meeting HM The Queen in 2009

In addition to Robert's chosen career to teach English at Oxford, my two daughters have also chosen to spend their working lives helping youngsters at important stages of their lives. Penny, the elder, took up the challenge while looking after two teenage boys as a single mother by going to Greenwich University in 2010 and obtaining a BSc in psychology. This was then followed by a Masters degree and is likely to lead to work where she will be able to help problem children. Lucy, the younger, has spent many years as a nursery nurse, where she is able to use her long experience and her own excellent education in helping very young children during their all-important formative years.

Bits and Pieces

During my life I've encountered a few injustices, of which the following are two typical examples:

Refrigerator doors. The difficulty of being able to buy a refrigerator that is made specifically for right-handed people (that is, one where you can retrieve its contents with your right hand having opened it with the door hinges manufactured on the left hand side). It seems that this ridiculous situation arises from the fact the inventor of the refrigerator happened to be left handed. All you will get from a salesman is 'there's no problem as most of the makes allow for doors to be hung on either side'. My point is, why on earth should right-handed people be inconvenienced by this absurdity when they represent approximately 90% of the population? I haven't researched it, but it seems probable that the inventor of the QWERTY keyboard was likewise left handed as I have discovered that over 3000 words in English can be typed using only the left hand on the QWERTY board as opposed to some 300 with the right hand and, overall, almost 60% of the keystrokes made when touch-typing on a QWERTY board are made with the left hand.

Immigration frustration. I feel bound to mention a second major grievance that I have had for some years. On arriving home at the end of a cruise, for example, there has never been a problem for me when suffering the rigmarole of being processed through Passport Control at Dover (or Southampton for that matter). What always annoys me, and I find utterly abhorrent, is when one arrives back in England at Gatwick Airport, for instance, and when, after enduring what is sometimes a considerable queue, one is confronted by someone of dubious ethnicity themselves who is evidently in the position of deciding whether or not I will be permitted to enter my own country. I have always found this situation to be most annoying.

Over the years, especially when on holiday, I used to find it complicated to try to explain what exactly it was that I did for a living. Should I just say 'painting contractor', fully knowing that this would not mean anything to a lot of people? (Over the years I have found that even professional firms found this difficult, judging by the number of letters addressed to us as 'printing contractors'). Given the number of specialist tasks I was expected to undertake - accountant, manager, director, insurance consultant, employment law specialist, etc - I decided that, in reply to the question 'What do you do for a living?', I would just say 'company collector'. Some people imagined that this occupation was akin to being a ticket collector or rubbish collector and took the matter no further. Others, however, would want to know more. 'What exactly is a company collector?' they would ask, and I would reply 'Some people collect stamps, some collect fine porcelain and others collect butterflies, for example. I collect small limited liability companies'. (For details of the companies I have acquired or started from scratch, please see Appendix E.)

During the period following semi-retirement, when I continued to hold a 20% shareholding in the holding company, I was often amused on occasions when I visited the FWA head office to be greeted in the reception area by a new employee who would ask 'Who are you?' Being someone who could never resist a pun, my reply would often be 'I'm the 'F' in FWA' with a slight emphasis on 'effin'.

APPENDIX A
The meanings of the abbreviation 'PC'

Painting contractor

Palliative care

Panama Canal

Paper clip

Parental control

Parish church

Passport control

Pasteurised cream

Peace corps

Penal Colony

Pencil case

Pension contribution

Pepsi Cola

Per capita

Per cent

Personal care

Personal computer

Petty cash

Petty crime

Phone call

Phone card

Phone connection

Photo copy

Physical contact

Pie crust

Pierre Cardin

Pin cushion

Pine cone

Plaid Cymru

Planning consent

Plant cell

Plaster cast

Platoon commander

Pocket calculator

Poet's Corner

Polaroid camera

Police car

Police constable

Policy committee

Pollution control

Pony club

Pop culture

Portable computer

Post card

Postal clerk

Postal code

Potato crisp

Potting compost

Power consumption

Power cord

Practical completion

Pre-cast concrete

Presbyterian church

Press conference

Press cutting

Pressure cooker

Pressurised container

Pre-stressed concrete

Price comparison

Primary care

Prime colour

Prime cost

Prince Charming

Prince Consort

Printed circuit

Printed circuit

Printer cartridge

Private citizen

Privy Council

Product code

Product codes

Production company

Production control

Professional computer

Profit centre

Protective custody

Provisional cost

Public company

APPENDIX B
History of Recessions and Difficult Trading Periods

1893

The Depression of 1893 was one of the worst in American history with the unemployment rate exceeding 10% for half a decade. There were repercussions in the UK from this.

1902

Difficult trading conditions following the end of Boer War. The recession came about a year after the American 1901Stock Market crash.

1914

Start of First World War and a major recession.

1922

Deflation of 14% caused major problems

Early 1930's

The Great Depression brought about by the 1929 Wall Street crash.

Early 1940's

Second World War making trading conditions very difficult.

Early 1950s

UK Government moratorium on spending badly affects construction industry.

Early 1960s

Characterised by very high inflation. Especially difficult trading conditions during the first few years of Harold Wilson's 1964/1970 administration.

Early 1970s

3 day week introduced at midnight on December 31st 1973 and 1973 oil crisis. Inflation reached 16% in 1974, peeking at 24.2% in 1975.

Early 1980s

High Inflation again, reaching 18% in 1980 and general trading conditions very tough

Early 1990s

A two year general recession with the UK's departure from the ERM – 'Black Wednesday' on 16th September 1992.

Early 2000's

For the first time for over a hundred years no serious recession for over 15 years, until 2008 when the biggest recession in living memory made up for missing one in the early 2000's.

APPENDIX C

A selection of some of the important buildings and locations where painting and maintenance work has been carried out over the years by the FWA Group of Companies

Alleyn's College
American Embassy
Australia House
Avery Hill College
Bank of England
Barbican Centre
BBC Broadcasting House
Bethnal Green Museum
Birmingham Civil Airport
Brighton University
British Telecom Tower
Broadlands Estate, Romsey
Buckingham Palace
Chelsea Barracks
Chelsea Hospital
Chatham Naval Dockyard
Clarence House
County Hall, London
Covent Garden market
Crystal Palace Stadium
Cumberland Hotel, Marble Arch
Dover Castle
Dulwich College
Dungeness Power Station
Eltham College
Eltham Palace

Eton College
Gatwick Airport
Goodwood Circuit
Hammersmith Bridge
Hampton Court Palace
Harrods Store, Knightsbridge
Heathrow Airport
Hendon Police College
Houses of Parliament
Imperial College, London
Imperial War Museum
Kings College Hospital
London University
Mount Pleasant Sorting Office
National Maritime Museum
National Portrait Gallery
New Scotland Yard
Paddington Station
Palm House, Kew Gardens
Pentonville Prison
Public Health Labs, Porton Down
Queen's Flight Hangar, RAF Benson
RAF Station Biggin Hill
RAF Station Lakenheath

RAF Station Mildenhall
Royal Air force Museum
Royal Albert Hall
Royal Arsenal, Woolwich
Royal College of Surgeons
Royal Festival Hall
Royal Mint
Royal Naval College, Greenwich
Science Museum
Scotts Restaurant Piccadilly
Shell Centre, Waterloo
Somerset House
Southampton Technical College
Southampton University
South Bank University
St James's Palace
Tate Gallery
The Guildhall, London
Tilbury Power Station
USAF Base, Greenham Common
Victoria & Albert Museum
Waterloo Station
Windsor Castle

APPENDIX D
Humorous notices from around the world

Item in a Crawley Newspaper
'Gatwick Airport failed to return a hearing aid to its owner despite repeated broadcasts over the public announcement system'.

Sign outside a Hong Kong tailors
'Ladies may have a fit upstairs'.

Sign outside a tailor's in Greece
'Order your Summer Suit. Because is big rush we will execute customers in strict rotation'.

On a menu in an Alpine restaurant
'Our wines leave you nothing to hope for'.

Sign in a Copenhagen ticket office
'We take your bags and send them in all directions'.

In a Norwegian cocktail lounge
'Ladies are requested not to have children in the Bar'.

In a Vienna Hotel
'In case of fire do your utmost to alarm the Hotel Porter'.

Outside a Hong Kong dentist
'Teeth extracted by the latest Methodists'.

Advertisement in Shropshire Newspaper
'Holiday accommodation available in Welsh Farmhouse. Comfort and good food (except August)'.

In a Rome Laundry
'Ladies, leave your clothes here and spend the afternoon having a good time'.

In a Swedish Furriers
'Fur coats made for ladies from their own skins'.

On door of Moscow Hotel Room
'If this is your first visit to the USSR, you are welcome to it.

In a Japanese Elevator
'The lift is being fixed for the next day. During that time we regret that you will be unbearable'.

In a Bangkok Temple
'It is forbidden to enter a woman even if a foreigner is dressed as a man'.

In a Budapest Zoo
'Please do not feed the animals. If you have suitable food, give it to the guard on duty'.

Notice in a Doctor's Surgery in Rome
'Specialist in women and other diseases'.

In a Japanese Hotel
'Cooles and Heates. If you want just condition of warm in your room, please control yourself'.

Sign in a Tokyo Car Rental
'When passenger of foot heave in sight, tootle the horn. Trumpet him melodiously at first, but if he still obstacles your passage then tootle him with vigour'.

In a Bangkok Dry Cleaners
'Drop your trousers here for best results'.

In a Zurich Hotel
'Because of the impropriety of entertaining guests of the opposite sex in the bedroom, it is suggested that the lobby be used for this purpose'.

In a Prague Tourist Office
'Take one of our horse-driven city tours. We guarantee no miscarriages'.

Sign in a Thailand Donkey Hire shop
'Would you like to ride on your own ass?'

Spotted in a toilet of a London office
'Toilet out of order – please use floor below'.

In a Tokyo Hotel
'In case of earthquake, use the torch to pass yourself out'.

In a London department store:
'Bargain basement upstairs'.

In an office:
'Would the person who took the step ladder away yesterday please bring it back or further steps will be taken'.

In a Laundromat
'Automatic Washing Machines: please remove all your clothes when the light goes out'.

In an office:
'After tea break, staff should empty the teapot and stand upside down on the draining board'.

Sign outside a secondhand shop
'We exchange anything – bicycles, washing machines, etc., why not bring your wife along and get a wonderful bargain?'.

Seen in a conference hall:
'For anyone who has children and doesn't know it, there is a day care room on the first floor'.

Notice in health food shop window
'Closed due to illness'.

Seen in a West Country Holiday Brochure
'West Dorset – where to eat street maps'.

From the Aberdeen Press & Journal:
'A group of youngsters who fled in a mini-bus were caught yesterday after a sharp-eyed member of the public spotted the vehicle 50 miles away'.

In Greenock, by a subsiding embankment, stands a sign
'Danger, Keep Out – Dangerous Banking'. Right opposite are the local offices of the Clydesdale Bank, the Bank of Scotland and the Royal Bank of Scotland.

From an advertisement in Classic Car Magazine:
'Ford Granada Hearse, 2.8 auto, 90,000 miles, superb engine and gearbox, body in good condition.'

Seen on a vehicle parked in Boston, USA:
'This vehicle is protected by Anti-Theft sticker.'

Sign outside a United Methodist Church:
'Don't let worries kill you – let the Church help.'

Seen outside a restaurant in Yorkshire:
'Today's Special – Buy one Fish and Chips for the price of two and receive a second Fish and Chips Absolutely Free!'

APPENDIX E

Admatch
Beaver Decorating & Cleaning Co. Ltd
Beaver Office Cleaning Ltd
Bulfords (Builders) Ltd
Fairhurst Guncrete (Gibraltar) Ltd
Fairhurst Pippard Ltd
Fairhurst Ward Abbotts Ltd
FWA Estates Ltd
FWA Holdings Ltd
FWA West Ltd
Group Twelve Advertising Ltd
Group Twelve Decorations Ltd
Group Twelve Ltd
Group Twelve Membrane Coatings Ltd
Hugill Windows Ltd
J Smith (Chislehurst) Ltd
John Fairhurst & Sons (Southern) Ltd
John Fairhurst & Sons Ltd
John Fairhurst (London) Ltd
Kaytherm Services Ltd
Moderngood Flooring Ltd
Pietro Properties Ltd
R L Ruggles & Son Ltd
Saxon Plant Hire Co.
Southern Decorating Supplies
Southern Paint Services
Ward Abbotts Painting Ltd